Permitted and Prohibited Desires

$\mathcal{P}$ermitted and Prohibited Desires

Mothers, Comics, and Censorship in Japan

Anne Allison

WestviewPress

A Division of HarperCollins*Publishers*

Copyright © 1996 by Westview Press, A Division of HarperCollins Publishers, Inc.

Published in 1996 in the United States of America by Westview Press, Inc., 5500 Central Avenue, Boulder, Colorado, 80301-2877, and in the United Kingdom by Westview Press, 12 Hid's Copse Road, Cumnor Hill, Oxford OX2 9JJ

A CIP catalog record for this book is available from the Library of Congress.
ISBN 0-8133-1698-7—ISBN 0-8133-3127-7 (if published as a paperback)

The paper used in this publication meets the requirements of the American National Standard for Permanence of Paper for Printed Library Materials Z39-1984.

10   9   8   7   6   5   4   3   2   1

In memory of
Lawrence True Allison

Contents

Figures

Acknowledgments

There are a number of people who have variously supported and assisted me in this project. I would like to offer my appreciation to them all: Katherine Ewing, Marro Inoue, John Comaroff, Katherine Murawski, Jennifer Hirsch, Kristina Troost, Kären Wigen, Andrew Gordon, Eiji Yutani, John Solt, Greg Leupp, Naomi Quinn, Mack O'Barr, William Kelly, Brett deBary, Harry Harootunian, Steve Snyder, Linda White, Susan Erikson, Sawa Becker, Miriam Silverberg, Margaret Lock, Arif Dirlik, Anne Imamura, Dennis McGilvray, Paul Shankman, Tani Barlow, Susan Napier, Lori Gruen, Jean O'Barr, and Nancy Rosenberger. I would also like to thank people at Westview Press who have been tremendously helpful in the book's production. Kellie Masterson, who subsequently left, first inspired me to do this project with Westview; Gordon Massman later became my editor; Connie Oehring has been project editor; and Diane Hess was an expert in copyediting.

Orin Starn has been a special colleague and friend, and for his constant input and support, I thank him deeply. My children, Adam and David, have lived through this project with me, from eating the *obentō* I made for them in Japan to the long months enduring my distractions and moods while writing it here. Their enthusiasm for my work, despite its definite "oddity," I appreciate tremendously.

It was my partner, Charlie Piot, who first suggested this book, and he has been tireless in offering assistance and encouragement of all kinds throughout its production. It is he who has wrapped its everyday labors within joys both profound and mundane. I have no words to express my feelings and thanks.

Lastly, I dedicate this book to my father, Lawrence True Allison, who lay dying as I started the last chapter (Chapter 1) in the room next to his in June 1994. My project of desire and the everyday became crystallized in its final moments of being written as I interacted with my father, who, stricken with brain cancer, had become largely disengaged from "reality." It was in this state that I read to my dad from a book he requested, Norman Schwarzkopf's autobiography, which I imagined he would hardly comprehend. As I read, his eyes would barely move and eventually close. Often I read when I thought he wasn't listening. Then I would read some more before tiptoeing away to continue the stories I was crafting next door about floating breasts and Japanese psychoanalysis. I kept expecting the two different endeavors I was immersed in, with their different sets of stories, to feel radically dissonant, even surreal. Yet, curiously, they never did, just as my prediction about the incomprehensibility of the book to my father was not borne out. Occasionally he would remark on what I had read, and always it concerned the same part—stories about Schwarzkopf's childhood, particularly his mother.

Desires somehow emerge out of life, even the life of someone who is dying. And they involve realness as much as fantasy. I learned even more about this when I returned at the end of June to my home in Durham, which was empty; my sons were with their dad in New York and my partner with his daughter in Colorado. All alone, I worked on Chapter 1. And every night at 11 I called my father, who had moved to a hospice. As a result of new pain medication, my dad had become reenergized and reconnected somehow to the world. He also had rediscovered the taste for food, which gave him the delight of a new discovery. We had long, engaging conversations in which he would tell me the details of each meal, lingering over its pleasures and, sometimes, its disappointments. And he always asked about my work, wondering how the chapter was coming and encouraging me with his interest. By the end of the month, it was the desire to answer my father's question about whether the chapter was done that inspired me to finish it.

I saw my dad again in August for the last time. The desires and grace with which he laced the last days of his life and which he was able to not only share with me but also connect to my work have left an indelible memory. I feel blessed to have this as well as a mother whose image of strength and beauty in the endless labors of love she extended to my father as he lay dying will inspire me forever.

Anne Allison

Introduction

Desire is both of and beyond the everyday. In an ad for running shoes, for example, the figure of a man jogging at dawn on the Serengeti Plain both evokes a fantasy of escape and invokes a disciplinary norm to stay fit. The bottom line for the ad, of course, is to create a desire to consume, the promise being that with the purchase of these shoes, the consumer can realize yet also transcend the daily exhortation to perform.

To say this differently, there is something both real and phantasmic about desire. Yet this notion seems contradictory. Isn't there a difference between the desire to be fit, for example, which is realizable, realistic, and, in these senses, real and the desire to escape routine everydayness, which, for most of us, is inescapable most of the time? But is exercise real or phantasmic? Certainly not everyone works out, and even those who make exercise a part of their reality may do so in order to pursue a fantasy about themselves. And are escapes from daily routines phantasmic or real? An escape from the everyday is far more realizable for some people than even fitness. But here too what is fantasy blends into (and becomes indistinguishable from) the real: A vacation away from work may be a means of ensuring a higher level of work performance when one returns.

Looking back at the ad, we can see that the desires structured here reflect a certain perception and experience of the world: one that demands hard work, values high performance, and pleasurizes the foreignness of other worlds. It is in terms of this worldview that the desire to run hard is not so distinct from the desire to travel to the Serengeti Plain. One involves a daily workout, the other large sums of money acquired from years of saving or a high-powered job. Both are signs of hard work that, captured through desire, suggest both the realization of a fantasy and the phantasmal quality of the real.

❧   ❧   ❧

My objective in this book is to contemplate how desire as something that segues both into and out of the realities of everyday life is configured through relations of production and consumption in late capitalist Japan. Specifically, I am interested in one domain of productivity: the home, where women, as mothers, have been major contributors, albeit "indirectly," as Mary Brinton writes (1993), to the economic success story of postwar Japan. It has been the role of stay-at-home mothers (not a viable option for all families, of course) to oversee and therefore ensure the high performance of Japanese youth as they labor through the ranks of a highly regimented and competitive school system. In this educated and disciplined body of the child are rooted the labor force and consumer population of the Japanese state. In both cases, what is demanded is "the production of an exceptionally competent society whose members work remarkably well but do not, should not, produce spectacle as individuals" (Field 1995:26).

What children learn in Japanese schools is far more than the academic skills they are world-renowned for mastering. More important is an attitude toward work: a willingness to bend to the authority of the school system and an ability to mimetically reproduce its structure of endless surveillance, constant exams, and habitual memorization. As Foucault (1980) has written about the shift in western sexuality from something that once was a mere act to something now thought to constitute the very foundation of the "true" self, the postwar educational model in Japan exceeds being "merely" a school system and extends into a regime of test-taking that produces and centers the Japanese self. In what is called Japan's *gakureki shakai* (academic-pedigree society), the schools one attends almost totally determine one's future career. In turn, admission into high school and college is determined by performance on entrance exams, the rigors and stakes of which are well known to even preschool-aged children. In the name of offering preparation for these tasks, a whole industry of supplemental training—cram schools (*juku*), preparation schools (*yobikō*), written guidebooks, and sample tests—has built up since the 1960s and further encases children in work schedules that leave little time for anything else.

In such a society, where children must labor as hard as adults and adults must work hard just to monitor and pay for their children's education, what has emerged is a "new continuity between childhood and adulthood through technocratically ordered labor" (Field 1995:68). One significant effect of this continuity, Norma Field suggests, is the disappearance of childhood and play in contemporary Japan. What she means, in part, is that for children desire has become either absent or contained. "Perhaps even more important than training students in specific skills is ensuring the formation of an attitude that will tolerate a lifetime of arduous and/or dull tasks. Hence, the significance of establishing a horizon of desire and a range of sensibility in early childhood that will be compatible with such a life course" (Field 1995:58).

Despite Field's illuminating insights about labor, I disagree with her assessment of the place that desire consequently assumes in such a social order. My view is that even in such a performance-oriented world, desire is not something that can be partitioned behind a "horizon" that serves to delimit it, if not eliminate it altogether. Such a suggestion implies a pure realm of play, desire, and childhood that could or did exist in a society not dependent on relations of late capitalist labor, as is the case in contemporary Japan.[1] I would argue instead that play and desire are always interconnected with the paths people assume to make a living, reproduce a community, and move from childhood into adulthood. In this sense, desire is not reduced or repressed as much as it is actively produced in forms that coordinate with the habits demanded of productive subjects. The "dullness" and "arduousness" of the tasks Japanese must execute over a lifetime, starting in childhood, are made acceptable not by the mere threat or force of an external structure (fear of failure on exams, for example). More powerful is the internalization of a different sort of process, one based on sets of desires that make the habitual desirable as well as making escape from the habits of labor seem possible through everyday practices of consumptive pleasure.

Mothers are doubly critical in such a process. They must ensure, on the one hand, that their children are working hard enough to realize their performative potential. Various strategies are used to achieve this end, including monitoring how children study at home, selecting supplemental education, and investigating the best school to fit a child's particular aptitudes. Throughout, women use maternal love and domestic space not, or not only, to provide a haven for children to escape from the labors demanded of them elsewhere, such as school. Rather, they suture home and motherhood to the very regime of a child's performativity, insisting that performance continue, even intensify, on familial turf.

On the other hand, the figure of the mother also appears, albeit in various guises, as a dominant motif in escapist leisure products, which are used, often continuously, by children as well as adults. This point is one of the main theses of this book: that the repetition and fetishization of certain motifs in mass culture— the infantilization of female sex objects (the *shōjo*, or young-girl phenomenon), voyeuristic peeping up skirts, sexual and sexist dominance, hugely sized phalluses, hidden pubises, eroticization of (female) underpants, breasts that alternate between being hidden and exposed—reflect, at least in large part, the desire to escape the performative ethos so insistently and incessantly demanded of contemporary Japanese and taught them, figuratively and usually literally, by mothers. I lay out the ways in which these fantasy configurations frame and reframe relations with mothers (who both metaphorically and metonymically stand for, or alongside of, wider economic and social relations) at great length in a number of the chapters in this book. Here, though, I would like to preface these later discussions with a word about why I find this terrain significant in terms of Japanese postmodernism, the state of gender politics and ideology today in Japan, and the combination of these two in what I will argue is a non- (or not strictly) phallocentric economy.

◦　　◦　　◦

Karl Marx wrote in the midnineteenth century about the phantasmic quality of commodities. Commodification transforms not only labor but also products of labor into "mysterious" and "enigmatic" things. "The form of wood, for instance, is altered by making a table out of it. Yet, for all that, the table continues to be that common, every-day thing, wood. But, so soon as it steps forth as a commodity, it is changed into something transcendent. It not only stands with its feet on the ground, but, in relation to all other commodities, it stands on its head, and evolves out of its wooden brain grotesque ideas, far more wonderful than 'table-turning' ever was" (Marx 1978:320). Once the humanness and particularity of our work is measured by a common standard, not only is the former eclipsed under the latter but also the latter assumes godlike power. Money can buy anything; hence, it is the possession of money, more than anything else, that determines the "properties and essential powers" of individuals (Marx 1978:103). Under capitalism, money serves as the medium of all value, though in and of itself it is nothing and its meaning resides in being a condensation and symbol of something else (labor). That people are mystified by this process, believing that the power of money exists as a natural property immanent in money itself rather than as its embodiment of labor and social relations, Marx referred to as the fetishism or reification of commodities. For him, this meant that the basis of a capitalistic economy and social order is a fantasy, one that turns "an image into reality and reality into a mere image" (1978:105).

Slavoj Žižek, writing in the late 1980s of what he calls the "post-ideological world" (and what I assume others such as David Harvey and Fredric Jameson mean by postmodernism), also speaks of commodity-based economies in terms of fantasy. The false consciousness of which Marx earlier wrote, however, has now disappeared, meaning that "when individuals use money, they know very well that there is nothing magical about it—that money, in its materiality, is simply an expression of social relations" (Žižek 1989:31). This does not mean that Žižek finds people today somehow more insightful about the illusory nature of commodification than they were at an earlier stage of capitalism. Rather, the point at which the "fetishistic illusion" sets in has merely shifted; now people know money is no more than an image and yet engage in its economy where use-values have been increasingly replaced and displaced by images (one of the primary definitions of postmodernism) all the same. For Žižek, then, the reality that Marx believed had an existence despite its distortions by fetishistic ideology no longer exists (if it ever did). Hence, images are (already) reality, and the real is (also) imaginary. Or, to say this better perhaps, the real and the phantasmic are so intertwined as to have become indistinguishable.

In Japan, the same process is at work, but with a particular twist. Under postwar conditions, it is academic performance that has increasingly become the common standard of value in the economy. This means that in the marketplace of careers and jobs, it is the test scores and schools attended as youths that operate as the currency of exchange for adults. There is nothing particularly magical about this. Almost none of the Japanese—children, students, mothers, housewives, white-collar workers, government officials, even teachers—I have ever spoken to about the *gakureki shakai* system believe that the inherent worth of an individual is ultimately measurable by how one performs on academic tests. There is a general consensus, in fact, that too much weight is placed on academic success in Japan, that too much of its schooling is geared to test-taking, and that too much pressure is placed on Japanese children to study. The fixation on exams, then, is seen as both excessive and arbitrary: the means adopted by the government and the economy to determine who in society should get the best jobs. Despite the ability to stand back, as it were, and critically assess the narrow and rigid fetishization that exam-taking assumes within the schools and society at large, however, there is a general acquiescence among Japanese to the *gakureki shakai* system in practice. I constantly hear Japanese speak of it as *"shikata ga nai"* ("that's life," "there's nothing one can do about it," "that's the way things are") and witness how central its rigors are in the lives of my friends.

This willingness to live by the rules of a system in which one does not fully believe is what Žižek means by living in a postideological world. "People no longer believe in ideological truth; they do not take ideological propositions seriously. The fundamental level of ideology, however, is not of an illusion masking the real state of things but that of an (unconscious) fantasy structuring our social reality itself" (Žižek 1989:33). For Žižek, there is a fusion between what is real and what is phantasmic; despite knowing that exam scores are merely an artificial and arbitrary assessment of value, one acts as if they were real anyway. We have become "fetishists in practice, not in theory" (1989:31) and engage in what he calls "ideological fantasy." This notion of the ideological fantasy strikes me as particularly apt for discussing Japan's economy based on the academic performances of test-taking. Further, it offers a way of talking about gender politics in Japan and what is distinct, if not altogether unique, about such politics in Japan's site of advanced capitalism in the postwar era. Namely, women are both discriminated against and pivotal to an economy so dependent, as is Japan's, on the academic performance of its children. It is women, as mothers, who not only oversee the educational regimens of their children but also, and more importantly perhaps, fuse these closely with practices of maternal nurturance, indulgence, and love. What is, on the one hand, ideological—that test scores are a sign of and for economic value—becomes sutured to and blurred with what is, on the other hand, a fantasy of imaginary union with mother. When mothers I knew, for example, played for hours with their children in ways that would also (and continuously) stimulate intellectual skills, this was a practice in which ideology and fantasy, work and play, discipline and desires became melded and blurred.

Only within the subject position of motherhood, however, linked as it is to both heterosexuality and family, are women assigned such a central role within the economy. In other spheres, namely the labor market and education, women do not receive parity with men. This inequity exists despite the fact that gender discrimination has been outlawed both in the school system (by the democratic constitution of 1947) and the labor market (by the Equal Employment Opportunity Law [EEOL] passed in 1986) and despite the realities that more women than men continue on to secondary education,[2] and 40.8 percent of the total Japanese workforce is currently[3] female (Buckley 1993). That is, although women are very much present in the spheres of both school and work, their presence is shaped by an ideology that considers their so-called real (or what Žižek means by fantasy) role to be raising families and managing homes.

To start with school: Although more women than men acquire a secondary education, far fewer women enter four-year universities (only 482,844 of a total of 1,861,306 entering universities in 1988), and far more are entering two-year junior colleges than are men (out of a total of 444,808 in 1988, 402,265 were women) (Buckley 1993). These statistics reflect the Japanese opinions gathered in surveys that it is more important and desirable for sons to attend university than daughters (44.9 percent for sons in contrast to 18.6 percent for daughters, according to a 1982 survey). The link between school and future career seems weaker for women than men, or, more accurately, the link between type of schooling and type of career is different. Indeed, Japan is the only industrialized country where education has a negative effect on women's employment (Tanaka 1995). The more educated a woman, the less likely she is to enter full-time employment and the shorter her average periods in the workforce (Buckley 1993). As many of my friends have told me, however, this does not mean that the education a woman gains has no value. Rather, it increases her desirability in marriage for, among other reasons, the skills it gives her as an "education mother" (*kyōiku mama*).

In the labor force, 50.7 percent of all women aged fifteen and above are employed in wage labor (Kawashima 1995), and they are working at older ages (the average age of female workers is midforties), beyond marriage (the majority of working women are now married), and for longer periods of employment (an average of 6.3 years of continuous employment in comparison to 11.3 for men) than ever before (Buckley 1993). Still, women's wages average only 60.7 percent of men's, 29.3 percent of women are working at part-time rather than full-time jobs (Kawashima 1995), and only 28.9 percent see their wages as supporting a household rather than supplementing its income[4] (Buckley 1993). Women definitely seem to be on a different track in the work world, yet such differentiation can no longer be officially mandated by employers. The Labor Standards Act has been dismantled that, by outlawing certain jobs and hours as "dangerous" to women and by securing maternity and menstrual leave, worked in the postwar era, as Sandra Buckley (1993) has noted, to protect the reproductive functions of women workers more than the workers themselves. Since the imposition of the EEOL, companies cannot restrict employment choices to women by enforcing, for example, mandatory retirement upon marriage or the birth of a child (as was common company policy before). Many workplaces have subsequently introduced a two-track system that allows women the choice between the *sōgōshoku* (career track leading to managerial positions) and the *ippanshoku* (secondary track). It has been found, however, that few women choose the former, and when they do, their attrition rate is 50 percent (Kawashima 1995).

Some feminist labor observers (Buckley 1993; Uno 1993; Kawashima 1995) explain the reluctance of Japanese women to choose career paths within the workforce as a factor of the masculine model on which those career paths (and the entire workforce itself) remain based. This model of working hard at a job to which one must be primarily and constantly committed is unacceptable for some women not only because it is difficult to maintain while also managing a household (for those who want to marry, which still includes the vast majority of adult women despite the fact that they are marrying later and having fewer kids[5]) but also because it is thought to be grueling, inhumane, and distasteful in its own right. None of the mothers I interviewed for a postdoctoral project on urban middle-class women longed for the work worlds their husbands inhabited that demanded long days of work, nights out drinking, and an obsequious demeanor in front of bosses. What they did admit, nonetheless, is that without a paycheck equivalent to that of their husbands, their life choices remained limited (divorce wasn't a possibility, for example, because financial independence would be so difficult) and their social status lacked the weight of that of a wage earner, particularly one who could support (rather than merely supplement) a household.

In a capitalist economy where money is the common standard of value, gendered ideologies have often operated to differentiate between the wage-earning labor of males and the unpaid domestic labor of (primarily) women in ways that come to be symbolized in a sexual language of phallic power. As feminists (see

Hartmann 1981) have long pointed out, the logic of commodity fetishism at work in capitalism all too easily fits and breeds a logic of phallic fetishism at work in an ideology of masculinism. Under both systems, one particular part of a much wider system comes to stand for primary value. For capitalism, this item is money, which condenses larger relations of production and reproduction into a single object. For masculinism, this object is the penis, which condenses wider relations of gendered work, family, sexuality, and procreation into a single body part. In both cases, there is belief in a hierarchy, in a value that supersedes all others and is used to judge everything else as subordinate. When both money and men are given such authority, a chain of social and economic relationships is likely to develop. For example, the domestic work of reproducing the labor force is kept unpaid, women are assigned this work and men are largely excused from it, wage labor is given more symbolic capital than domestic labor, and males have a social power and dominance that females lack.

Although all of these relationships are certainly present in contemporary Japan, I argue that the capitalistic phallicism they so strongly suggest is complicated by the presence of an additional social and economic fact: the value placed on academic performance and the central role assigned mothers in its production. But if women are so crucial in Japan's postwar socioeconomic formation, we must nevertheless be cautious in applying a "separate but equal" model that implies that domestic (by primarily women) and wage labor (so masculinized that women earn only 60.7 percent the wages of men) are equally valued. Such a model, put forth to describe Japan by some Japanese (including some feminists such as Iwao Sumiko), overlooks some key facts, including the powers and authorities that constrain women's full entry into the labor market; keep men from assuming domestic responsibilities (and also keep them increasingly from home altogether); require that more women seek employment to help defray children's educational costs but restrict these jobs to low-paying, part-time ones that can accommodate the management of home; and retain an ideological notion of male dominance that breaks out in patterns of wife abuse, sexual philandering, and macho aggression. The very ideology of marriage and family, in fact, particularly when encased in the rhetoric of Japanese cultural values with their demand for supreme self-sacrifice on the part of mothers, appears to embed women in an economy in which their value remains forever subordinate. Even as "education mothers," after all, the role assigned women is to oversee the movement of a child, particularly a boy, into a labor market to which full access is denied to women themselves.

This situation represents a tension or contradiction in the gendered embodiment of Japan's postwar economy. Although maleness and money still carry a primary value, the production of each is critically dependent on mothers. This means that although there is still some belief in the superiority of maleness, which leads to a fetishization of the distinguishing male body part, the penis, the "phallus" that emerges is also marked, sometimes scarred, by its dependence on female mothering. Therefore, in order to speak about the desires and fantasies that arise out of this complex set of gendered labor and familial relations in contemporary Japan, we cannot rely on a model of phallocentrism that treats the phallus as a pure and simple homologue to capitalist currency (as, for example, Goux does in a brilliant but Eurocentric discussion [1990]). By this line of reasoning, males seem to have direct access to power, while the bodies and labors of women are regarded as mere "lack."

Neither of these premises works in explaining the popularity of a recent bestseller whose central character is a young woman, Mikage, who loves to cook in a postmodern kitchen set up by her friend's mother, who was the father until his sex-change operation after the death of his beloved wife. The blended parent, Eriko, plays a key role in the story, but her identity is clearly as mother, albeit one whose adoption of this role has required that he get rid of his penis. This novel, *Kitchen*, is interesting not only for the portrayal of its three main characters, who are all ambiguously gendered and form a nonconventional family unit, but also for its author, Yoshimoto Banana, who self-identifies as a *shōjo* (young female) and crafts her writing style to be popular culture rather than high literature. Of even greater interest, given these two facts, is the choice of *Kitchen* by Japan's Foreign Ministry to dispense to all its international guests attending the G-7 (leading industrial democracies) summit held in Tokyo in 1993 as a way of informing them about the current (postmodern) state of Japanese culture (Treat 1995).[6]

In John Treat's analysis of *Kitchen*, he notes that "masculinity of any sort seems lacking in this novel, as does the sort of femininity predicated on an essential difference from masculinity" (1995:291). Further, he points out, there is an absence not only of explicit gender differentiation but also of sex. In this context, Treat characterizes the entire novel as suffused with the warmth and nurturance that emanate from the hearthlike kitchen and center the narrative even though the kitchen here is full of commodified contraptions that make it as much a fantasy of late capitalist consumption as anything "real." Linking this central trope of kitchen to the lack of gender contrast and sex, he argues that *Kitchen* presents "an anti-Oedipal scenario, one in which the kitchen and Mikage's recipes have superceded the traumatic conflicts that Freud predicts for us; in which *Kitchen*'s warm and fuzzy feelings have replaced the struggles that 'normal sexual development' mandates" (1995:291).

What can it mean that a novel whose only male adult has been dephallicized and transformed into a mother and whose primary character is a woman who shows love for others by preparing and serving them food has been selected by the Foreign Ministry as an exemplar of Japanese culture today? What it suggests to me is a highlighting of how central the role and figure of mothers is today in Japan and how downplayed, even problematic, the place of men and masculinity (as well as genital sex, but that's a matter more for the rest of this book) has simultaneously become. It further encodes an emphasis on the relations between people rather than on the individuality or individuation of particular persons. This feature of interrelationality resonates with what many scholars and officials have called Japan's "particular characteristic" of postmodernist capitalism. In Prime Minister Ohira's 1980 plan, for example, to "transcend the modern" by returning to a foundation based on Japanese culture, the invocation was made to a "restoration (*kaifuku*) of warm family relations in family, workplace, and local regions" (quoted in Harootunian 1989:80). Though Ohira was calling for the return of something he believed to be an old cultural pattern—the value of relationalism (*aidagarashugi*), which privileges the relations between human and human and part and whole—he was asking for this pattern to be channeled to the buildup of a new economic order. As Harry Harootunian has pointed out, this principle of relationalism intended as the undergirding of the Japanese cultural form of late-stage capitalism resembles a game of "scissors, rock, and paper" in that it opposes binary oppositions and is the opposite of a structure in which "sharp distinctions between two things" are made (Harootunian 1989:80). The latter structure is thought to characterize western thought and culture, of course; it is also the description given the phallus by such western psychoanalytic thinkers as Sigmund Freud and Jacques Lacan. Lacan, for example, treats the phallus as a signifier for power (the paternal signifier) that cuts off the imaginary merging between mother and child and forces the child (through the threat of castration) into the symbolic realm of language, rules, and taboos. In this model, the phallus is a social force that demands individuation of children away from others, especially mothers.

This phallic model is at the root of what Asada Akira calls the "industrial 'adult' capitalism"[7] that dominates in the west. Individuals internalize the phallic threat issued by the father, both his sternness and the fact that he is seen as a rival by the child. In doing so, they begin to compete with themselves and become workers who can labor independently with motivation that comes from the self. This construction of labor relations in the west (which borrows from Deleuze and Guattari) is strikingly different from the capitalistic model at work in Japan that Asada calls "infantile capitalism" and characterizes in the following way: "The Japanese family is an essentially maternal arena of '*amae*,' indulgence, and both the father and family are softly wrapped in it. . . . In Japanese companies, the clever management, rather than mobilizing the entire company around its positive leadership, functions as an apparently passive medium which prompts agreement to be spontaneously formed from the bottom up" (1989:276).

Once again, then, we've returned to mothering as the key, "indirect" as this may be, to the economic productivity of Japanese capitalism today. And once again, we hear it spoken of in terms of desires that "softly wrap" Japanese subjects within regimes of work that are expected to yield high performance. How to treat this model of mother-dependent economic values in a symbolic currency of sexual desires is the project of *Permitted and Prohibited Desires*.

❧   ❧   ❧

I would like to say a brief word now about the chapters that follow and their organization. Each is informed by the set of material relations in postwar Japan that I have laid out in this introduction, and each is driven by my aim to question how these relations are organized, escaped, contested, revealed, and problematized in forms of desire that are at once permitted and prohibited. By these descriptors, I mean to show how desire is something that is constructed both as a part of our everyday work worlds (hence, permission) and as something that takes us beyond to a place that feels refreshingly transgressive (prohibition, often staged).

Given the nature of my own desires in this project, to both understand something of the terrain from which desires are being produced and pursued in the Japan of the 1980s (my main historical focus, which bleeds both forward to the 1990s and back to the entire postwar period) and come up with analytical means by which to make critical sense of these behaviors, I am faced with a major and certainly unwieldy task. I also feel that there are few, if any, models I can follow. I am dealing with a place that does not fit easily or cleanly (as perhaps no place does these days) into any one theoretical or ethnographic paradigm. Japan is non-western but no longer "traditional"; it is at a late stage of capitalism but in a form that is recognized by many to be culturally "Japanese"; sexuality assumes patterns here in sites as different as the family and mass culture; and gender relations are incredibly complex in ways both real and phantasmic. To deal with such complications, I have made choices in both the parameters of my study and the methods I have adopted in carrying it out.

First, I pursue common themes in my study of gender and sexuality that are traced throughout all the chapters and therefore provide a common focus. These include looking at escapist and work-oriented desires that are embedded in an economy that values money and hard (i.e., academic) work and that accompanies a sexual symbolics that resists rigid characterization as either phallocentric or matricentric.

Second, the research methods I use are both varied and experimental. I rely on the anthropological conventions of fieldwork and ethnography in only two of the chapters, which draw on a postdoctoral research project I conducted in a Tokyo neighborhood among middle-class Japanese mothers in 1987–1988. In the other chapters I look mainly for sites or practices of cultural behavior that I analyze as being paradigmatic of wider relations involving labor, performance, desire, and fantasy. Many of these are texts, such as particular kinds of stories, scenarios, images, or gazes, that I argue are especially good arenas for studying desire, which is itself elliptical, indirect, and symbolic. I thus try to blend here methods of analysis that are both textualist and anthropological. The former I cull from film theory, psychoanalytic theory, feminism, and cultural studies, and I sometimes scrutinize a particular theoretical concept such as "the male gaze" for its applicability to a nonwestern setting such as Japan. For the latter, which demands an attentiveness to the everydayness of people's lives, relationships, and cultural categories by which certain texts acquire both meaning and pleasure, I experiment with a number of strategies. I use Japanese scholarship, research, and lay commentaries on material such as comic books; consider both the specific and general dynamics of social/economic/familial relationships that contextualize the reading of the stories I examine; and refer to discussions, observations, and knowledge I have acquired in the field concerning pleasure, desire, play, and fantasy. I have been unable to conduct surveys or interviews with audiences of specific texts, but, given the nature of my interest in fantasy and desire, I am not altogether convinced of the reliability of such a research technique.

In Chapter 1 of the book I lay out my scholarly position in terms of the academic fields within which I work: Japanese studies, anthropology, feminism, and cultural studies. Looking at the various academic blind spots I have had to navigate in doing this project—against theory in Japanese studies, for example, and sexuality in anthropology—I make a case for studying sexuality even in a nonwestern culture with a version of psychoanalytic theory.

In all of the following chapters, I look at ways in which everyday labors and performances are enmeshed within stories or fantasies of desire. Sometimes these fantasies appear to invert or disassemble labor sites; at other times they are worked into a form of labor as if to lace and embroider the latter with design. The former pattern is the one I trace first. In Chapters 2 and 3, I examine sexual motifs in the mass culture of *manga* (comics) and *anime* (animation). In Chapter 2 these are a form of male gazing found in cartoons and comics targeted to children. The look is fashioned as coming from male watchers, and the objects of the look are females who are either naked or eroticized at particular erotogenic zones (breasts, genitals, buttocks). Mothers whom I have spoken to find this form of presentation relatively harmless and view it as an acceptable forum for escapist leisure that takes children away from the hard work that otherwise consumes their lives (especially those of boys). Keeping in mind Field's observation of the continuity in labor between childhood and adulthood in contemporary Japan, I see in this child's practice a phantasmic practice of leisure that continues into the adult media I examine in Chapter 3. Here I focus on *ero manga* (erotic comics for men) with their dominant tropes of sadomasochism, macho dominance, analism, and deferral from genital copulation, which I read in terms of the consumptive patterns by which *manga* are engaged (typically outside the domains of home and work and in ways that make the reading compulsively fast). I suggest that part of the fantasy at work here is positioning readers in relations of voyeurism, fetishization, and consumption that permit but also contain the illusion of escape that is being fostered. That the stories highlight violence in ways that continually allow the violator to remove himself from the softly rounded body of a female I also read as a desire to extract oneself from mothering, both real and metaphoric.

In the next two chapters (4 and 5) I look at practices that build desirability into habits of everyday performance. Both of these chapters are grounded in the particular site of nursery school, specifically the nursery school my son attended in Japan and that I observed. In Chapter 4, I analyze the lunchboxes mothers make with great artistry and elaboration for their children to take with them to school and the contents of which children are required to eat in full as part of the disciplinary habits they must adopt at school. Mothers are thus expected to teach and encourage children with the aesthetics of food, and children, it is ideologically hoped, will consume rules and school order along with the scenarios of rabbits and bears designed in their lunches. In Chapter 5, I extend this analysis into other habits of labor and love that mothers are asked to perform for their nursery-school children. Throughout, the message is to utilize pleasures the mother is best able to provide toward the end of getting children to perform certain tasks. Making everyday work both habitual and desirable for children is the ideology of motherhood women are asked to uphold.

In the rest of the book (Chapters 6 and 7), I extend and problematize the linkage between performance and desire that I have treated more as two separate patterns in the earlier chapters. In Chapter 6, I look at a host of stories about mother-son incest that were faddish in a spectrum of the mass media in the late 1970s and early 1980s. In all, the elements of the narrative were so consistent as to form a mythic pattern: Boys, at the point of studying for entrance exams, become sexually distracted, which prompts their mothers, all following the model of the good "education mother," to assist them with sex. Except for the incest, all of these stories are realistic in the normative sense of children and mothers forming a labor team to study for exams. Troubling therefore the very meaning of normativity as well as transgressiveness (as incest would otherwise appear so clearly to represent), these stories point to both the phantasmic quality of the real and the real quality in fantasies. Chapter 7 concludes the book and is a multilayered analysis of Article 175, the law against obscenity that has remained basically consistent since its inception during Japan's period of modernization. Its injunction against the realistic depiction of genitalia (including pubic hair) seems mysterious given that, under the same law, almost every other sexual or bodily depiction, including sadomasochism and analism, is permitted. I question the notion of "obscenity" here, tracing how it allows for a very real policing of mass media at the national and public borders of Japan as well as produces pubic fantasies in very particular forms. My conclusion is that these sexual fantasies that circulate as mass culture wind up protecting and, in some sense, reinscribing a "real" center to the home. Mothers, of course, are who and what I see as occupying this center.

❧   ❧   ❧

At the end of all this, I feel my work has just begun. The story of *Kitchen*'s Eriko stays in my mind as that of a figure who represents a new kind of mother with ever new possibilities for sexual and gendered configurations. Here is a mother who has emerged out of a man. Elsewhere in the mid-1990s landscape of mass culture in Japan, there are increasingly such blended, rearranged, multiply constructed, cyborglike models of gender that defy any neat differentiations between femaleness and maleness. Ranma 1/2, for example, is a popular cartoon figure who, though a boy, morphs into a busty female when splashed with cold water. Does this mean there is a woman inside of every man—a mother, perhaps? Women are changing too. More female superheroes are stars now, some (Sailor Moon, for example) far more popular than any male superhero.

However, until men assume the responsibilities of child-raising and home care more than they have in the 1990s, the figure of primary childcare provider, with the ties this role has to academic performance, will remain gendered as mother. And along with this social fact will be the circulation of desires that both reframe this reality and promise its phantasmic escape.

❂ 1 ❂

Different Differences: Place and Sex in Anthropology, Feminism, and Cultural Studies

I begin this book with two stories. One is mine as I embarked upon a postdoctoral research project on Japanese motherhood in 1987; the other is of a Japanese professional as he embarked upon his career in 1932. I return to them throughout the book as a means of commenting on my project: to examine divergent, multiple, and sometimes inconsistent constructions of gender and sexuality in contemporary Japan and to test various theoretical strategies for understanding the specific conditions for, and operations of, gendered and sexual behaviors in Japan today.

Story 1

One morning as I was watching television with my children in Japan, the following scene caught my eye. Cartooned breasts, naked, rounded, and full, were rising slowly in a space resembling a sky. The context was a song about mothers, sung sweetly in the high-pitched voice of a young woman; the words about devoted mothers who tirelessly and selflessly tend to their children were printed at the bottom of the screen. As each verse of the song was sung, more realistic sketches of mothers were shown in various acts of taking care of and nurturing their children. Yet the floating breasts returned for every chorus, accompanying the refrain about motherly gifts for which children were told to be grateful.

I was struck, of course, not by the motherhood theme itself but by the device used to represent it: breasts. And they were not depicted as they might be on a show such as *Sesame Street* in the United States—by realistic photography in which a mother is seen discreetly nursing her child without revealing much, if any, breast—but rather cartooned and crafted to be explicitly naked and boldly displayed. These breasts lingered in my mind, fascinating to me in a way they

1

obviously were not to my Japanese friends. Most of those I asked, also mothers of nursery school children who watched *Ponkiki* in the mornings, had not even noticed the breasts. Those who had found them unremarkably "cute" (*kawai*). Yet as I reflected further, their unremarkable cuteness was what I found to be so striking—naked breasts standing for motherhood on a show targeted to young children.

Such a convention of representation was different from those with which I was familiar in the country I had just left, the United States. Granted, breasts generate no less interest or attention in the United States than in Japan, but the fixation in the United States is exclusively sexual, particularly in the medium of public or mass culture. This fixation undoubtedly accounts for the discomfiture that surrounds even the inadvertent slippage of maternal breasts into public view. It was not until summer 1994 that women succeeded in getting legislation passed in the state of New York to stem the discrimination they constantly face when nursing in public. Exposing their breasts was said to be inappropriate and unseemly, and women were told to vacate the places they were patronizing—stores, boutiques, restaurants, even alternative bookstores. One doubts that any of these women would be similarly challenged were their breasts revealed through sexy dressing.

In maternal representations across such U.S. media as television, cinema, magazines, and advertisements, mothers are invariably clothed. Their bodies are covered—and much noted when not, as when the pregnant Demi Moore posed nude on the cover of *Vanity Fair*—and their motherhood is largely conveyed through such depictions as hugging, reading a book to, or making breakfast for a child. Would the gaiety and fleshiness of the bouncing breasts on *Ponkiki* be regarded in the United States as offensive or just strange? Would such a depiction amount to a transgression of the boundaries by which motherhood is marked and womanhood differentiated? Turning from such thoughts on that morning, I focused my attention again on the screen. The breasts were uniformly shaped—beautifully round, filled full like balloons, with nipples erect—and each was moving with the gracefulness of a cloud gently percolating in the pastel, skylike background. What were these figures signifying of motherhood to the children parked in front of their screens? As objects, their qualities were mixed: firm yet light, full yet soft, steadfast yet playful. So too was the image projected of mothers: tender and sweet yet confident, commanding, and tough.

Significant as well was the fact that each breast was separate but indistinguishable from the others. This was a pattern of social organization I had noted at my son's nursery school, where crayons, for example, were not communally shared; each student was required to purchase crayons, and they had to be the same kind as every other student's. All the floating breasts in the mother-song cartoon were exactly the same; none was smaller or bigger than any other and each moved at exactly the same speed. Was the message one of uniformity of motherhood or uniformity of the mother-child relationship or uniformity of children's behavior as they enter the institution of school (or all or none of the above)? Or perhaps these repeated and duplicated images reflected the never-ending presence of a mother in her child's life.

The breasts were designed to both stand apart from and stand for the realism of motherhood. Crafted as self-propelled and disembodied automatons, they were larger than life as well as reductive—distilling mothers to their breasts but making these breasts-mothers into the very essence of life itself. Imaginary, these mounds were meant not only to represent mothers, as they unambiguously did in my mind, but also to elicit the response by my neighborhood friends that they were charmingly "cute." And then, of course, they were naked and drawn not with a staidness that muted or veiled the flesh but rather with a joyousness that celebrated and highlighted it. These were breasts that resembled apples—fresh, rounded, and firm. Wholesome but sensuous, they were a somewhat different evocation of motherhood than that triggered by the imagery of apple pie.

Story 2

In 1932 Kosawa Heisaku[1] traveled to Austria to deliver a paper to Sigmund Freud. Kosawa, the founder of psychoanalysis in Japan, was meeting Freud for the first time and presenting to him a theory he imagined the master would receive with great interest. Labeled the Ajase complex, his concept was built on the Freudian premise that children become adults by assuming their place within a social order whose rules and norms are internalized to shape the psychological desires and motivations of the self. Although Kosawa agreed with the assertion that a process of this kind is universal, he disagreed with the notion that it necessarily takes the shape of what Freud termed the Oedipus complex. The latter assumes a familial scenario in which the father's role is central: By threatening castration, he compels the child to individuate from the mother and form an identity and love object apart from the family (Freud 1964a; 1964b; 1975). By contrast, Kosawa argued, socialization in Japan proceeds according to a different set of family dynamics. Dyadic rather than triangular, the family centers almost entirely on the relationship between mother and child, and there is a gradual development of this bond rather than an abrupt disrupture at the time of adolescence. In a process that barely involves the father, maturation is marked by the child's ability to not break from the mother but remain bonded to her while recognizing her as a person rather than an omnipotent ideal and while overcoming the feelings of resentment this recognition initially engenders (Okonogi 1978, 1979).

Kosawa developed his theory of the Ajase complex to explain facts of Japanese social life different, he believed, from those implicit in Freudian concepts such as the Oedipus complex. He argued that these differences principally lay in three areas: dominant social values, family structure, and construction of self. Further, these areas intertwined, in Japan's case, in a complex of psychosocial behavior regulated by a maternal principle rather than a paternal principle, assumed to be universal by Freud. In this context Kosawa presented the tale of Ajase—the Japanese version of the Indian prince Ajatasatru, a contemporary of the Buddha whose legend appears in Buddhist scriptures—as paradigmatic of the process of identity formation in Japan. The story, briefly told, is of Queen Idaike, who desires a child as a means of keeping her husband as she ages and loses her beauty. Consulting a seer, she is told that a sage living in the forest nearby will die within three years and be reincarnated as her son. Unable to wait, however, Idaike kills the seer and bears a son shortly thereafter. But the queen's happiness is short lived, and fearful of being cursed by the dead sage, she tries twice to kill her desired child. Unsuccessful, Idaike accepts her fate and becomes a loving and dutiful mother.

Happy as a child, Ajase learns the history of his birth (and near death) at the time of adolescence. Disillusioned with the mother he has idealized, Ajase attempts to kill her. Failing, he is wracked with a guilt that brings on a disease so offensive that no one will approach him. His mother, however, stays by his side and attends to him with such love and devotion that Ajase loses his resentment of her. Idaike, too, forgives him, and the two reunite in a bond of mutual forgiveness.

As analyzed by Kosawa, the Ajase myth is a morality tale revealing the path a boy must take in order to mature into a man. According to Freud, of course, the Oedipus myth tells the same story, yet as Kosawa aimed to point out, the two versions are significantly different. In the Ajase myth, morality is reached through both guilt and forgiveness. Kosawa labeled Ajase's type of guilt penitence. He argued that penitence forms the basis of Japanese morality and suggested that it differs from the kind of guilt motivated by fear of punishment as modeled in the Oedipus myth and incarnated by Freud in his doctrine of the castration threat. Boys, according to this model, obey the social law tabooing sex with their mothers (incest) because they fear being castrated by their fathers. In the Ajasean paradigm, by contrast, boys are compelled to abandon not eroticism for their mothers but hatred and resentment, and they are motivated to do this by a mother's forgiveness rather than a father's threat. Although in both cases a loss ensues, its nature is different. Losing his mother as an eroticized object, the oedipal child starts to individuate from his family and separate more definitively from his mother. For the Ajasean child, the loss is of mother as an idealized figure, and this loss enables rather than obstructs the continuation of the mother-child bond.

The Ajase myth encodes a social value of interrelatedness and mutual forgiveness that is conditioned by a family scenario in which mother is dominant and father, almost irrelevant. This social value is productive of a self that is defined and developed in terms of social relationships. The psychosocial complex crystallized by the Oedipus myth is quite different: Social law is based on a set of clear-cut, incontestable rules (incest taboo), enforced by the phallic authority of fathers in families where mothers are mere objects of desire, and constructive of a self individuated from others.

The theory Kosawa crafted with the Ajase tale was intended, in part, as an application of psychoanalytic methodology to a cultural area where it had not yet been applied. In part as well, however, it was a treatise on difference, on the patterns of psychosocial behavior in Kosawa's part of the world that did not correspond to those described by Freud as being worldwide. And in this observation of cultural difference, Kosawa implicitly launched a challenge to the universalism and objectivism claimed by Freudian science and to its ethnocentrism and biases. Yet in Kosawa's mind at least, he was not contesting at all the value of psychoanalysis, and he remained until his death in 1968 a devoted practitioner and teacher of psychoanalysis in Japan. Still, what he sought from Freud in the 1930s—recognition of the validity of the Ajase complex and admission that different cultures organize the socialization and construction of the psyche differently—was never granted by Freud himself and was also not granted, for close to forty years, by members of the international community of psychoanalysts.

Divides Between Theory and Ethnography

I started with the stories of animated breasts and contested theories for several reasons. First, I wish to address at the outset the issue of positionality and the thorny and problematic enterprise of studying culture, particularly in terms of differences. In this age of multiple posts—postmodernism, poststructuralism, postcoloniality, postcritique anthropology—there are those who no longer recognize the presence of entities bounded by history, geography, and customs that can be properly identified and differentiated from others as cultures (West 1992; Ferguson 1992). "Properly" is the key word here, for no one is blind to the fact that people everywhere identify themselves in terms of communities that share forms of language, everyday practice, and sets of meanings. The objection to the word "culture," however, is to the tendency to reify and essentialize it. That is, to see behavior conditioned by a number of factors such as history, politics, and race as being only and thus unalterably cultural. "Culture," in other words, is a simplified and reductive descriptor; it hides complexities of realities whether intended or not.

One corrective to such myopia, of course, is to abandon using "culture" altogether. Another is to refocus attention on those ways in which cultural borders are crossed, transgressed, or made fluid: transnational globalisms, intercultural contact zones, people who have either multiple cultural identities or none (Gupta and Ferguson 1992). Still other scholars, those active in the debates about multiculturalism, for example, speak directly about difference and position: Multiple cultures are gathered within boundaries of nationality or have been seized under colonialist or imperialist ones (Spivak 1988; Mitchell 1995; Bhabha 1992). Within hegemonic power structures, different cultures are assessed and treated differently, and power compels the production or obstruction of cultural identities every day (Gates 1987) and in every part of the world, as we all are keenly aware from recent events. That culture must be studied within the context of power is almost a commonplace these days. Also, attention is increasingly placed on differences within groups or categories of people such as African Americans, women, homosexuals, and the U.S. middle class (Lorde 1992; de Lauretis 1987). The positionality each of us assumes in different groups is also critical: We all are products of multiple factors, histories, and relationships that affect our experience of and treatment within (not so) shared identifiers. Thus from many different schools of thought and many kinds of political activists we hear that identities, including those recognized as somehow cultural, are shifting and unstable rather than timeless and fixed, and differentiated and power-laden rather than singular, unified, and pure.

None of the foregoing is new, of course, but I am coming to the first point I wish to make with my stories. Namely, being an anthropologist these days or one who is committed, for whatever reason, to studying the behavior of people who share some, and to some degree, common boundaries is exceedingly tricky; those of us who proceed anyway do so warily, as if there were land mines on our path ready to detonate at any minute. As I choose an image from a Japanese children's show and use it to ponder conventions of representation, meanings of the female body and nudity, and practices of motherhood in a land where I am considered by everyone around me a nonnative and outsider (*gaijin,* a term that means literally outside person and one that even the women I became closest to never fully abandoned), I am faced with the possibility that I am just making up a story. I see in these breasts something paradigmatic of what my later research revealed of mothers, motherhood, and mothering in the Tokyo neighborhood I studied, yet these breasts shaped a story for me in a way they did not for my Japanese friends.

I could call this story the art of anthropology—seeing and depicting human behavior in novel ways that open up understanding—and yet this art is uncomfortably close to what Malinowski called the anthropologist's "magic" (1922): the wand we wave that clarifies the realities of others based on our training as anthropologists and our skills as ethnographers. Malinowski has been rightly criticized for the arrogance of what Clifford calls his assumption of "ethnographic authority" (1988): speaking for a group of which we are not a part and with a representation that is crafted by us and neither solicited nor necessarily approved of by them. Anthropologists have been heavily bombarded by both internal and external critiques since the early 1980s over just such issues as the position we take in studying cultures and cultural difference (Clifford and Marcus 1986; Marcus and Fischer 1986; Said 1978, 1989; Alcoff 1991). As a result, many have taken a turn toward reflexivity, studying ourselves and the groups of which we are members or, when studying others, inserting ourselves clearly and visibly in the process.

Yet in such trends as turning away from other cultures and turning more toward ourselves, we run the danger, of course, of slipping back into the ethnocentrism and cultural narcissism we had intended to escape. We study ourselves so as not to impose our categories onto others, but then we produce and use theories that reflect only our own realities and retain rather than challenge the old power structures. Cultural difference, that is, stays at the periphery of theory. Feminists of color, for example, have noted that although their work is increasingly assigned in women's studies classes in universities across the country, it is included much more for the worlds they describe than the theories they present.[2] These works are brought into the curriculum to overcome and correct for cultural bias, but differences (racial, ethnic, cultural, gender, sexual) are often simply reghettoized rather than integrated into theory.

Feminist anthropologists (Babcock 1993; Behar 1993, 1995; Lutz 1990, 1995) have similarly noted that the theoretical canon taught in graduate programs of anthropology rarely includes the works of women such as Ruth Benedict or Elsie Clew Parsons and even more rarely the works of such interesting minority women as Zora Neale Hurston and Ella Deloria. As Behar further elaborates, Margaret Mead, one of the most popular anthropologists, who found a way of making cultural difference interesting and relevant to the masses of nonacademics, is typically taught in introductory classes. Because she is categorized as a good ethnographer or good crafter of ethnographic stories, her work is relegated to the backwaters of theory. Such is also the fate of others similarly categorized. For example, Laura Bohannan, also known as Eleanor Bowen, adopted a style of imaginary realism in the 1950s that is thought to be quite chic today. Her ethnographic novel *Return to Laughter* is also a staple in introductory classes.

My point is that we need to find and explore new paths in integrating cultural studies (meaning here the study of culture[s] whether in anthropology, cultural studies, or other disciplines) and theory and that as cautious as we need to be, we also need to take risks. I feel this need to be particularly pressing in my own specialty, Japanese studies. As Kosawa discovered more than half a century ago, Japan is all too often relegated to a case study from the viewpoint of western academics. Freud read Kosawa's paper on the Ajase complex not as a theory, as Kosawa had intended it, but as an account of behavior so different that it was dismissed as theoretically irrelevant. As the Japanese psychoanalyst Okonogi Keigo wrote in the late 1970s about Kosawa's theory of guilt based on penitence, "To the eyes of Western people under the sway of the paternal principle, this Japanese type of mentality naturally appears to be an emotionalistic subjectivism lacking in social ego" (1978:98). Difference gets translated as lack.

In my own discipline of anthropology the study of Japan has been positioned primarily by lack as well. Japan remains far more peculiar than mainstream, and the works of our practitioners are considered far more as contributions to the ethnography of Japan than as contributions to the theories of anthropology. There are historical reasons for the antipathy toward integrating such studies into the theories advanced in this discipline. Scholars of Japan, as of other cultural areas such as South Asia and China, have been traditionally trained in area programs emphasizing the study of the culture's language, history, and literature and deemphasizing theoretical or disciplinary training. Yet in Japan's case, there are other resistances. It lacks the scholarly prestige of cultures such as India and China for reasons not altogether clear to me, and as an economic superpower that is racially and culturally nonwest, it sits uneasily in the popular and academic imagination. It is neither third world as we have come to define it nor first world when this is categorized as the United States and Western Europe.

Thus Japan needs to be studied and complexified beyond the stereotypes imposed by popular culture and the press,[3] and such studies can be used to challenge an outdated world order that lingers in the theoretical trends of the academy. As I discovered when working for my Ph.D. in a top-ranked anthropology department known to emphasize theory, work on Japan was not encouraged, and the area itself was considered almost innately or automatically uninteresting. As many of the faculty told me over the years, no anthropologist of Japan had yet made a valuable contribution to anthropological theory except for Ruth Benedict, who, due to the exigencies of war when conducting her research, never even set foot in Japan.[4] One professor refined his view to state one day that anthropology should be training students to study Japan, but he specified that what was needed in this area was "village studies"—that classical trope of anthropology that denotes the study of "primitives" (and one this particular anthropologist had never pursued). What a misreading of Japan today, I thought, and what an interesting commentary on anthropology.

Now, more than ever, is the time for the study of Japan to break outside the boundaries of parochialism and area studies to become a subject that challenges old theoretical and ethnographic borders and helps produce new ones. Kosawa addressed this need in one way; I attempt to do so in others.

Divides Between Gender and Sexuality

There are other reasons I began this book with the stories of motherly breasts and rejected theories. They raise issues about different borders: those involved in the study of sexuality and gender in a milieu that is nonwest and those concerning my multiple identities—feminist, anthropologist, mother, scholar of Japanese studies, Anglo academic. In this case, I lay out the terrain first and return to the stories at the end.

Within the field of Japanese studies the subjects of gender and sexuality are new, though the research on gender and feminism has progressed solidly and vibrantly over the past few years. This research includes the work of Jennifer Robertson on the all-female theater revue, the Takarazuka (1989, 1991); Miriam Silverberg on the café waitresses and *moga* (modern girls) of the 1920s (1993); Sandra Buckley on Japanese feminism and gender-bending in popular culture such as karaoke and comic books (Mackie and Buckley 1985; Buckley 1991, 1993); Kathleen Uno on the ideologies of "good wife/wise mother" (1993); Margaret Lock on women's life cycles, medicalization, and menopause (1990, 1993); Vera Mackie on feminist history (Mackie and Buckley 1985; Mackie 1988); Robert Smith and Ella Wiswell on the sexualized lives of rural women in the village of Suye Mura (1982); and my own study of corporate entertainment and the staging of masculinity in hostess clubs (1994). Within some of these works and those of a few others, sexuality as the way in which people organize, imagine, and experience sensual relations has been a subject given initial recognition. As an area of research, however, it remains underdeveloped; treated by Japanese scholars almost exclusively within the framework of reproduction and physiology, sexuality has been neglected by most scholars in the United States, who see it as a peripheral, irrelevant, or suspicious scholarly subject, as I have discovered from reactions to my own work.

This disregard of sexuality is not limited, of course, to the field of Japanese studies. Even within feminism and gender research, sexuality is sometimes ignored or minimized. For example, in two recent books identified as studies in feminist anthropology—*Gender at the Crossroads of Knowledge: Feminist Anthropology in the Postmodern Era*, edited by Micaela di Leonardo (1991), and *Feminism and Anthropology* by Henrietta Moore (1988)—the subject of sexuality barely comes up (Ann Stoler's article "Carnal Knowledge and Imperial Power: Gender, Morality, and Race in Colonial Asia" in the *Crossroads* volume is the one exception). In neither volume is there a heading for "sexuality," "sex," or "desire." In Moore's book the topic is subsumed under "sexual division of labor" (with references to "changes under socialism," "capitalism," "origins," "inheritance/descent systems," and "as defined by state"(245) and in di Leonardo's, under five headings: "sex differences and primatology," "sex-gender system" (a reference to Gayle Rubin's terminology and referring here to only one page), "sexism" (by far the most comprehensive heading with thirteen subheadings and multiple references), "sexual division of labor," and "sexual orientation" (two references)(418).

By contrast, in two other recent books—*Dirty Looks: Women, Pornography, Power,* edited by Pamela Church Gibson and Roman Gibson (1993), and *Sex Exposed: Sexuality and the Pornography Debate,* edited by Lynne Segal and Mary McIntosh (1993)—both volumes of essays by feminists in various fields and disciplines,[5] the focus is on pornography because, as both characterize it, this is *"the* feminist issue of the decade" (Clover in Gibson and Gibson:1). Here the authors write explicitly and primarily about sexuality, which they study and theorize through such arenas as identity, race, gender, fantasy, power, pleasure, censorship, sadomasochism, performance art, cinema, representation, and commodification.

As stated by Segal and McIntosh in their introduction to *Sex Exposed,* the aim of the authors is to question why recent feminist debates so persistently return and reduce to the topic of pornography and use feminism to obstruct rather than advance sexual research. Speaking for western (and, one might add, primarily white and middle class) feminism, they argue that the subject of gender became mired in a politics and polemics over pornography in the early 1980s following a number of significant moves by leading feminists. These centered around the issue of the imbrication of power and gender that operates in a society-politics-economy of male domination and female oppression such as is found in the United States.

The focus was originally not on pornography but on rape, which Susan Brownmiller (1975) argued was more about violence than sex in the 1970s. This position was soon modified, however, by feminists such as Andrea Dworkin (1981) and Susan Griffin (1981), who believed not only that all rape is about sex but also that all male sexuality is about violence. In the 1980s Catharine MacKinnon extended this argument further, writing that sexuality is the vehicle by which men oppress women and women become alienated from themselves: "Sexuality is to feminism what work is to marxism: that which is most one's own, yet most taken away" (1982:515). In her highly influential work, MacKinnon stressed that it is sexuality that shapes gender and not gender that shapes sexuality. By sexuality she meant specifically male sexuality, a construction of sexual desires where only men are subjects and women are only objects. Within this asymmetrical power relationship, women acquire their gendered identity: "This, the central but never stated insight of Kate Millett's *Sexual Politics*, resolves the duality in the term 'sex' itself: what women learn in order to 'have sex,' in order to 'become women'—woman as gender—comes through the experience of, and is a condition for, 'having sex'—woman as sexual object for man, the use of women's sexuality by men" (531). The motto "Pornography is the theory; rape is the practice," coined in 1979 by Robin Morgan, reflected the view that pornography is the everyday practice that most visibly and concretely embodies the eroticization of male sexuality and female oppression at the core of gendered relations in U.S. society today.

Since the mid-1980s feminists have aligned themselves differently and often oppositionally on the issue of whether this assessment of pornography is an accurate one and whether, accordingly, censorship of pornography should be demanded or resisted.[6] The point I wish to raise here, however, concerns less the history or politics of this debate and more the meaning it gives to sexuality. How is this term used and why is it so central to gender discourse in some schools of feminism and not in others? One difference between the orientation of the authors in the two sets of books I mention is that in *Dirty Looks* and *Sex Exposed*, the cultural context is entirely the United States and Western Europe; in *Feminism and Anthropology* and *Crossroads* it is cross-cultural with western cultures barely represented. Is the difference, at base, then one of geographical and cultural (what anthropologists would call ethnographic) site? Certainly the empirical observation that Segal and McIntosh use to introduce their volume—"Pro-sex or anti-sex, Western cultures remain sex-obsessed. This is why the issue of pornography just won't go away" (1993:1)—is far different than the statement of purpose advanced by Henrietta Moore: "Anthropology is in a position to provide a critique of feminism based on the deconstruction of the category 'woman.' It is also able to provide cross-cultural data which demonstrates the Western bias in much mainstream feminist theorizing" (1988:11).

In her book and di Leonardo's *Crossroads*,[7] emphases are on division of labor, kinship, and the state (and, in di Leonardo's book, colonialism and colonialist histories). Gender is located within those relationships that organize who labors at what; with what respective values, authorities, and constraints; under what controls by the state; and with what patterns to descent, marriage, and family. In both books as well, weight is placed on overcoming the biases that westerners have applied in analyzing the lives of (nonwestern) others. Moore writes that the confluence of these interests has characterized feminist anthropology from the start, an anthropology that, apart from a few early pioneers (such as Margaret Mead and Ruth Benedict), began in the early 1970s with the two groundbreaking anthologies *Women, Culture and Society*, edited by Michelle Rosaldo and Louise Lamphere (1973), and *Toward an Anthropology of Women*, edited by Rayna Reiter (Rapp) (1975).[8] In both these volumes, the authors aimed to write women into an ethnographic record that, produced by a male majority and masculinist bias in anthropology, had hitherto privileged the social lives, labors, and roles of only men. This stage of what Moore labels the "anthropology of women" was critical, but it was more "remedial than radical" in her estimation, and more ethnographic than theoretical.

Given that so much feminist scholarship of all kinds has been ghettoized or disregarded in anthropology on the basis of its "ethnographic" associations with women (Behar 1993), Moore's distinction is troubling. Her point, however, that this earlier work adopted rather than challenged anthropological conventions in its study of women is correct. Yet if it added little to the theoretical development of anthropology, feminist anthropology in the 1970s was at the forefront of feminism, a status it can no longer claim. Reflecting that decade's social and feminist interests in the issues of gender and power, the so-called ethnographies of women provided cross-cultural data and social scientific, mainly materialist, analyses of what the editors of *Woman, Culture and Society* stated to be the "universal subordination of women." Conducting fieldwork in specific locales, these feminist anthropologists studied the roles and positions women assume in production, reproduction, ritual, education, kinship, storytelling, leadership, and decisionmaking. Based on their findings, they developed models explaining and predicting the conditions under which female oppression is most likely: when the domestic and public spheres are most segregated; when women are isolated within homes and from one another; when males don't participate in childraising and the female assumption of this responsibility is culturally devalued; and when women lack control over the products of their labor and lack access to social arenas such as law, education, and politics.

The tendency of this earlier work to generalize or universalize relations of gender asymmetry on the basis of localized fieldwork has been heavily critiqued and largely overcome in feminist anthropology of the 1980s and 1990s. Further, scholarship has advanced in two main directions (which, being more theoretical in Moore's mind, she labels "feminist anthropology"): (1) gender has replaced women as the object of inquiry, and (2) the practice of anthropology is no longer adopted as is but remapped according to a critique and deconstruction of its various biases (ethnocentrism, sexism, heterosexism, academism) and omissions (power, gender, sexual orientation, race). Beyond this there has been diversification and difference: Some advocate the pursuit of feminist ethnography (i.e., Abu-Lughod 1990), and others question its viability (i.e., Stacey 1988). Some adopt postmodernism in their feminism (i.e., Kirby 1989, 1993; Haraway 1991), and others caution against it (Mascia-Lees, Sharpe, and Cohen 1989). Some use transcultural methods and theories to study gender cross-culturally, and others argue that such usage is inevitably Eurocentric (Strathern 1987b). As with trends elsewhere in academia and feminism, there is also the move away from collapsing and homogenizing such identities as women, men, and gender and such relationships as oppression, dominance, and power.

Not all feminist anthropology in the 1980s and 1990s has been devoid of broad-based schematizing, but it has been developed more productively in other directions, namely toward finely tuned analyses of specific historical and cultural settings where gender and power are given a careful, complicated account that in turn challenges tendencies in western feminism to essentialize, reduce to, or universalize Eurocentric categories of gender. The articles compiled in the di Leonardo collection all follow this trend or that of deconstructing anthropological paradigms for their biases (hence the comprehensive "sexism" heading). Moore takes this direction as well by emphasizing change and variation in her study of the intersection of cultural constructions of gender and relations of economics, politics, and intercultural contact in a number of societies at different historical moments. She sees trends (similar responses to similar conditions of industrialism, colonialism, and capitalism) but also particularities (differences of culture, history, race, class). In both the di Leonardo and Moore volumes the authors concentrate on the politicized relationships of production, reproduction, and kinship (the main words in Moore's chapter headings are "kinship, labor, and household," "status," "position," and "women's lives"; and in di Leonardo's, "gender" coupled to each of the following: "kinship," "reproduction," "cultural politics," "labor," "colonial history," and "anthropological discourse"). Both authors also concur with a position voiced powerfully by Michelle Barrett (a sociologist whose feminist materialism is highly anthropological) that since forms of patriarchy have both predated and outdated capitalism, sexism is a behavior that has both cultural and economic determinants and cannot be reducible to mere material conditions (1988).

Still I am left with the question, Why is the subject of sexuality so underrepresented and understudied in these works by feminist anthropologists? It is not totally absent, of course. In the genre referred to by Moore as "anthropology of women" there are several ethnographic accounts in which women's sexuality is explicitly covered. *Nisa* by Marjorie Shostak (1983) is memorable in part because of the openness with which it gives voice to Nisa's sexual histories—an aspect of the book not unrelated, I imagine, to its popularity in introductory classes. Margaret Mead as well, of course, wrote numerous ethnographies—*Sex and Temperament in Three Primitive Societies* (1963), *Coming of Age in Samoa* (1928)—describing and analyzing the sexual trysts, maturations, and relationships of various peoples. Even in what Moore considers to be the genre of more theoretical work, that which is more deserving of the descriptor "feminist," there has been scholarship on sexuality: Esther Newton's *Mother Camp* (1972); Gayle Rubin's "Traffic in

Women" (1973) and "Thinking Sex" (1984); Carole Vance's edited volume *Pleasure and Danger* (1984) and her work on the Meese Commission and obscenity laws in this country (1990, 1992); Peggy Sanday's *Fraternity Gang Rape* (1990); and the various studies stemming from mainly culturalist, structuralist and interpretivist perspectives analyzing the sexual in codings of cultural meanings. These latter studies include *Sexual Meanings: The Cultural Construction of Gender and Sexuality* (1981), edited by Sherry Ortner and Harriet Whitehead; the prolific scholarship by Marilyn Strathern (1984a, 1984b, 1987a, 1987b, 1988); and *Nature, Culture, and Gender* (1980), edited by Carol MacCormack and Marilyn Strathern.

There is also burgeoning research in the area of lesbian and gay studies in anthropology, led by such scholars as Kath Weston (1993), Elizabeth Kennedy (1995), and Gayle Rubin (1973, 1984). These works, though compelling, are few and far between (and almost totally ignored by Moore and di Leonardo in the histories they write of feminist anthropology). Why is their attention to sexuality so exceptional, and why is there this apparent chasm between feminist anthropologists who tend to exclude sexuality in their studies of gender and feminists in other fields (in the *Sex Exposed* and *Dirty Looks* volumes, contributors come from such fields as film studies, literature, English, psychology, psychoanalysis, journalism, political activism, and cultural studies) who have so eagerly taken it up? The difference cannot be due simply to the place of study. A recent anthropological volume focusing entirely on the cultural context of the United States—*Uncertain Terms: Negotiating Gender in American Culture* (1990), edited by Faye Ginsburg and Anna Tsing—for example, includes only one out of nineteen essays that specifically deals with the matter of sexuality (significantly, it is authored by Carole Vance and concerns pornography). The rest address such topics as abortion, evangelism, amniocentesis, the workplace, and reproductive ideology; these articles include references to sexuality, but their primary foci are elsewhere.

Perhaps, as the literary theorist Eve Sedgwick puts it (1990), the study of sexuality is simply not coextensive with that of gender. Although sex and gender are related, she notes, they are not the same thing; and whereas in some ways they are intertwined, not all aspects of sexuality reflect back on gender (some aspects are determined more, for example, by race or class).[9] Gayle Rubin has made the same point. After advocating for the linkage of the study of sex(uality) and gender in her 1973 article "Traffic in Women: Notes on the 'Political Economy' of Sex," she reversed this position in 1984 (in "Thinking Sex: Notes for a Radical Theory of the Politics of Sexuality"). Here she writes that a radical theory of sex is inhibited by certain cultural assumptions about sex that are common among westerners, namely that both conventional genital intercourse between heterosexuals and nonconventional sensual behavior between same-gendered individuals are gendered acts. Yet sex, Rubin argues, involves other factors that have little or nothing to do with gender, such as erotic tastes in position, mood, and activity. She therefore concludes that whereas feminism is aimed at the study and eradication of gender oppressions, it is less attuned to the presence of sexual oppressions and, moreover, adheres to a gender politics that actively militates for a sexual correctness experienced as oppressive by some feminists including herself. As Sedgwick also states, feminism may not be the best site for studying sexuality.

Disciplinary and Theoretical Divides

If sexuality is not the shared feminist issue that gender is, then those who study it are motivated by something besides mere feminism per se: political activism, for example, or disciplinary orientation. It is the latter I am interested in here. Is there something about not only feminist anthropology but anthropology more broadly that inhibits research on sexuality these days? Anthropology has certainly not always been so reserved on the subject. In the late 1800s and early 1900s it was widely included in the grand typologies that sought to document as many behaviors of as many people worldwide as possible and to categorize them according to evolutionary stages or cultural types (e.g., Frazer's *Golden Bough* [1959] and the Human Area Research Files[10]). In the smaller-scale ethnographies of localized groups begun at the turn of the century as well, sexuality was routinely included in the shopping list of social facts to be described about a particular people. And in certain cases the ethnographic lens was turned entirely on sexual behavior, as in Bronislaw Malinowski's memorably entitled *The Sexual Lives of Savages in North-western Melanesia* (1929). Yet recently, apart from those studies already mentioned and work in the singular paradigm of psychological or psychoanalytic anthropology (the research of Gananath Obeyesekere and Gilbert Herdt is notable here[11]), sexuality as a subject of inquiry noteworthy for the ethnographic research it yields and cutting-edge theory it provokes is practically dormant in anthropology.[12]

What accounts for this lack and why is the situation so different in fields such as cultural studies, film studies, English, and literature, where the work of scholars like Eve Sedgwick, Kaja Silverman, Judith Butler, Slavoj Žižek, and Linda Williams richly proliferates around the subjects of desire, fantasy, sexuality, and sexual identities?[13] I suggest that there are two major reasons: ethnographic (geographical and cultural locale), as already discussed, and theoretical (an aversion on the part of anthropologists to psychoanalytic theory, which is the primary paradigm for the study of sexuality by western scholars today). Simon Watney, for example, cites psychoanalysis as the framework guiding his analysis of the mass mediazation of AIDS (*Policing Desire: Pornography, AIDS, and the Media* [1989]). As he puts it, psychoanalysis is attentive to the unconscious and the disjunctures between what we speak literally and the symbolic meanings of our speech (10). Watney, a lecturer in the history and theory of photography at the School of Communication, Polytechnic of Central London, and an AIDS activist, also writes in this context that the relation between anthropology and psychoanalysis should not be a "boundary dispute." He argues, following Paul Hirst, that the issue should not be determining "where 'the psychic' ends and 'the social' begins" because "social institutions and cultural formations by no means exhaust the sphere of the social. . . . There are socio-cultural forms which are a part of the psychic domain and parallel and intersect with other social relations" (Hirst cited in Watney:xi).

As stated here, Watney's position would not seem radical or even objectionable to most anthropologists. Any graduate student who has been schooled in the canon of Émile Durkheim, Max Weber, Marx, and Freud, after all, has been taught the significance and nonliteralness of symbolic behaviors as a commonplace. The resistance to psychoanalysis lies elsewhere, occurring less because of its recognition of the psychic domain and more because of its construction of this psyche in terms of a western self. More accurate perhaps, the two become conflated and the theory as a whole gets rejected because of its Eurocentric orientation. To use psychoanalysis on a nonwestern culture is deemed a form of anthropological colonization, as seeing others in terms of a concept of self that is (only) western. And as Foucault has importantly pointed out (1980), the belief that sexuality forms the core of our identities as individuals is the result of a particular chain of developments in western history. And as unique to the west as this history is, so is the cultural formulation of sexuality—what Foucault branded "scientia sexualis." Sexuality becomes the object of multiple scrutinies—medical, administrative, moral, scientific, personal—that encourage an autodiscursiveness about sex that not only situates the "truth" of the self but also hegemonizes a social politics that people internalize through the body talk we westerners (mis)recognize as speech from and about ourselves. Psychoanalysis has been a part of this history and continues to support this ideology: roles, Foucault notes, which are naturalized under the rubric of western scientism. The suspicion with which he treats psychoanalysis is widely shared by many in the social sciences, including anthropology.

I sense that in my field anything to do with psychoanalytic theory is widely regarded as politically incorrect and narcissistically irrelevant. It is regarded not only as Eurocentric but as too "self" centered, too individualistic, too interpretive, too speculative, and, to be redundant, too psychological. As if psychoanalysis is the epitome of touchy-feeliness, endless graduate students have disclaimed to me any interest in psychoanalytic theory, refuse to consider its utility, and even question how the category of the unconscious could have any place in anthropological research. Those who study it—once a vibrant subdiscipline and still pursued by a small but active contingency within the discipline, including scholars such as Mel Spiro and Obeyesekere, who have attained disciplinary prominence—are marked by its peripheral status in anthropology, and those who do not take measures to distance themselves from its very language, as did one keynote speaker recently in a national anthropology conference. She used the concept of fantasy in her talk but borrowed its definition from the *Random House Dictionary*. The judgment is that using a psychological-psychoanalytic framework precludes analyses that are political, materialist, and historical. For example, the scholars versed in psychoanalytic theory in fields such as cultural studies, media studies, and film theory are often criticized by anthropologists for their analyses of popular or mass culture (movies, comics, books, television shows) and are said to be inattentive to such materialist and political questions as: Who produces these texts and for whom and with what agenda(s)? Who are the various consumers and under what varied conditions do they consume? What are the political and social milieus of a text's appearance and circulation? and How do the representations in a text resemble or deviate from the lives, experiences, and identities of the viewers away from their viewing of the text?

Yet does the adoption of a psychoanalytic perspective necessarily block the tracking of these other concerns? Further, why does the study of sexuality need to be dominated by or collapsed into the paradigm of psychoanalysis, making anthropologists so phobic of both? Also, why can't sexual research, both inside and outside a western context, learn from nonwestern scholars, utilize a mixture of paradigms, and adjust psychoanalytic theory to correct for its Eurocentrisms and limitations?

These, of course, are the challenges I face in developing my own work on gender and sexuality in contemporary Japan. And once again, the path feels treacherous. On the one hand, I share the concerns of anthropology, particularly as they have motivated research on gender—the material and political relations of reproduction, production, and kinship. I am interested in who labors at what in Japan, who reproduces whom, and how the institutions and conditions of the state, economy, and localized environment (including those of race, class, and ethnicity) interact with cultural practices and meanings to affect the ways people live their lives, relate with others, and identify themselves. I pursue these issues in terms of gender; I do so as well in terms of sexuality, but here, on the other hand, the directions taken by anthropology serve me less well.

Movements in other fields have been far more useful, namely those that have studied desire, fantasy, images, and representations as vehicles that form and inform the channels by which persons interact with each other and assume identities and activities they recognize as sexual. Much of this work analyzes, as I do, a society situated in what Jameson has called late capitalism. In such a society, the currency of economic exchange is increasingly that of commodities and images that, as W. F. Haug has pointed out (1986), borrow on and produce sensual illusions and pleasures. Accordingly, as Baudrillard has also noted about such societies widely categorized as "postmodern" (1981), there is the propensity toward "simulacra": We invest (socially, economically, and psychically) more in the fantasies with which we represent, imagine, and escape our realities than in the realities themselves. This is the Disney World syndrome—a made-up world that becomes more compelling and believable than the so-called real world that exists outside its gate. And this simulacrum signifies not only a disjuncture between the materiality of the relations by which we live, labor, and reproduce and the images by which these are represented but also a tendency for the latter to take on a life of their own, becoming a crucial determinant of who and what we are.

Given such material conditions, the study of fantasy and imagery becomes socially critical rather than whimsically playful. The best work along these lines, as far as I'm concerned, explores the issues of representation, identity, and desire in terms of historically and socially specific contexts. This work is, in other words, as attentive to relations of power and materiality as to symbolic imaging. These works include bell hooks's *Black Looks* (1992), on the ways that race, desire, power, and culture intersect in the racialized setting of the United States today; Susan Bordo's *Unbearable Weight: Feminism, Western Culture, and the Body* (1993), on anorexia and body imageries in the contemporary United States; and Simon Watney's book that I have mentioned already, *Policing Desire: Pornography, AIDS, and the Media* (1989). Unlike all three of these works, however, mine is situated in a culture that is nonwestern and that, although sharing forms of political economy and the prominence of fetishized commoditization with countries like the United States, has had cultural traditions and social histories that are very different. The question here is, Can any usage of such terminology as "fantasy," "desire," "imaginary," or "identification"—developed as it has been within western theorizing as particularly if not exclusively psychoanalytic—be applicable to a cultural setting other than that for which it was originally conceived? That is, despite the empirical fact that "sex" (variously named in Japanese as *sei,* which is an all-encompassing word including the meanings of both gender and sexual activity; *seiyoku,* which means sexual desire; *yokubō,* which means desire; and *sekusu,* which comes from the English word and is a more direct word for sexual acts) is publically discussed, imagistically evoked, and widely commodified in a presence that often feels ubiquitous in Japan, how can one even call this "sexuality" let alone ruminate on its constructedness in a language that assumes a construction of sexuality and self that is western? With these questions, I at last return to my stories.

Toward the Bridging of Divides: Playing with the Phallus

Ponkiki was not the only children's show I watched while living in Japan. Years earlier I viewed a cartoon series called *Machiko-sensei,* which was targeted to an audience of young teenagers and featured a junior high school teacher named Machiko-sensei. An attractive unmarried woman, Machiko-sensei is a conscientious teacher whose devotions congeal around a group of male students who endlessly and variously require her help. During one show she disguises herself as a professional wrestler in order to save one of her students who has decided to quit school and enter the ranks of wrestling. By the end of the program she has accomplished her mission, yet in the course of events her shirt gets removed three times, showing her exposed breasts to the eyes of all. Machiko-sensei is embarrassed each time this occurs and looks down. By contrast, those who see her, including spectators to the wrestling, some of her colleagues, and her group of favored male students, all gaze at her breasts greedily. Instantaneously, Machiko-sensei covers herself, removing from sight a part of her body that ought, as her gestures tell us, not to have been seen.

This combination of showing but not showing female flesh, or revealing it but only through a display or look that is constructed to be socially illegitimate, is one that I saw repeatedly in a variety of media in Japanese popular culture aimed at both children and adults. For children, this display was featured in television shows and in *manga* (comic books). In, for example, the program *Doraemon,* aimed at children as young as three, a robotic cat (Doraemon) lives with a well-meaning but socially awkward boy, Nobita-kun. In one show Nobita uses a special telescopic machine given him by Doraemon that he can use to see far distances and through walls. Its viewfinder focuses inadvertently on Sakura-chan, the only girl in his gang of friends, who is standing naked before she enters her bath. Nobita gasps and sweats profusely before Doraemon sensibly turns the viewfinder away. The show's viewers have been given a peek at Sakura-chan's naked body, but the look is constructed to be surreptitious—not Nobita's right and against Sakura-chan's will—much like that of a Peeping Tom. So too are the displays of female flesh in a number of children's comic books I examined for the chapter in this book entitled "A Male Gaze in Japanese Children's Cartoons." Bodies of females are presented provocatively, either without their clothes on or through clothing as if it were being imagined away. By strategies in both the imagery and narratives, girls are scanned up their skirts to show panties; sketched in ways that exaggerate buttocks, crotches, or breasts; and situated in stories of violation, duplicity, or force by which their clothing is removed and their nakedness seen. These girls may be attacked, but the attack comes almost invariably as the means by which to remove their clothes; once naked, the girls are rarely attacked further or touched in any sexual manner except by sight. Once again, we are allowed to look, but the look is figured to be somehow sneaky, transgressive, illicit, or circuitous. It also stops rather than precedes further activity and is over almost as soon as it is begun.

In media aimed at older audiences as well, a similar construction persists. Naked breasts are an image that circulates widely and openly in popular culture. They peek through sheer blouses on the women drawn to sell products on public billboards and in advertisements; are revealed on the models posed in glossy photos appended at the front and back of news magazines; get pulled out of the clothing worn by actresses in the course of being raped or pursued on prime-time television shows; and are paraded in the multiple places that categorize themselves as overtly sexual—the "sex page" in sports newspapers, handbills for call girls, photographic advertisements for various sex services, articles in entertainment journalism about the sex trade, late-night "adult hour" on TV, and sexually explicit magazines. In such urban centers as Tokyo, in fact, breasts are visually inscribed almost everywhere. Yet despite this visibility, the inscription often seems qualified, as if permission to view or disrobe has not exactly been given after all: Women who strip are in a dirty place and are dirty themselves; those who show their breasts in "respectable" venues smile girlishly and sweetly as if they are not exposed at all; and females who wind up with their clothes off in movies, television shows, and particularly *manga* (here I am referring more to the comics read by teenage and adult males, as covered in Chapter 3) do so overwhelmingly as the victims of attack, violence, duplicity, or rape.

The contrast between these breasts and those that float so cleanly but assuredly across the frame of *Ponkiki* is striking. Besides unambiguously projecting goodness, the motherly breasts display their nakedness directly and invite a view that is unobstructed, permissible, and prolonged. By contrast, those shown on programs such as *Machiko-sensei* and *Doraemon* or so excessively in erotic comic books and on late-night TV are constructed as if looking at them is not quite allowed. Whatever meaning and pleasure these breasts hold is conditioned by this seeming ambiguity: A sight is both revealed and concealed in almost the same instant, and a look is split between seeing freely and being forbidden from seeing at all. Set against the fleeting or contorted visions—the woman tied from head to foot and whose breasts stick up between two segments of rope—the breasts on *Ponkiki* appear accessible and whole.

There is another difference. The breasts on *Ponkiki* stand alone, whereas characters to view them are added in the rest of the examples. In *Machiko-sensei* these are the spectators; in *Doraemon,* the boy Nobita; in erotic comics, the various watchers, desirers, and violators of women. In *Ponkiki,* by contrast, the breasts appear comparatively unmediated, closing rather than opening the distance between object (of sight) and subject (who sees the object.) Drawing in a viewer, by contrast, emphasizes not only the viewer-viewed relationship but also the very act of viewing itself. Obviously, the children watching *Ponkiki* can only view the breast image, yet the impression of a relationship not limited to the visual is at least created. Even more important, when viewers are included in the image, they are almost always and exclusively males who look at bodies whose nakedness exposes them to be invariably female. Looking at breasts, then, has become an activity and relation that is not only situated by gender but also differentiated by it: Males look; females are looked at. Of course, even girls watching a show like *Machiko-sensei* can see the teacher's breasts, but to look at them with the desire and interest exhibited on the faces of the spectators in the show, they need to identify as male.[14] By contrast, whereas the breasts themselves are obviously gendered on *Ponkiki* their viewership is not. Anyone, is the suggestion, can relate to and find pleasure in a mother's breasts.

Moving from *Ponkiki* to *Machiko-sensei* and *Doraemon,* we see a move from one type of breasts to another, from one kind of viewing to a different kind, and from an audience that is gender neutral to one that is gender marked. This change reminds me (with resonances as well as dissonances) of the story told by Freud and retold by Lacan and psychoanalytic feminists of gender formation in the west in which penises and phalluses figure centrally. Against this story and the one I have crafted with the breast images in contemporary Japanese popular culture, I wish to consider whether there is merit, and if so what kind and what degree, to Kosawa's assertion of a maternal principle at work in Japanese culture. My aim is smallscale rather than broadscale; I am attempting not to develop a major thesis as much as to give play to an idea that, in the course of getting played out, will point to one way in which a study of subjects so fractured and inhibited by the divisions I have pointed out (ethnography/theory, gender/sexuality, Japan/the west) might be better integrated.

The Freudian-Lacanian story, briefly summarized, goes as follows.[15] Children are raised primarily by mothers. Children love and depend upon their mothers but also come to resent them for the independence with which they come and go and for the fact that they provide but also deny caregiving. This relationship is central to how children develop, how they imagine their bodies, conceptualize the outside world, and navigate a course between the two. Increasingly, what type of body parts a child has (most critically, whether there is a penis or vagina) will affect how the outside world and her or his choices within it are perceived. Also, relations with the mother come to depend upon and differ according to a child's anatomy, which determines what positions are assigned the child both inside the family and later outside in society. These assignations, formed and informed as they are by mother-child relationships (and the rules, losses, and taboos surrounding them) will condition the identities children assume as gendered adults, and the constellation of desires and fantasies that shape their sexualities.

In Freud's version of the story, adopted and modified by Lacan and his followers, the most crucial part of psychosocial development comes with the chain of events he referred to as the Oedipus complex. As discussed earlier in relationship to Kosawa, these are developments that start between the ages of three and five and are precipitated by the child's desire to genitally engage and satisfy the mother and by the social prohibition, the incest taboo, that this desire triggers. Though this is not the first constraint to the satisfaction of desires the child has encountered, the incest taboo is different: It is instituted by social law (versus a mother's refusal to nurse, for example) and enforced (symbolically if not literally) by the figure within the family given social authority—the father. The threat made "in the name of the father" and by the "paternal signifier" of the phallus is castration of the boy's penis.

Coincidental to this developmental moment is a significant look (Freud 1961) made by children in the direction of someone who is differentially gendered to themselves: Girls see fathers or brothers; boys see mothers or sisters. According to Freud, the girl understands immediately the significance and signification of the penis; she lacks it, wants it, and knows it is superior to what she has (Freud 1964a). From this point on she develops an envy of penises based on the recognition that a penis both satisfies mother (unlike what she has can) and stands for a social power females lack (as true for her as for her mother). As a result, a psychic "wound" of inferiority is formed like a "scar." In this state girls enter the phase of the Oedipus complex wherein castration, as Freud puts it, has already occurred. By contrast, a boy's awareness of gender difference comes later, cushioned as he has been by his penis, which he, like the girl, has already come to associate with the phallicism of the social order (feminists such as Jane Flax [1990] and Jane Gallop [1982, 1985] have noted the importance of this recognition and pointed out that it precedes rather than accompanies the Oedipal moment with the implications this bears for gender formation). It is only with the threat of castration that he "sees" the genitalia on a female for the first time, and he interprets what he sees less as a matter of gender difference than as the absence of a male penis. Projecting his own body onto hers, in other words, he sees "lack," a "terrifying sight," in Freud's words, that compels him to both look away and retreat from his incestual desires. He assumes a position of phallus-in-waiting, identifying with his father and biding his time until he can take an object choice outside the family whom, as feminists have pointed out, he will be able to dominate more than he could his own mother.

What is critical to this story, no matter the version or the telling of it, is the importance of the phallus even when feminists such as Jessica Benjamin (1988) and

Nancy Chodorow (1989) dispute the signification given it by Freud or Lacan. For both of the latter, the phallus, in its absence or presence, is what distinguishes and therefore constructs gender. And for both, this construction is not a pre-given but comes about at the developmental point in the child's life when she or he confronts castration: The girl realizes that she is already castrated; the boy faces the fear that he might become so at the hands of his father. Whereas Freud associates the symbolic meaning given to the phallus with the anatomical organ of a penis, Lacan disclaims such a connection: "The phallus . . . is not a fantasy. . . . Nor is it as such an object. . . . It is even less the organ, penis or clitoris, which it symbolizes" (1977:79).

In Lacan's mind, the phallus is a signifier that is "intrinsically neutral" (Ragland-Sullivan 1982:10) and is not just any signifier but the signifier par excellence; it signifies signification itself and the entrance of a person into the realm of the symbolic, which conditions sociality. To become social entails a loss—a "pound of flesh," Lacan calls it at one point, referring to the "realness" of any bodily need, part, or function. And from the stage of the "real" to the "imaginary," in which the child imagines a closeness to mother and a satisfaction of needs and demands that cannot be sustained, he or she enters the "symbolic," a third stage wherein the duality of mother-child is broken. In this stage, it is the phallus, operating as what Lacan calls the third term, that ruptures the imaginary and illusory identity between mother and child and comes to represent the pursuit of that which can compensate for ("petit objet à") this loss as well as loss and lack in general; that is, each child strives to be social, a condition that can never, in fact, be attained. Whereas everyone, as a member of society, is equally "lacking," people play their lack out differently on the basis of gender: Males disavow their lack and displace it onto women (being allowed to imagine that they lack "lack"), and women symbolize lack for men (imagining that their "lack" can be filled only by a male phallus). The phallus in the symbolic, then, acts as both sign of gender difference and signifier of (the object of the other's) desire (Grosz 1990).

Feminists have critiqued both the Freudian and Lacanian theories of the phallus on various grounds: They place too much importance on the oedipal and post-oedipal stages of development with an emphasis on the role of the father and too little on the preoedipal stages, where the mother's power and influence is primary; they describe as universal and socially necessary what are behaviors, relations, family structures, and sexual orientations unique to the social and historical context of western societies today and, in doing so, naturalize and endorse a model that is heterosexual, heterosexist, masculinist, and individualist; and despite Lacan's insistence to the contrary, phalluses refer far more to the penises of men than to the vaginas or clitorises of women (Flax 1990; Cixious 1980; Irigaray 1985; Benjamin 1988; Chodorow 1989). Few critics, however, have denied that there is a descriptive accuracy to the phallocentrism theorized by Freud and Lacan. We do live in a social world where males have more political power and authority than do females; where male identity, more so than female, is configured in terms of an autonomy and individuality that demands separation from mother and a repudiation of the femininity she represents; and where males are encouraged to be active, aggressive, and dominant in sexual activity. Women are positioned to be more passive and to be objects rather than subjects in sexual relations. And penises are a symbolic marker of phallic power just as the lack of a penis denotes the respective absence of this power granted women.

Can these same characteristics describe a society such as contemporary Japan, which is often portrayed as equally, if not more, chauvinistic, patriarchal, and oppressive to women than a society such as the United States? I would say broadly that male economic and political privilege and male sexual rights apply but not the renunciation of motherhood and individuation from mothers/others.[16] But whether penises are symbolic markers of power is the question that most interests me. Children in Japan are not required or even encouraged to pull away from their mothers at the stage of developing their social identity nearly to the extent that they are in western societies such as the United States. Further, such is particularly true for boys: In Japan, boys feel greater pressures to succeed academically and thus their need to rely upon mothers for assistance in the long years of their studies is greater as well. Two chapters in this book ("Producing Mothers" and "Japanese Mothers and *Obentōs*") deal with the relationship between mothers and children and how an ideology of motherhood as well as institutions such as the school system materially as well as symbolically produce and monitor the identities of adult women as devoted, loving, self-sacrificing, and "good" mothers. I also question the gendered and sexual implications of an intensified mothering in the lives of specifically boys at the time of adolescence in the chapter "Transgressions of the Everyday."

Another social fact critical to the manner in which Japanese children mature and develop their identities is that adult men, particularly in the middle class, are increasingly absent from the home. As many studies have shown (e.g., Yuzawa 1982), their social roles are deemphasized within the sphere of domestic life, where mothers, by contrast, assume the position of authority. Thus women are the primary caregivers not only in a physical sense but also in a social and psychological one and not only when their children are little but also as they grow into adults. Of course, as numerous western feminists such as Chodorow (1989) and Dinnerstein (1976) have pointed out, such a division of labor that assigns women to the primary role of caregiver is often connected to the devaluation of women and femininity in a society. Whether or to what extent this is true in Japan has been debated extensively both by feminists studying Japan, such as Vera Mackie and Sandra Buckley (Mackie and Buckley 1985; Buckley 1993), and by Japanese feminists such as Ueno Chizuko (1987), Mizuta Noriko (1995), Aokī Yayoi (1986), and Tanazawa Naoko, Horiba Kiyoko, and Takayoshi Rumiko (1988). Yet it must also be pointed out that mothering is given much recognition and value in Japan, far more so than in the United States, for example. Coupled to this is the relative absence, both physical and symbolic, of fathers. Relatively absent as well, then, is the phallus bearer so essential to the psychoanalytically inspired theories of western identity formation and male dominance, particularly in comparison to the intensiveness and extensiveness of the mother's role in Japan. There, the mother's presence is compelled not only by cultural values and social traditions but by the school and exam systems.

Does this mean that Kosawa was right when he wrote, over fifty years ago and long before the competition surrounding the educational structure and the demands this places on mothers had escalated to the degree they have today, that Japan is a culture based on a maternal rather than paternal principle? In his scenario of the symbolic and the child's passage into it, it will be recalled, there is no mention of phalluses, the disrupture of the mother-child bond, an incest taboo enforced by father through punitive threats (castration), or females psychically wounded because they lack a penis. Rather, the one social rule the child must learn is how to accept the mother as a human being with desires and behaviors that exclude or decenter the child. Thus the child must abandon narcissism: There must be a readjustment of the idealization of mother as omnipotent and totally self-sacrificing and a willingness to remain bonded to her anyway. This stage of development, as Kosawa also stressed, is triggered by acts performed by the mother, who exhibits devotion and forgiveness toward her child, rather than by the father, who threatens punishment in his role as social and phallic authority. And as a result of successfully resolving what started as a rage against mother for her fractured mothering, the child emerges as a socially appropriate adult: one not individuated into an autonomous individual but rather a person who identifies and acts on the basis of social interrelatedness.

Rather than try to deal profoundly or in any sense absolutely with Kosawa's thesis and how relevant it is to describing social and political realities operating in Japan today, I merely question whether western-based psychoanalytic theory with its articulations of concepts such as the phallus can be meaningfully applied to a cultural context such as Japan. And to ask this I consider only breasts and the persistence with which they are fetishized in the mass culture of 1980s and 1990s Japan. What do they mean in terms of gender and sexuality? In particular, I am interested in the partial, fractured, and obstructed display of this common fetish. Always somehow veiled (even when naked), these breasts are popularized as an ambiguity; they are disclosed, yet the disclosure is qualified or immediately revoked. Breasts may be no more than implied or momentarily glimpsed before hiding again behind a shirt. Or if they are fully seen, the look is somehow halted or blocked or, just as likely, presented as a voyeuristic transgression that follows some form of accident, violence, violation, or deceit. In this configuration, not seeing is as crucial as seeing, and hiding the flesh is as critical as exposing it.

Interestingly, ambiguous is also how Lacan describes the role the phallus plays as the signifier supreme (1982:74–85): It symbolizes both loss (the "pound of flesh" one loses upon entry into the symbolic) and the substitute for what is lost (a simulacrum that is bigger and better than any "real" penis could be). Freud speaks similarly of what he calls the fetish (1961): what is used by a boy to turn his glance away from the mother on whose body the lacking penis has just been noticed. The fetish, like the Lacanian phallus, is a "compromise": It is an artificial substitute for what was never real in the first place. And as Freud stresses, the fetishist both knows and disavows its artifice. Yet even in this ambiguity—the substitute both is and is not what it stands for—the fetish acts as a "safeguard" against the threat of castration, compelling the subject into the symbolic and forever leaving its mark as the condition for being (westernly) social.

What is the parallel mark left on the Japanese subject as the condition of sociality? Is it that which compels the proliferation of breasts that now you see and now you don't and that differ from the visually consistent breasts shown on *Ponkiki*? If the latter are configured in some sense as imaginary, having an imagistic appeal that is immediate and direct, as if there is little separating the viewer from the breast, the former are marked by an intrusion—the sign of being ordered and monitored by a set of rules. What is this grammar and where is it coming from? I suggest that it derives from a pair of related prohibitions: not the taboo against sexually copulating with one's mother that is installed by the threat of castration but (1) that against expecting maternal indulgence and omnipotence beyond the age of narcissism and (2) that against the aggressive impulse, triggered by the first prohibition, to hurt or turn away from the mother/other. The latter, of course, is what Kosawa argued is the penultimate challenge facing a child as she or he acquires identity as a Japanese adult. And the reality in contemporary Japan, where the pressures to perform in an increasingly competitive school system are not only intense for children but intensify around mothers, whose role in supporting educational imperatives is so highly prescribed by the state, is that not all children succeed. Acts of violence by children against parents, typically the mother, are far more common in Japan than the reverse, and incidents of mother-beating intensify around the time of exam-taking, when the attentiveness of mothers is aimed at extracting a performance from the child. Other forms of child-perpetrated violence have become even more disturbingly commonplace, most notably, bullying (*ijime*): A group of kids targets, usually, one child who is younger or different (in ethnicity, background, physique, economic status, intellectual ability). The aggression leads, on occasion, to injury, murder, or suicide.

Rage and violence are often scripted into the scenes of fetishized breasts. Overwhelmingly (if not exclusively), the female is the victim and the sketched-in (male) viewer, the perpetrator. This violence, in its phantasmic transgression, represents one of the prohibited behaviors mentioned earlier.

The desire, however, to be completely and narcissistically indulged by the object of one's desire, is realized only with ambiguity. This desire is given form as the fantasy of seeing female breasts, but it is the incompletion of this wish that is so regularly and compulsively repeated; the female is distracted or disinterested, her breasts are shown but then covered, she is exposed but never possessed. Of course, the impression of indulgence is given: The imagery of even momentarily exposed breasts is so pervasive that the sight of naked breasts is a commonplace. Still, figured into the exposure is the persistent obstruction: the giving yet taking away that makes this image less a given than a compromise, and the look it engenders, one that is marked by forbidden desires.[17]

"Desire," as theorized by Freud and Lacan (and by Marx as commodity fetishism), is characterized by such impossibility. It cannot be realized as long as one remains within the parameters of sociality (the "symbolic" in Lacanian terminology, capitalism in Marxian). Yet the grammar of desire that emerges—conditioned as it is by the materiality of everyday life and the cultural and familial nexuses that inform what paths what people take to make what kinds of lives—does not prevent the production of pleasure as much as pattern it in terms that reflect rather than inhibit social taboos.

Such a statement is as true for people living in Japan as anywhere else, so the answer to my question about whether psychoanalytic theory (as well as other western-based theories) has applicability to a milieu such as contemporary Japan is yes. But the application is tricky. "Desire," "fantasy," "gender identification," "sexual aim," are the types of concepts that do not or should not free float over borders where differing sets of cultural categories and material conditions exist. Neither, however, should these concepts remain grounded and exclusive to one place, particularly if that place is the west.[18]

So rather than hesitate and fixate too long over the endless problems that adhere to a project such as mine, I choose to go forward. My main agenda of examining gendered and sexual behavior in contemporary Japan orients all the work in this book. In the following chapters I have tried a number of tactics, both theoretical and ethnographic, to accomplish this goal. In the process, I have also sought to tease and test the categories and techniques used by those of us who study these issues and, more important, to discover how they can be used most effectively.

❧ 2 ❧

A Male Gaze in Japanese Children's Cartoons, or, Are Naked Female Bodies Always Sexual?

In a cartoon show targeted to young children, a boy peeks at a female friend as she stands naked before entering the bath. In a cartoon aimed at older children, junior high school boys stare at their teacher's breasts as they are accidentally but repeatedly exposed. In a printed comic magazine geared toward junior and senior high school students, a girl's jeans are pulled down against her will and her body is gazed at by an entire auditorium of boys and men. In a comic book for teenagers, a girl is stripped of her clothes and hung outside a window to be viewed by a crowd of onlooking boys gathered below.

Within the genre of children's *manga*—animated cartoons and comics—in Japan, the image of males gazing at females who are either naked or shown in their underwear is a common motif (see Figure 2.1; also see Chapter 7, Figures 7.2, 7.3). Although this depiction could not be said to dominate comic imagery for children—not all *manga* include it, for example, and in those that do it may be central or only subsidiary—it appears consistently. Basically this image is structured as follows: A female who is a girl, a woman, or a girl transiting to womanhood has her clothes fully or partially removed, usually by a male. This male and often others—a group, crowd, even an auditorium of onlookers—then view the female's body, positioned as it has been by both the events of the story and its illustrations to be on display. Occasionally no clothes are removed at all and the viewers peep up a skirt at panties or see a close-up of breasts or buttocks whose contours are visible through clothes. The female typically reacts with embarrassment if she realizes she is being looked at, and with humiliation if her clothes have been forcibly removed. The male's reaction is one of transfixion and immobilization; sweat pours down his face and he rarely does more than just stare. The scene ends here, crystallized into a still shot of male looking and female being looked at that almost never develops into further action or bodily contact.

FIGURE 2.1   The pervasive peepshot. Underpants, seen voyeuristically here, are
highly fetishized in Japan's sex industry and popular culture.
SOURCE: *Manga Goraku* (Manga Entertainment), December 9, 1994 (Tokyo: Nihon
Bungeisha), p. 42

In this chapter I examine two aspects of the previous image: its location within
a genre explicitly intended for children and its structure of a look at fetishized female bodies by male viewers whose gaze is illicit, coercive, and voyeuristic. Specifically my question is, Given that looking at female body parts is an act, relationship, and construction prominent in many other media and practices in Japan
where its meaning is clearly sexual, what meaning does this image have when its
context is a children's *manga*? Is the signification similar (and if so, what does this
say about sexuality in Japan) or different (and if so, what accounts for this difference)? In the medium of *ero manga,* for example—written *manga* also labeled
adult comics or men's comics—the imagery of female bodies displayed to empha-

size naked flesh is the most dominant depiction.[1] Almost as common is the addition of male characters who adopt various strategies (coercion, coaxing, affection, deception, abduction, violence, rape) and apparatuses (knives, cameras, binoculars, rope) to position the female, often unwillingly, as the object of their gaze. The look itself is characteristically drawn out as if frozen or in slow motion—frame after frame of a woman tied up, for example, with barely any change in the composition.

The meaning of such images is subsumed under the *ero manga*'s categorization as erotic (*ero*), which tallies with its objective of being a masturbatory device, according to one researcher (Ishikawa 1983),[2] and a device that "substitutes for real sex" when the latter is unavailable, according to another (Go 1981:261). One difference between the imagery of male gazing and female fetishization in *ero manga* (and in a new erotic comic genre for women called ladies' comics)[3] and children's *manga* is that only in the former may these images be followed by ones depicting sexual penetration, release, or intercourse. Even in the adult comics, however, still shots of naked female bodies being scrutinized, photographed, and leered at by gazing males often stand on their own, developing no further into a narrative of genital contact or climax.

My own interest in this phenomenon began in 1981 when I viewed an episode of a television cartoon called *Machiko-sensei*. In this show about a female junior high school teacher (Machiko-sensei) and her male students, the teacher is repeatedly shown in a state of partial nudity that draws the eyes and attention of her students. The scenes of female nudity and male looking in *Machiko-sensei* resonate with key elements in what was then a popular theory (in large part made so by Laura Mulvey's important article "Visual Pleasure and Narrative Cinema" [1975]) in western feminism, film theory, and art criticism generically referred to as the "male gaze."[4] According to this theory, the positioning of males (by cinema, pornography, advertising, art, capitalism, political relations, social practices) as the viewers of female nakedness has three critical components: (1) gender: the positions of looking are conditioned by and are the condition for gender difference (men look, and women are looked at); (2) power: positionality in looking encodes a power differential (lookers are empowered subjects, and the looked at are disempowered objects); and (3) sexuality: looking is stimulated by and the stimulant for sexual desire (looking produces sexual pleasure, and being looked at produces someone else's sexual pleasure).

Concurrent with my viewing of *Machiko-sensei* and exposure to western "male gaze" theory was my research on two adult practices in Japan that similarly raise the issue of how gender, power, and sexuality are both constructed and intertwined. One involved *ero manga* and their typically being read by teenage and adult males when they are away from home—when they commute to work on trains, take time off from jobs to eat noodles or drink coffee, or stand in a bookstore on their way to school or cram school.[5] The violence and obsession with control (silencing, restraining, immobilizing women) encoded in the sexual imagery of the *ero manga* are related, many have argued, to the manner in which they are read and the purpose they are, in part, expected to serve; that is, they release tensions from work and school and provide an alternative "text" (or "fantasy" in Kaja Silverman's use of the word[6]) for lives in which Japanese are heavily controlled by performance demands not of their own making.

These demands may also account for the fact that genital exchange, penetration, and release do not necessarily accompany acts of sexualized looking in adult sex comics. *Manga* and their deemphasis on genital copulation and orgasm are mechanisms that accommodate the commitments to perform at school and work at the same time they displace them. A *manga* can be read on the way to work, for example, and the looking it structures (consuming the text by reading, acting sexually within the text largely by looking) interferes far less with the performance demanded of a student or worker than would other formulations of sexual behavior.

The practice of Japanese corporations entertaining their male white-collar workers in places such as hostess clubs, where men talk sexually with women but where genital or ejaculative sex is deferred, is the second area I have researched that impinges upon issues explored here. In what are called *settai* (company outings) or *tsukiai* (get-togethers), men with an intracompany or intercompany connection pursue collectively an activity of play or pleasure as a means of solidifying their work relations. When such parties convene at a place with female servicers, there is much (hetero)sexual banter and allusions to or requests for further sexual intimacy. These imagined encounters are rarely realized; they are contained instead in talk, in references to how the eye/I of man sees woman. "Your breasts are big," "your legs are long," "what a pudgy body you have," "do you have any breasts at all?" punctuate and sustain conversation as a recurrent and ritualistic trope. Sexual interaction formulated as talk serves the business agenda of *settai* by providing a conduit for male bonding. Rather than being distracted by personal and physical intimacies with women, men (homosocially) focus on one another. Further, according to my research, flirting with women with whom genital contact is ultimately tabooed serves not only the interests of business but also the desires of men from various backgrounds, classes, and jobs.[7]

I argue in this chapter that there is a continuity between the images in children's *manga* of male looking and female display and the patterns of (hetero)sexual interaction in certain practices connoted as sexual and targeted to adult males (such as corporate entertainment and *ero manga*).[8] More specifically, I suggest, the continuity resides not only in the organization and meaning of sexual imagery but also in the positioning of males to be masterful viewers but passive and consuming actors—a position that feeds into relations of production and consumption assumed by adult Japanese males and a position to which Japanese children are being introduced, prepared, and schooled with the naked female imagery in the *manga* they consume as breaks in their early regimens of study and homework.

To make this argument I divide the remainder of the chapter into two sections. In the first section I examine western "male gaze" theories to understand what they say about the relations and structures that both compel and are affected by practices of male looking. Much of this theory is sophisticated and provocative and is useful in the examination of children's *manga*. Still, as I discover in this process, theoretical paradigms crafted in one cultural setting bear the imprint and specificity of that culture. Much of "male gaze" theory carries western assumptions about the construction of sexuality, subjectivity, and family dynamics whether these assumptions are stated explicitly or not (and they are usually not). My aims in analyzing this body of theory are to point out this constraint and to ask seriously how useful western-based theory is to those of us who study nonwestern cultures. My own field of Japanese studies has suffered, in terms of academic recognition as well as scholarly sophistication, for its deemphasis of theory. To abandon western theory altogether, then, is to lose not only symbolic currency but also exposure to important knowledge, research, and critical methodology. What of "male gaze" theory is culturally transportable? What questions are raised and what gaps are found when this theory, often treated as universal, is applied to a different cultural setting?

In the second section I consider certain stories and images in children's *manga* that situate boys to look at naked females. Deconstructing the relations and acts of viewing, I note structural consistencies: Boys look; females are looked at. Looks often follow action (violence, coercion) but rarely lead to more action (that is, to further bodily contact). Looking is both passive and aggressive. I also consider how and in what sense these structures define gender, sexuality, and power. These three components emerge from "male gaze" theory as critical to practices of male looking and are similarly relevant to looks in Japanese children's *manga;* but I argue that the construction of sexuality central to this theory is not necessarily applicable to the cultural context of Japan. Male looks in children's *manga* are sexual, I conclude, but the meaning and place of this sexual practice is acceptable for children in Japan and is continuous with practices adults assume in later life. Both these conditions challenge the construction of sexuality grounded in "male gaze" theory. As an exercise in the dialecticism between theory and practice, Japanese children's *manga* inspire a rethinking of theories on the male gaze. And an examination of one image in a medium used as diversionary, pleasurable play for children, reveals male looking in children's comics as having meanings for relations of production and consumption in Japan as well as for constructions of gender and sexuality.

Sights/Sites of Gender and Sex:
Western Theories of the Male Gaze

Freud, in his *Three Essays on the Theory of Sexuality* (published originally in 1905), treated scopophilia, or a pleasure in looking, as a normal aspect of sexuality. In children, whose sexual instincts are present but not yet directed to a sexual object, looking is one of several sexualized activities that is situated in the eye, one of many active erotogenic zones. Infantile sexuality is characterized by polymorphism and multicenteredness. At the time of puberty, the genital area emerges as the primary erotogenic zone, a sexual object is developed,[9] and sexuality is experienced differently according to gender (Freud 1975:73). Freud discusses scopophilia at this stage of sexuality—a sexuality now organized and unified under genital control—in terms of normalcy and perversions.[10] Measured by a standard of sexuality based in one's own genitals and directed toward the genitals of a gendered other, looking is a normal prelude to heterosexual intercourse and genital release. When scopophilia becomes itself an act of sex, however, Freud termed it perverse.[11]

Freud followed his discussion of scopophilia with one on sadism—the desire to inflict pain on others—which he considered the most common sexual perversion. Rooted in aggression, which is common in all humans, normal sexuality includes an aggressive component that, upon exaggeration, becomes sadistic and perverse. According to Freud, males are more sexually aggressive than females and far more likely to become sadists—defined as those who need to overcome the resistance of the sexual object by a means other than "wooing" (Freud 1975:24). Females whose sexual inclination is more toward masochism—turning the aggressiveness of sadism in on the self—tend to be objects rather than subjects of a sadistic sexuality in which scopophilia can be used as one method of generating pleasure out of pain extracted from another (23–26).

Looking, though a normal part of sexuality, becomes perverse, then, under two conditions, according to the Freudian model: (1) when it hegemonizes a sexuality that is supposed to be hegemonized by genitals and genital intercourse, and (2) when it is used aggressively and nonconsensually on a sexual object whose pain conditions one's own sexual pleasure.

The "male gaze," though not a Freudian term, refers to a process of looking that, like scopophilia, is sexualized and based in a relationship of dominance and inequality, if not necessarily sadism as clinically defined by Freud. The term has been employed by western feminists, film theorists, and art historians to refer to a process in which males are positioned to look at females who are positioned as the object of a male look. As stated by John Berger in his characterization of western nude painting, where only women are drawn naked, "Men look at women. Women watch themselves being looked at" (1972:47). Noting that the women are traditionally drawn with their eyes either averted or looking out, Berger argues that their nakedness is fashioned as a construct—what he calls "the nude"—that is intended to be pleasurably viewed by not the woman herself but an imagined male viewer. A woman is thus positioned as a passive object whose appearance inspires the active viewing and pleasure of a man. In this there is both a process of eroticized looking and a relationship of gender and power. He writes of the nineteenth-century painting *Les Oreades,* an oil pastiche of naked female bodies floating up to heaven who are turned (frontally) toward the viewer just as the bodies of the three male satyrs watching these females are turned (genitally) away: "Men of state, of business, discussed under nude paintings like this. When one of them felt he had been outwitted, he looked up for consolation. What he saw reminded him that he was a man" (57).

Berger, like other theorists of the male gaze, adopted the structure of Freud's model for scopophilia. Where some differ, however, is with the Freudian assumption that scopophilic practices stem from impulses that are ultimately biologic and in this sense both universal and eternal.[12] For certain scholars the stress is placed rather on constructions and the constructedness of looking. The argument is made that looking becomes a practice embedded with sexual and gendered meanings only within specific cultural and historical settings. Linda Williams, for example, in her book entitled *Hard Core,* observes that the pioneer motion picture photographer Eadweard Muybridge filmed women and men in strikingly different poses for his eleven-volume opus *Animal Locomotion,* published in 1887. In this work, a pictorial study of naked men, women, children, and animals performing short tasks and filmed in a series of instantaneous shots, the men are shown executing their routines in a perfunctory fashion with a minimum of accoutrement. Women's bodies and movements, in contrast, are supplemented by a series of props, gestures, and dramas. They are asked to move, for example, by blowing kisses, flirting with a fan, or twirling their bodies around in a dancelike motion (Williams 1989:41–42).

Thus although Muybridge considered his project scientific—recording the minute movements of the human body—he couldn't help recording also, according to Williams, social constructions of both body and gender that in the nineteenth-century United States fetishized the female but not the male body as an object of a sexualized look. As Williams points out, however, the new technology of the motion picture projector not only reflected an apparatus of looking that was already established but also enhanced and stimulated it (1989:46). In her view, shared by many film theorists, the technology of film, which is a technology of image making and illusion, advances mechanisms for looking at the same time it multiplies the pleasures produced by looking. As scholars such as Laura Mulvey have also argued, the spread and sophistication of, particularly, cinematic film gave impetus to not only a practice of visual pleasure but also the politics of gender and sexuality embedded within this practice (1975).[13] Males, positioned to look, are empowered by the proliferation and advancement of viewing technologies. Females, positioned to be looked at, are weakened by technologies that make images increasingly perfectible and the scrutiny and judgment of women as images increasingly harsh.[14] It is this power relationship that grounds and is grounded by cinematic viewing, according to Mulvey, and it is this power differential that stimulates pleasure—a pleasure in viewing that is or that can become sexual.

A wide range of feminists and scholars of various orientations and fields working in the west agree with parts of Mulvey's thesis.[15] The so-called antipornography contingency of feminists spearheaded by Andrea Dworkin and Catharine MacKinnon, for example, emphasizes the inequality of gender relations, which they argue is the very condition of and for heterosexuality as constructed in western societies. Never explaining the origins of either gender inequality or of a sexuality premised on this inequality, they nonetheless treat pornography as a representational format that literally and insidiously perpetuates both. When men look sexually, by this argument, they are likely to act sexually in a violent or degrading fashion. When women are looked at sexually, by this argument, they become victims in a construction of sexuality that can only hurt them (Dworkin 1981; MacKinnon 1979, 1984).

Feminists such as Dworkin and MacKinnon treat pornography as real. They argue that as a format that institutionalizes a scopophilia for men at the expense of women, pornography is a source of implanting relations of gender inequality within the society. Other theorists such as Kaja Silverman (1981), Mary Ann Doane (1983, 1990a, 1990b), and Teresa de Lauretis (1984, 1986, 1987) speak increasingly against such a reductionist position, crafting their own analyses of other forms of institutionalized looking, mainly film, as attempts to understand rather than merely condemn the mechanisms by which male looking becomes both pleasurable and erotic. Approaching film in terms of symbolism rather than realism, feminist film theory uses psychoanalytic models to argue that cinematic viewing is a process that builds on, exaggerates, and temporarily denies preexisting constructs of sexual difference. Although the arguments are highly sophisticated and dense, the basic starting point is an adherence to the Freudian paradigm of the Oedipus complex.

As Freud argued, a person doesn't assume or internalize a gender identity until this stage, when sexual development has advanced to being dominated by the genital area (1964a). Desiring, now genitally, the parent of the opposite sex, the child learns two social facts: (1) parents share a relationship of mutual desire and genital intercourse from which (2) the child is excluded. The child's place in the family is no longer centered by the mother's attentions and is now decentered by the parental bond of sex; subjectivity starts at this moment of genital awakening, gender beginnings, and the cultural imposition of the incest taboo.[16]

Though many feminists dispute the biological inevitability that Freud imputes to the Oedipus complex, many agree that as structured within western culture at least, a process such as the Oedipus complex establishes gender identity and does so on a principle of difference. As Freud states it, the anatomical differences between bodies have been seen but not perceived, particularly by the boy, until this time. Now males see the nakedness on a female for the first time as it were, and they both recognize and desire what is different about female bodies. Significantly, a boy's desire for his mother is both genital and genitally tabooed at this stage, and it is the father, with a penis larger than the boy's, who is the object of the mother's sexual interest as well as the social authority who enforces the taboo against mother-son incest. All of these desires, prohibitions, and recognitions become conflated at this point, according to Freud, and most important for both boys and girls is the recognition that fathers have a social power that mothers lack and that males have a penis that females don't (1964a).

This theory of the female lack—lack of social power coupled with lack of male genitalia—is the premise and foundation of much western theorizing on the male gaze, even though the stance taken is that this lack is a social and political construct rather than a biological fact. Further, although few feminists agree with Freud's thesis that females experience this lack as penis envy, most do agree that males experience it with a mixture of feeling superior and fearing castration. In the Freudian model this ambivalence is stated as a realization on the part of boys as they look at their mothers' genitalia during the oedipal stage that to be without a penis is to be feminized and socially disempowered. Thereafter, when males look at women and are exposed to the evidence of their sexual difference, they feel both a desire for this other and an anxiety about themselves. The male pleasure that is produced by cinematic viewing, by this theory, comes from the reassurance men feel about their own phallic integrity when it is threatened by the dephallicized presence of females.

As theorists such as Stephen Heath (1981; de Lauretis and Heath 1980), Laura Mulvey (1975), and Christian Metz (1974) have argued, three processes involved in looking produce this reassurance. One is voyeurism, in which a distance is maintained between the spectating subject and the spectated (specular) object. By this technique a man is distanced and thus protected from the woman who, with her lack of phallic genitalia, threatens him with castration. The second process is identification, where the distance between subject and object is closed; a male spectator identifies with a strong and powerful character on the screen, for example, who himself exerts control, authority, or moral superiority over the female character. This strategy is common in film noir and reassures men in their phallic identity. The third process is fetishism, by which the female object is fetishized into a phallic substitute, thereby turning the male's attention away from the lack *in* her body and toward the fetish that is made *of* her body. With fetishism, a female is made over as it were; her lack of a penis is concealed by the fetish that phallicizes and becomes her body. As Linda Williams, among others, has pointed out, however, this fetish can never completely cover up that which it lacks. By definition, although it is a substitute for the penis, it is not a penis (1989:40). Hence it is as both a presence and an absence—a part that is male with which men can identify and a part that is female from which they can remain differentiated and distant—that the fetish works to reassure men and give them pleasure.

Western theories of the male gaze are varied, sophisticated, and complex, and my presentation here is too brief to give all these intricacies full play. Nonetheless, I would like to consider the utility of such theories for examining male gazes in different cultural settings by assessing the assumptions, parameters, and conditions by which the western male gaze has been theorized. I offer three comments:

1. One of the most productive aspects to come out of male gaze theorizing is its emphasis on structures of looking that become institutionalized within relations of power, economics, and politics. The Foucauldian use of "technologies" to investigate historically and culturally specific institutions of looking has particular value for societies such as Japan that share in the late capitalist proliferation of visual apparatuses for producing and consuming images. To what extent late capitalism breeds an economy of images and gazes that is transcultural must be investigated, but it cannot yet be assumed that such an economy is always embedded with the same sexual and gender constructions as in a western context. Hence although the work of Norma Field (1991), among others, has recorded the proliferation of viewing technologies that have intensified the scrutiny of, for example, a now secularized emperor in postmodern Japan, the issue of how embedded these technologies are with codes of gender and sex must be explored rather than assumed.

2. The concepts of power used in male gaze theory are provocative but problematic. Implicit if not explicit is the argument that practices of spectatorship, pleasure, and sexuality are wedded to and embedded in relations of power. So as Mulvey for example, argues, cinema viewing not only produces pleasure but reproduces a political and gendered order (1975). Connecting the position of viewer within such scopophilic practices as cinema and pornography to subject positions within other social institutions employs concepts of hegemony, ideol-

ogy, and power that are commonly used and accepted in the social sciences today. What is less acceptable, however, is the rather homogenized and simplified assumption that men are empowered when looking at women and that women are disempowered when they are looked at by men. Work is being done that examines nonheterosexual forms of gazes or gazing by women as well as the potential for pleasure that not only looking but also being looked at may produce.[17] Yet the assumption is still widely shared, if lamented, that when men in a patriarchal society are positioned to look at women, the look is charged with power.

The problem with this position, as I see it, is that power is defined in jural-political terms that leave out forms of power, influence, and authority that real women and real mothers in society exert. Such power includes realms of the sexual, reproductive, and maternal that may be conditions for the manner in which females are represented and objectified even for the so-called male gaze. As a few theorists such as Karen Horney have suggested, fetishization of women not only disavows any "lacks" they have but also, and more importantly as far as she is concerned, discredits any power that they do possess (1967). In her language, men dread women and fear their vaginas, and as Bruno Bettelheim has stated it, men envy the reproductive abilities that only women have far more than women envy the penises only men have (1962).

Although many feminists, such as Luce Irigaray (1985) and Julia Kristeva (1980), have examined how woman's bodies, their mothering, and their forms of sensuality do not and cannot be represented in languages that privilege men and mute or silence women, few consider how a phallocentric social order also puts burdens on males. When men look at women in pornography, argues Susan Lurie, they are seeking reassurance against phallic lack not in women but in themselves (1980).[18] It is their own feelings of insecurity and fears of inadequacy, particularly in a society that has made the penis such a symbol of and for phallic power, that activates the pleasure taken in viewing women as objects. Lurie's position, and Horney's, are infrequently taken but are refreshing in a discourse where female lack, even when opposed, is such a given. These positions also problematize the concept of power and question the assumption that men are necessarily empowered as voyeurs in a fetishistic gaze.

3. The third parameter of much western theory on the male gaze that affects its applicability to other cultures is the assumption of a particular construction of sexuality and its linkage to subjectivity and the person. As Foucault has deconstructed this tradition of western sexuality, it is one where sexuality becomes a signifier for the ultimate truth of the individual (1980). As Freud has not only described but prescribed with his theory of sexuality, psychoanalysis is the procedure of uncovering the self by telling and revealing sexual histories. By this construction, sexuality is serious because it is the most important determinant of

gender, identity, and social place. Whereas feminists increasingly argue that the dimensions of class, race, culture, history, and nonheterosexual-, nongenital-based sexual practices should be factored into this privileging of (hetero)sexual-ity,[19] theories of the male gaze are heavily grounded in the psychoanalytic assumption of sexuality as central and centrally constitutive of subjectivity and the self.

Quite apart from the question of whether this assumption still holds true in the United States and Western Europe and if so, under what conditions, with what relations, or for what subjects, its truth cannot be assumed for cultures outside the west. Theories of the male gaze are culturally bounded, in other words, and can be applied only by taking this into consideration.[20]

Machiko-sensei and the Male Gaze in Japanese Children's Cartoons

Machiko-sensei, on which my analysis of the male gaze in Japanese children's cartoons is largely based, is a cartoon show I viewed during two stays in Japan—one in 1980–1982 and one during 1987–1988. The one show I will detail here was shown on a Thursday evening at 7 P.M., 1981, and lasted for thirty minutes. The following is its narrative.

Machiko-sensei (*sensei* is the appellation of respect accorded teachers as well as doctors, politicians, executives, etc.), a junior high school teacher in Japan, is young, attractive, and very devoted to a small group of male students. The standard plot involves a misadventure one of these students has fallen into and Machiko-sensei's efforts to disentangle and thereby save him. The first scene is a professional wrestling ring where Machiko-sensei has agreed to participate in an exhibition wrestling match for her school. She is shown competing against a male wrestler she's defeating, but the man pulls out a pair of scissors during the match and cuts the strap of Machiko-sensei's top. Her breasts fall out and she is immobilized. The match stops, Machiko-sensei looks down in embarrassment, and all those watching from the bleachers (her male students and colleagues) turn with eyes transfixed on her breasts. No one comes to Machiko-sensei's assistance, and the scene ends.

The next scene starts at the school, where one of the boys informs Machiko-sensei that another in the group has decided to drop out of school and become a professional wrestler. Machiko-sensei is alarmed and rushes out to the wrestling ring. There she sees the boy wrestling against a professional female wrestler who is beating him. In an effort to disarm his opponent, the boy mimics the scissors routine he witnessed earlier against his teacher and cuts her bra strap. Though her breasts immediately fall out, this woman doesn't flinch. She keeps pouncing on the boy with the added assistance of another female wrestler who has jumped in the ring to help her friend. At this point Machiko-sensei, disguised as a professional, enters the ring herself and takes the place of the boy. She succeeds in beating her opponent, thereby winning the match.

The final scene shows Machiko-sensei being chased around the ring by the wrestling coach, who is urging her to give up teaching and become a professional wrestler. In the chase the man tugs on her clothes and reveals Machiko-sensei's breasts once again. With this the show ends.

The image I focus on in this show is the partially unclothed Machiko-sensei, who becomes the object of a male gaze almost exclusively fixated on her breasts. The spectators are various male figures: the male coach and Machiko-sensei's male students and male colleagues. To be very explicit, this image of female nudity does not represent all sexual images found in Japan or all images found in *manga*. Yet this fetishized construct—I use fetish here in the Freudian (1961) sense of a fixation on one part of an object and in the Marxian (1978:319–329) sense of reifying a human or social relation by a concrete object—is an image found commonly in both children's *manga* and various other media not explicitly child oriented, such as adult pornographic comic books, photos appended to news magazines, and mainstream shows on prime-time TV.

As located within children's *manga*, the imagery of female body parts inspires and is inspired by particular looks. As Christian Metz has written about cinema (1974), these looks come from three sources: the instrument projecting the images, the characters who form part of the imagery, and spectators who are viewing the images. In the case of *Machiko-sensei*, for example, the exposed breasts are drawn in by the *manga* artist, gazed at by characters within the cartoon, and viewed by those who watch *Machiko-sensei* on TV. All three looks, by those producing as well as consuming this imagery of female nudity, are predominantly male: More *manga* artists of all genres are male than female, more of the characters gazing at these images within the *manga* are male than female (Schodt 1986), and more of the audience for a show like *Machiko-sensei*, I have been told (although I would need to do further research to verify this statistic), is male than female. Therefore, the imagery made out of female body parts in a *manga* such as *Machiko-sensei* is constructed both as gender coded[21] and as scopophilic.

Other children's *manga* in which I have examined similar images of female nudity situated by looks that are by, or intended to be for, predominantly males share these two characteristics in addition to a third: the inconsistency or incongruity in the positioning of the male looks. On the one hand the looker displays aggressiveness, boldness, and a sense of entitlement in looking. In *Machiko-sensei* the male characters, who include fellow teachers as well as Machiko-sensei's students, stare directly at her breasts with no attempt to either hide their staring or help her. On the other hand, however, the males look passively, or better stated, *as* lookers they become passive, making no attempt to extend their looking into bodily contact.

Of course, whether looking in any sense can be adequately described in terms of active or passive is problematic. Freud argued that scopophilia, particularly when it is aggressive and exacts pain or discomfort from the object being looked at, is conditioned by the desire to exert mastery over the other (1975:23–24). Adopting this Freudian position, western theorists on the male gaze such as Laura Mulvey (1975) likewise assume that when practices of male looking are institutionalized and acceptable, males look actively and with control over the objects of their gaze. In children's *manga*, however, there is an obvious split in the looks taken not by the *manga* artist (which are in some sense active) or by the *manga* viewer (which are in some sense inactive) but by the characters internal to the *manga* script itself. Often, if not always, this split occurs when males stop a female's action and she becomes an object or image for male viewing. However, once the female has been inactivated to form a spectacle, the males also become immobile.

In another *manga*—the December 1991 issue of *Shōnen Sandē*, a written comic book aimed toward junior and senior high school boys—the same structure of male viewing is displayed. The narrative is as follows. Two hockey teams are playing a match, and one team is losing badly. The captain of the losing team notices that two of his opponents are lasciviously eyeing a female friend of his who is standing by the rink. In an effort to distract these opponents, the captain pulls the girl over and pulls down her pants, thereby exposing her pubic area to the entire auditorium. The next scene shows all those who are spectators to the game and those on both hockey teams (all of both are male) gazing at the female with eyes abnormally distended. All the males are also doubled over in the attempt to hide their erections, which have immobilized all the hockey players. The female, though angry, takes no further action except to move away. The final scenes show the ice operator in his booth with an erection that has accidentally bumped the handle of the ice-making machine and turned it off. The ice in the rink begins to melt, and the game is called off.

In another written *manga* entitled *Yarukkya Knight*, a paperback book issued by Jump Comics and geared also to junior and senior high school boys, the stories are repeatedly fashioned with narratives of boys who either inadvertently or purposely remove the clothing of females. One boy, rock climbing with a female friend, is below her on a cliff when he loses his balance. Reaching out to grab her leg, he grabs the girl's underpants instead and pulls them off. The boy's reaction is one of embarrassment but pleasure, and as the beads of sweat pour profusely from his forehead, his eyes dart back and forth in a look depicted as pleasurable but illicit. In another story three boys remain masked as they forcibly abduct girls, taking them to an auditorium where they are ordered to remove their clothes. The girls are then forced to pose for a camera that will be used, the boys state, to produce a pornographic film for distribution in the city. The girls are humiliated in this exposure and filming of their body parts, but their bodies are only looked at, not touched.

This behavior is repeated in another story in which a girl is hung outside the window of a high-rise building and her underpants pulled down. A crowd of spectators on the ground look up at the image constructed of female flesh, but even though this imaging of her has been done savagely, the savaging does not include actual penetration of her body or further touching once her body has been arranged to be a spectacle. Likewise, in a story where boys remove the clothing of a girl and put her on a cross with the words "look at me" underneath, the girl is severely embarrassed and pained. As she is set out in the schoolyard to remain naked overnight on the cross, she is hurt because, and as, she is made into an object for male viewing. No males, however, touch her further.

How powerfully transfixing the looking at female nudity can be for males is demonstrated in another story where it is the girl who shows herself to a boy. When she lifts her skirt to exhibit underpants, the boy reels back in a hyperbolic response: Sweat streams off his face, his eyes are so distended that they have actually left his face, and some form of excretion is pouring out of his nose. Needless to say, the boy doesn't move an inch. This immobilizing effect is also figured into *Machiko-sensei* when the spectators at the wrestling ring only stare when the teacher's breasts are exposed. Likewise, in the *Shōnen Sandē* comic, the male hockey members, ice operator, and spectators are literally stopped in action by the sight of female flesh. And in the cartoon show *Doraemon,* already mentioned in Chapter 1, when Nobita sees the naked Sakura he gasps but doesn't move.

In all these examples of male gazing at female body parts in children's *manga* there are three shared structures: (1) looking positions and is positioned by gender (males look and females are looked at), (2) looking often follows action but rarely leads to further action, and (3) the position, particularly of males, as lookers, splits between one that is permitted and controlling and one that is illicit and immobilizing. It is in terms of these three structures that I will explore the meanings of and for sexuality and gender in this form of male gazing in children's *manga.*

To preface this exploration, I would like to acknowledge two limitations to my analysis. The first is the absence of interviews with consumers and producers of children's *manga.* Although I have discussed the sexualized element running through children's comics with a number of Japanese mothers and have read analyses of it by Japanese feminists and *manga* artists,[22] my aim here to do an anthropological study of popular culture rather than a merely textual one would be strengthened by the type of formal interviewing I have not yet been able to conduct in Japan. The second limitation is my focus on a structure of male rather than female gaze and my concentration on how this affects mainly male rather than female viewers. It is obvious that there are many practices and activities today in which females are not only allowed to gaze but also specifically targeted as gazers (for example, there are girl comics and girl superheroes who look admiringly at both boys and other girls). Further, there are forms of consumership in which females become the subjects of gazing far more than do males.[23] Nevertheless, my subject in this chapter is one particular relationship of looking that has connections, I will argue, to other patterns of voyeurism and sexual commodification that remain masculinized in Japan today.

In the gazing I have described in children's *manga*, the structure is both voyeuristic and fetishistic in ways that are congruent with scopophilic practices in the adult landscape. Females are fetishized in terms of specific body parts—breasts, pubises, and buttocks—and, in this fetishization, they are constructed as objects to be looked at and enjoyed by primarily males. Images, sketches, cartoons, photos, toys, paintings, and drawings of either females who are naked or naked body parts proliferate in Japan with little official regulation. Censorship laws (somewhat lifted since 1991; see Chapter 7) prohibit the display of pubic hair and penises (Kimoto 1983), but airbrushed pubises and imaginary phalluses are as acceptable as exposed buttocks and breasts (Buckley 1991). All of the previous, but particularly breasts, appear in anything explicitly coded as sexual—adult pornographic magazines, x-rated movies, strip shows, and late-night adult TV, for example—as well as in media and forums whose subject is overtly something other than sex, such as police shows during prime-time television, photos appended to news magazines, public advertisements for whiskey or cigarettes, and call-girl fliers deposited in residential mailboxes. As many friends and informants, both female and male, have told me, such display of female flesh is appealing to men even when not directly connected to sexual acts. One word used in this context is *tanoshī*—pleasant, joyful, or happy—a word men also commonly use when referring to diversionary or recreative activities such as reading a book, watching TV, listening to the news, or getting drunk with a friend. And in this connection many male informants equated looking at naked females—whether they are on a screen, in a magazine, or stripping on a stage—with other relaxing or idle pursuits. When I questioned one man as to the juxtaposition on late-night adult hour (on television) of segments on Buddhism and football next to ones of women's naked mud wrestling and stripping, he stated simply that all these stories and images were *tanoshī*.

Gazing at female bodies is constructed both as diversionary and recreative for males and as sexual, though these two constructions are not always conjoined. As mentioned previously, in the hostess clubs where white-collar men are taken to have fun and build bonds at company expense, a constant staple in their conversations is references to the body parts of the women who are pouring their drinks. As I discovered when doing fieldwork as a hostess in one such club, men continually speak of the women at the level of their bodies, particularly their breasts. When commenting on the size of a woman's breasts or when wondering aloud whether apparently beautiful breasts are actually fakes, the men typically refer to themselves as *sukebei*—lewd, lecherous, or horny old men. These men only rarely proceed toward a sexual liaison with any of the hostesses. Therefore, some of my informants, men as well as women, claimed that whatever takes place in such an establishment—looks, flirtations, talk—is not about sex. Others disagreed, however, saying that it is sexual even if no acts of genital intercourse or release take place.[24]

Japanese writers, scholars, and clinical practitioners who write about adult sexuality similarly fluctuate as to whether genital release or intercourse becomes the definition of what is sexual. Go Tomohide, in discussing erotic comic books, for example, characterizes them as *iyarashī*, or offensive, which, he adds, is not intended as criticism. Rather, offensiveness is the very objective of *ero manga*, as it is of eros more generally, according to Go (1981:260). By this formulation, the aim of the *manga* artist is to represent as realistically as possible real penises and vaginas and real contact between these organs, and the aim of the *manga* reader is sexual excitation or genital release. A sociologist who conducted a survey on males who purchase pornography with photographic rather than cartoon images confirmed this connection between looking at fetishized females and genital release. According to the responses of over 1,700 males, 100 percent declared their objective was masturbation (Ishikawa 1983:232–233). By contrast, Ōshima Nagisa, the director of many films including the sexually explicit *In the Realm of the Senses* has argued that viewers of *pinku eiga* (pornographic films) are using watching itself as a form of sexual release. Though watching may be more a substitute for than a prelude to other sexual acts, Ōshima still refers to this type of scopophilia as sexual (1983:58).

It is Ōshima again who has written that sex has become increasingly commodified in the posteconomic boom of late 1960s Japan.[25] Speaking mainly of men, Ōshima argues that long and demanding work schedules allow workers no other time or space for sex than as a commodity (1981:39). Men buy pornographic magazines, visit strip shows, or enter a soapland[26] or *pinku saron*,[27] where the sexual services one receives depend on the price the consumer is willing to pay. Of course men and women can always engage sexually as married couples, but much in the literature points to a cultural and ideological distinction between procreative sexuality (conducted at home, with a spouse, in the context of family, and with an association more female than male) and recreative sexuality (conducted away from home, apart from responsibilities, and with an association more male than female).[28] Thus when men want recreational sex, they tend to look for it away from home. As one of my interviewees stated regarding his preference for prostitutes over his wife, there are no commitments attached and the woman handles everything. And as another man explained the pleasure men take in being serviced by hostesses with whom the service does not include sex, "Men are all *sukebei* [lewd, lecherous], but they don't have the time to find women on their own with whom they can flirt."

It is in the context of recreative, nonprocreative male sexuality that structures of fetishism and voyeurism not only appear in Japan but are almost hegemonic. Looking with various forms of voyeuristic distance maintained between subject and object is a convention, for example, in most clubs in the *mizu shōbai*—the entertainment domain of bars and clubs, whose service includes women. In *nōpan kissa*,[29] a fad a few years ago, customers could watch but not talk to or touch waitresses who served the food without their underpants on. In *nōpan* karaoke clubs now, customers can sing music along with women who are not wearing underpants. In *nozoki* clubs—*nozoki* is also the word for Peeping Tom—men can look up the skirts of women who sit in a simulated subway car above a glass ceiling. In strip clubs, men watch women strip; in *shirū pabū* men watch naked women swimming around in fish tanks; and in photo clubs, men pay to take pictures of women posing. In other establishments such as soaplands and *pinku saron*, looking at females may be less important than other services the male receives, such as assisted masturbation (*hassha no tedasuke*), intercourse, oral sex, or having his drinks poured and cigarettes lit. In these places as well, however, some form of distance is maintained between subject and object, even if it is not one that is structured primarily through looking.

In the *mizu shōbai*, in fact—a domain that costs money but that informants, both blue collar and white collar, corporate and noncorporate, say they frequent when they can afford it (Gendai Hyōronsha 1980; Kobayashi 1970; Narabayashi 1983)—a distance is maintained through the women's status as social other. Although I have been told that this stigmatization has eased somewhat in recent years, women in the *mizu shōbai* are still categorized as social peripherals. Women no self-respecting man would marry, these females are dirtied by the sexual use to which they are put by men. They are retained as nonmothers and nonwives, and it is this otherness that men value for its sexual and recreative currency. As others, women become fetishized into objects and constructs that serve men. And as fetishes, women become desirable but also distant, a structure that positions men, in their desire, as voyeurs, fetishists, and consumers.

I don't mean to totalize with these statements and assert that the previous description is the only construction of sexuality in Japan. Yet there are institutional conditions that support and are supported by a construction of recreative sexuality in which females are fetishized for the consumption and gaze of primarily males. These institutions, I would argue, are primarily three—industry, education, and the family—and they all are conditioned by and the condition for a gender division of labor. Females manage the home and raise the children even if they are also nondomestically employed. And males work at jobs that they make their primary commitment even when they have families and wives who remain at home.[30] Industry, particularly but not only in the case of white-collar workers, supports this division of labor through such practices as paying for corporate entertainment that extends the workday into night.[31] Men are kept from home by long work schedules and work-related activities all the while women are tied more closely to home by the duties of house and child management. The institution of education supports this assignation by relying on mothers to ensure that their children are studying hard. In the increasingly competitive educational market, one's adult career depends almost entirely on one's success with entrance exams while still a youth. The mother is pivotal in this process, supporting the child but also goading him (the education-career link applies particularly to males) into an educational success on which Japanese political leaders say their economic success depends.[32]

Both industry and the school system support families based on the reproductive labors of mothers and the productive labors of men, whose main duty as fathers and husbands is to bring home the paycheck. Gender distinctions are critical to and critically enforced through all three of these institutions—industry, education, and the family—and a construction of recreative sexuality in which the players are male and the played with are female reinforces this model of gender distinction even as the increasing infusion of women into the labor market is at odds with it.[33] Such a construction of sexuality does more, however; it also organizes sexual energies and desires to fit in with and not disrupt the gendered expectations for male workers and female mothers in postmodern Japan. By borrowing on cultural traditions—such as the history of a demimonde where men have been socially permitted to play with women not their wives—and a religious and mythological acceptance of sex as a matter of nature rather than morality, guilt, or sin, contemporary practices that allow and encourage males to fetishize females as social and marital others have real and practical effects. The first is that because males are encouraged to pursue forms of sexual recreation outside the home, the home and marriage remain grounded in notions of duty and gendered role expectation that are more stable than the far less stable ones of romance or sexual compatibility. Further, because marriage is thus stabilized and sanitized, marriages are less likely to demand commitments of time and energy that would distract men from their jobs or women from their mothering.

Second, because pursuits of sexuality outside the home are permissible but seen as recreative, males are reminded of the social peripherality of sexuality and the social centrality of other activities, namely those involving work, family, and school. It is from these realms that males will acquire social place, status, identity, and in these senses, subjectivity.[34] Sexuality, although conceptualized as part of the male nature, makes no contribution to the social persona of worker and family provider, by which the adult male will be primarily and socially identified.

Third, because male recreative sexuality is socially sanctioned but peripheral, there is a contradiction, or split, that positions males as sexual subjects but also as voyeurs, consumers, and fetishists. Males are thus titillated but satisfaction is deferred. Needing to go back for something they can never quite reach—a driving principle of capitalism—males are directed to practices of recreative sexuality that, although presented as a release or diversion from work, are increasingly work connected. A working man's visits to hostess clubs, for example, rarely lead to acts of sex, depend on his industriousness at his job, and will end when he retires.[35] And more generally, anything in the *mizu shōbai* or in the way of an extramarital affair, I have been told, costs money. So only those men who work hard will be able to afford sexual recreation outside the home, which is where male recreative sexuality is most profitably kept.

In these operations I see a consistency and continuity with the male gazes that are embedded in children's *manga.* I argue here not for a causal relationship but for an ideological compatibility: I believe that the imagery of naked female bodies is sexual but that it constructs male sexuality in such a way as to maintain the male's primary role as worker. Even as the five-year-old watches *Doraemon* and the twelve-year-old views *Machiko-sensei,* they are likely to be using *manga* as a diversion in lives that will be increasingly filled with study. As mothers with whom I discussed *manga* stated, comics and cartoons provide relief, and they dismissed the images of naked breasts as innocuous and harmless.[36] These images were also, however, seen as being for males: They are a treat that boys[37] digest as they study just as grown men read erotic comic books as they commute to work in the morning or visit a hostess club or a *pinku saron* after work is finished.

Encoded in scenes of boys gazing at female body parts there are thus messages that children's *manga* transmit about gender. Males and females are different, and this difference assigns social role and place.[38] Encoded as well is a formulation of sexuality that, as recreative, is for males but not females, is inscribed on female but not male bodies, and inscribes males but not females in positions of voyeur and consumer.[39] These codes apply to children as well as adults because sexuality, by this construction, does not radically change its form and meaning at puberty, the time when, Freud and western male gaze theorists argue, genitals dominate sexuality and order an emerging subjectivity.[40] Neither this western-based conception of subjectivity nor its construction of sexuality can be strictly applied, I argue, to Japan.[41]

This is not to say, however, that male gaze theory as postulated by westerners has nothing to say about Japanese practices of male gazing such as those found within children's *manga*. The insistence that scopophilic tendencies, particularly those that are institutionalized and structured, are ideological apparatuses prescribing formulations of sexuality, gender, and subjectivity is relevant to Japan as well. The content of these formulations differs in the two cultures, yet in Japan as well as the United States there are structures of sexuality, gender, and subjectivity being shaped through practices of scopophilia, and children's *manga* is one of these practices.

The fact that an image and a gazing I do believe is sexual, in terms of a Japanese construction of sexuality, is conveyed in a medium intended for children reveals a significant element in that construction of sexuality. Boys who are in some sense pregenital and in many senses still connected to mothers are introduced to a sexual looking conditioned by neither the sexual development of genitalia nor the development of subjectivity away from mothers, which is assumed to start at puberty by western male gaze theorists. Looking at naked females, by this western model, demands and is the result of psychic and social disruptures[42] in boys' lives. The sexuality of male gazing is consequently replete with meanings of psychic and social significance. I suggest that Japanese male gazing, by contrast, does not acquire such meanings associated with sexuality at the time of puberty and that it can be continuously voyeuristic as a result of its being introduced into children's *manga*. I therefore conclude that although sexual, naked female bodies carry different meanings in this Japanese context of children's cartoons. I also conclude that situating the male subject as a viewer and voyeur is not necessarily or unquestionably a practice of scopophilia that empowers him.

༄ 3 ༄

Cartooning Erotics:
Japanese *Ero Manga*

"Kaibutsu-sensei"[1] is the title of a comic strip in *Shūkan Manga Times,*[2] one of the many erotic comic books in Japan. The comic strip ran for six pages as part of a serialized story with the following narrative.[3]

A woman leaves the *sentō* (public bath) at dusk and cools off on a park bench with an ice confection on a stick. A man whose chest is bare pops over the hedge and asks the woman for her ice cream. The woman wonders aloud why she should give it to him, but the man says that he never assumed it would be free. He's willing to pay 500 yen,[4] which the woman accepts. Grabbing the stick, the man immediately plunges it into the exposed buttocks of a person crouched next to him whose face is never shown.[5] The man reacts with great glee at this; he jumps up and down and laughs hysterically. He also speaks to the first woman, who has been watching the entire scene. "She was too tight, so I figured the coldness would loosen her up. You really helped me out. Thanks a lot!"(see Figure 3.1).

The woman looking on is initially speechless; her eyes are cockeyed, a tear falls down her cheek, the word bubble contains only dots running off to the side. By the next frame, however, she appears mad and in leaving the park mumbles to herself: "Boy! That really surprised me. Males can do any number of things,[6] can't they?" At this point she sees a vending machine selling *manga* and muses to herself, "I wonder if *I* should do something as daring as buy a *manga*[7] once in a while." Examining one *manga,* she is startled—the word bubble is empty—and when she looks even closer, her eyes pop out of her head in astonishment. The cover she has seen is shown in close-up: "SM" is written at the top, and the cover sketch is of a devilish-looking man with bared teeth who is masked and naked. He holds a whip over a naked woman whose body has been tied both above and below her breasts and who is screaming.

The woman stares even harder at the *manga* and her reaction deepens: Teeth are gritted, eyes are bulging and red, and a tear falls from her face. By the next scene, however, it is obvious that she intends to buy this magazine, though she is

FIGURE 3.1   One page from the cartoon "Kaibutsu-sensei" in the comic book *Shūkan Manga Times*. (See the synopsis of this cartoon at the beginning of this chapter.)
SOURCE: *Shūkan Manga Taimuku* (Manga Times Weekly), July 27, 1979 (Tokyo: Hōbunsha), p. 109

drawn to show ambivalence: One side of her doubled self is composed and says, "Well I *did* just receive 500 yen"; the other side looks anxiously up and down the street to ensure that no one will see her (an empty word bubble is shown).

Having purchased the *manga,* the woman runs home. We see the house from the outside—darkness indicates it is evening—and then the woman inside, lying on her futon reading the *manga.* These frames are sketched from above so that the reader can look up the woman's nightgown at her underpants as she lies on her stomach. The comic she is reading shows three images: (1) a screaming woman tied with arms above her head, legs up behind her, and breasts roped in two places, both above and below, and a phallic-looking object lying in one corner; (2) what looks like hot wax being dripped on the woman as she lies on her back, legs thrust up; (3) a butt shot with buttocks roped in two places, ankles tied, and a crisscross bandage on one cheek.

The reader reacts with initial disgust; she covers her mouth with a hand, eyes are widened in shock, and she remarks, "What a scary thing [*osoroshī koto*]" and "This certainly is hell [*marude jigoku*]." Soon, however, we see beads of sweat emerging around the woman's underpants. She reaches under her nightgown and begins to masturbate, murmuring, "I wonder what this business of pain and hurting is all about anyway?!" Having fallen asleep—a prone figure with a drop of sweat on her face, an eggplant by her side,[8] and an empty word bubble yielding no answer to her question above her head—events take place, but whether they are in her dream or real is unclear. A close-up of a single breast is shown with an erect nipple and a hairy (= man's) arm and the suggestion of movement ("pa," an action sound, is written in large letters). Next two breasts are figured; both have sharply pointed nipples and are tied above and below with rope.

The following frame concludes the cartoon and is a scene between the woman and a burglar. A man dressed in patched clothes with a bag slung over his back has entered her house and is demanding "cash, cash!" The two are separated by a space—the man off to the right and the woman to the left—into which a knife has been stuck and where the woman's nightgown has fallen. The woman is now drawn in close-up: She sits on her futon with arms pinned to her body and breasts tied in the now familiar way, both above and below as to make them bulge. Her expression is filled with emotion; eyes are stretched wide, teeth are clenched, sigh marks emerge from her face, sweat beads fly from the head. Blood is also dripping from her nose. She speaks twice: "Won't you please beat me again because I'm imploring you do so do?" and "I don't have any, so I figured that's why you've tied me up." The cartoon states at the bottom, "To be continued."

With covers carrying such phrases as "Excite Eros" and "Manga for Men,"[9] erotic comic books, or *ero manga,* are one genre in a multigenred medium of comic book artistry (*manga*) that, vastly popular today in Japan, is also used for textbooks, traditional legends, and romance and *sararīman* stories. As a commodity, *ero manga* are cheap and as a medium, graphic and accessible. As such a product, *ero manga* circulate in an economy of mass culture where production and consumption are fast and transmission and reception are immediate.

In subject material, *ero manga* are hardly unique, sharing with an entire sex industry (*seisangyō*) the impulse to commodify sex. Unlike most of the other media through which eroticization is marketed and played out, however, *ero manga* are distinguished by the fact that they are commonly enjoyed in everyday life. Constraints such as the high price of even seedy sex establishments in the *mizu shōbai* (the "water trade") and restrictions on the sale, consumption, and display of photographic erotica do not apply in the case of *ero manga*, which are sold on practically every street corner and read in such open places and everyday circumstances as commuting to work on the trains.[10] The very pattern of buying an *ero manga* before a commute and throwing it away at the end[11] signifies how common a product an erotic comic book is and how commonplace its stories with their dominant trope of male conquest, rape, and female victimization.

In this chapter I examine *ero manga* as a form of popular culture targeted to males.[12] How are *ero manga* used, with what meanings, and with what effects on those who both consume them and do not? I write here as a feminist informed and also troubled by the pornography discourse that has so consumed the energies of western feminists in recent years. I am motivated, in part, by its inattention to nonwestern countries. Either such countries have been ignored or their practices and texts involving the representation, alteration, and aestheticization of bodies have been judged by western (or universalist) standards. I, like many others committed to looking outside the west,[13] foreground the local context in my analysis and attempt to understand behavior in these terms rather than those of a generalized pornography, female oppression, and sexual desire.

Of course, those of us who study the nonwest have not been alone in criticizing the generalizing and universalizing tendencies of the Dworkin and MacKinnon stand on pornography.[14] Their position, still considered hegemonic in feminism by one who opposes it (Kipnis 1992), essentializes both what pornography is and what it does: Pornographic stories and images of sex are premised on, and serve to literally (re)produce, male dominance over women. Speaking with the effects of postmodernism in us, we critics of this view[15] argue for multiplicity and complexity: There are many pornographies (not all are violent) with multiple audiences (not all are straight and chauvinist men) stemming from a plethora of circumstances (not simply male privilege) with effects and pleasures that are diverse, even contradictory (some women enjoy porno; some men do not). Most powerful have been the voices of those who speak as subjects, arguing that as feminists, they have found pleasure and empowerment in particular pornographies (lesbian, gay, sadomasochistic, the "female" pornography of Harlequin novels or soap operas).[16] Critiquing the Dworkin-MacKinnon position for not only its scholarly reductions but also its sexual politics, opponents have called for thinking about female sexuality not just in terms of victimization, which has the effect of moralizing against, rather than advocating, the sexual agency of women.

These moves have been extremely important to feminism and have oriented discourse on sexuality in the direction I think it needs to go, that is, in the direction of examining how a sexual practice or text may work *for* someone it gives pleasure to rather than merely *against* someone it ideologically oppresses. But I have noted that these developments rarely turn in the direction, importantly if problematically staked out by Dworkin and MacKinnon, of dominance. This issue is one that drives my own work here given that despite the fact that there are multiple differences in gender, sexual, social, and personal practices in Japan, male chauvinism remains ideologically dominant. This is true in both a so-called real sense—political rights, social opportunities, and labor practices—and the sexually symbolic one of the materials and arenas open to men for sexual play, release, and license. I could look at this situation from the perspective of how women (and other others) defy it. I choose rather to examine a sexual text and practice that confirms the dominant norm of masculinism (and whether such confirmation is its major "work" and the means by which it gives pleasure to male readers are issues I intend to question). I believe that as feminists, we need to understand such mechanisms far better and in far more complicated terms than we have in the past.

This is the terrain we should not abandon in the wake of our criticisms of Dworkin and MacKinnon even while we refuse their literalist, reductive approach. In my analysis, I follow the few but critical works by feminists on male-centered (hetero)sexuality: Kaja Silverman's on phallic imagery in cinema (1992), Linda Williams's on hard core pornography (1989), Laura Kipnis's on *Hustler* magazine (1992), and Duncan Kennedy's on the relationship between sexy dressing and sexual violence (1993). I also take Andrew Ross's plea seriously that it is time we considered (mainstream male) pornography from the perspective of what precisely it does to and for men. As one who is doubly excluded (as woman and non-Japanese) from the targeted readership of *ero manga*, I pursue this question of pleasure, meaning, and ideological and psychic work for the dominant reader as best and carefully as I can. I rely not on interviews with Japanese readers but on critical commentaries by Japanese (some who are *manga* aficionados) as well as two research projects I have conducted in what I believe to be related subjects.[17] In the next section I examine the representational medium of *manga* and in the following two sections I look at specific comics and relate them and *manga* in general to the social relations of family, work, leisure, and recreation. These relations are being worked and reworked, I argue, through the sexual storytelling of *ero manga.*

Manga: Comics of (not only) Play

Cartoon artistry is an expressive format that combines stylized and simplistic imagery with a laconic text. As a style of communication it is hardly unique, of course, to Japan. What is distinctive, however, is the degree to which *manga* has spread and diversified as a dominant (almost *the* dominant) medium in mass culture. In 1993, 39 percent of all printed publications in Japan were *manga* (Asahi Shinbunsha 1995; this 1995 figure represents a 10.8 percent rise over the previous year's). Comic artistry, in both written (*manga*) and visual (animation—*anime*) forms, is not only a huge industry but also a respectable art form, the technology and graphics for which Japanese artists and technicians are recognized worldwide. Significantly, cartoonery is viewed as neither a childish nor an impoverished textual medium in Japan, as it tends to be in the United States (Schodt 1986; Tsurumi 1987). Rather, it is valued for its own style and representational format. The coupling of word and image alters, and in ways extends, the use of either: Stories are told both visually and with (minimalist) text; there is a bending and blending of the borders between image and text (script is written with differences in size, shape, style, and syllabary,[18] and images such as a raised eyebrow are part of the narrative); meaning is compacted and direct; and storytelling relies on tropes other than realism to evoke,[19] escape, comment on, and unsettle that which is familiar. This description of *manga*—visual imagery into which a text has been melded and condensed—applies to the Japanese language itself; this similarity accounts, at least in part, for the ease with which *manga* has been established as Japan's national language of mass culture.

As in *manga,* visuality is highly stressed in many Japanese practices from aesthetics and cuisine to the teaching of traditional arts and interpersonal communication. As the film director Itami Jūzō noted (Canby 1989), it is telling that the Japanese often rely more on visual cues than on written or spoken explanations to learn, relate to the world, and interact with one another. Itami states that this principle guides his own filmmaking, as in *Tanpopo,* where multiple scenes jump-cut across, rather than toward, linearity and their dense visuality evokes meanings left unstated. In *manga,* the high degree of visual imagery lends itself to various uses. One is instructional; the image does not stand in for the text as much as complement it, thereby doubling the impact and speeding the reception of the message (or so it is hoped). Once fearful that the literacy of its citizenry would suffer as a result of *manga*'s spread, even the government now joins those who use it as an educational tool, printing directives and textbooks in *manga* as others do product manuals, economic and history texts, medical pamphlets, and warning signs. Such "work," however, is overshadowed by *manga*'s possibilities for "play," although the distinction between the two is becoming increasingly blurred in this age of late capitalism and image fetishism in Japan.[20] The cultivation in *manga* of a visual style that is intended not to mimic reality but tweak it creates a space that distances the reader from her or his everyday world and suggests various relationships between the *manga* scenarios and those of so-called real life. The *manga* can lampoon, satirize, romanticize, naturalize, eliminate, transcend, reimagine, ridicule, and essentialize the worlds in which people live. The same scenario, of course, can also be read differently by different readers or by the same person at different life moments. It is this quality of comic artistry that was developed by the first cartoonists in Japan, Buddhist priests who as early as the ninth century A.D. drew caricaturized sketches of themselves and animated drawings of skeletons and animals as a form of diversion and relaxation. The tone of these was typically humorous or satirical: self-portraits of monks with their physical characteristics exaggerated (large noses, engorged penises, glistening baldness) or posed in some earthy or ridiculous situation.[21]

Later, in the Tokugawa period (1603–1868), comic artistry was adopted by a number of famous artists such as Hokusai as a distinct and separate form of artistic expression. It was used, if not exclusively, to depict women and men at play in the pleasure quarters. The Yoshiwara was the section of Edo (now Tokyo) where prostitution, theater, and nonproductive (or nonreproductive) recreation was sanctioned and also contained by the government. This space had cultural significance: It was a realm set aside for play (*asobi*) where, as Buruma (1984) has put it, social regulations and hierarchies operating elsewhere could be temporarily suspended. Play, escape, and sexuality thus intertwined semiotically and were given symbolic form and expression in *manga* artistry during this time.

Manga continued and changed after the opening of Japan to the west in the mid-1800s. It incorporated European and American cartoon styles at the turn of the century, was used for propaganda during the war efforts of the 1930s and 1940s, and became a cheap and familiar entertainment (much like *kamishibai*)[22] in the poverty years following Japan's defeat in 1945. As an industry, however, it didn't take off until the late 1960s, when Japan experienced its first flush of postwar economic recovery. Since that time its growth has been exponential, in large part because of its adaptability as a mass medium. Because of its congeniality to adults as well as children, its utility for both education and entertainment, and the immediacy with which it can be consumed and yield instant gratification, *manga* has become *the* popular cultural form of postmodern Japan.

In 1993, 5,157 *manga* titles, in either book or magazine form (4,165 in magazine, 992 in book form), were printed in Japan. This constitutes almost half (39.3

percent) of the total volume of printed material published in Japan that year and 23 percent of the total revenue from printed matter ($2.41 million) (Asahi Shinbunstra 1995). This huge industry extends even further into supporting businesses that mass market television shows, animated films, live-show productions, and child-targeted commodities such as toys to dovetail with *manga* series. (Within the larger *manga* business, *ero manga* sell about 10 million issues per month with approximately 180 titles [Buckley 1991].) *Manga* are issued in either book or magazine form averaging 350 pages in length, are usually serialized (with some series lasting for years and endless volumes), and cost between 350 and 600 yen (80 yen = $1; each issue, then costs between $4 and about $7.50). They are sold ubiquitously—in newsstands, train kiosks, bookstores, convenience stores, and vending machines (although legislation has curtailed sales from the latter— and are often bought to accompany a long commute as well as stacked in *kissaten* (coffee shops) and eateries for browsing during lunch or coffee breaks. They are typically read quickly—about 18 minutes for a 350-page *manga* at roughly 3.75 seconds per page (Schodt 1986:18)—and packaged according to specific subjects (action, superhero, samurai, golf, mahjong, tennis, *sararīman*, erotica for males, erotica for females, romance, traditional legend) and distinct audiences (*shōnen* comics for boys, *bishōnen* and *shōjo manga* for girls, *ero manga* for men, ladies' comics for women). Despite these built-in differences, however, audiences cross over in their readership; there are boys and men, both gay and straight, for example, who read *bishōnen* and *shōjo manga* (Buckley 1991; Adams and Hill 1992). Also, readers may start reading a particular *manga* as teenagers and continue to read it as adults. This blending of audiences has been particularly noted for women who read *shōjo manga* (Buckley 1991) and for the comics that are read by both adult and adolescent males (*ero manga*, action comics) (Schodt 1986; Buckley 1991; Adams and Hill 1992).

Kusamori Shinichi, a journalist, describes his own addiction to mahjong comics in terms of the conditions of a busy urban life. His days are so filled with the demands of work and commuting that having no time for the mahjong he loves, he "plays" instead with a *manga*. Living in the postmodernist world of the simulacrum, he notes, "one might think that the popularity of mahjong comics would follow the popularity of real mahjong, but the opposite is actually true. Mahjong comics have become more popular with the actual decline of mahjong and, in this sense, *take its place*" (1983:235; my emphasis, my translation).

Freud has said (1961) that the fetish replaces what cannot be had but also does so in ways that phantasmically exceed the "real" thing.[23] Kusamori adds that a *manga* not only substitutes for real life but also perfects it. In actual mahjong, one needs four players, ample money, and the willingness to lose. In *manga* mahjong, by contrast, one can play alone for very little money and can identify with the winner. For these reasons, Kusamori turns to *manga* in order to play but also to work; every morning he reads one as a form of "brain training" to prepare for his workday as a journalist (1983:234–235).

Others have noted similarly that with the capitalist demands on production and consumption in Japan, there is little opportunity to play or relax except on the way *to* work or as a commodity bought *with* work. Oshima writes about these demands in terms of sex, arguing not only that the sex business is booming in Japan but that sex has become nothing but a business (1981:39). In the case of *manga*, it has been said that it serves a role much as does pachinko—a game that is mindless, solitary, and cheap and that players become so immersed in they wouldn't even notice if the person sitting next to them dropped dead.[24] In Tada's words, it is a "play that completely relaxes both body and mind" (1974:45). Pachinko parlors, like *manga*, are mundane rather than special and part of the workday rather than the time after five. They constitute play, but play that can be "worked" into a busy schedule and that breaks the boredom and relieves the stress of a wearying job.

Some commentators on *manga* say that it is the medium of *manga* that produces this effect and that the subject matter or genre is irrelevant. "I can't help but feel that action comics or baseball comics are not all that different [from *ero manga*]. In fact, they're the same" (Go 1981:261). Others argue that erotic comics are distinct. Kusamori finds that eroticism typifies *manga* and that sex fits the *manga* medium "better" than any other subject: "*Manga* and sex fit perfectly together; in this context sex and *manga* become synonymous" (1983:235). *Manga* and sex fit so well because the "offensive" (*iyarashī*) depictions—portrayals of sex as something "secretive and dark" (Kamewada discussing the *ero manga* artist Ishī Takashi [1981]), "violent and evil" (Sato 1981), illicit and transgressive (Ishikawa 1983:233), and (speaking of ladies' comics) "dirty and lewd" (Nakano 1990[25])—reflect common attitudes toward sex in Japan (see further on). Kusamori is careful to point out that this seediness of *manga* sex is not objectionable to him; it is precisely why he (and, presumably, any other consumer) buys *ero manga*. He is looking for this type of sex, escape, and play—something that is transgressive but whose transgressions can be printed and consumed in the popular medium of a comic book.

Given that the images of an *ero manga* are of naked women and the stories are of explicit sex, is the reading of an *ero manga* expected to lead to sexual release? Writers on *ero manga* are more elusive on this question than those discussing other erotic media. In Ishikawa's study of 1,767 adolescents who purchased photographic pornography at a vending machine, he discovered that 100 percent of them intended to use it for masturbation (1983:232–233). Oshima writes, by contrast, that viewers of *pinku eiga* (pink movies = pornographic movies) use movie watching as a sex act in and of itself (1983:58). Of course, the advantages offered by a *manga* are also limitations. One might masturbate to photographic sex at home, but one is far less likely to do so on a train while reading an erotic comic book. This does not mean, however, that the sex portrayed in a *manga* stays strictly on the pages; in, for example, a popular context for reading *ero manga,* commuter trains, illicit groping and touching (*chikan*) have become such a commonplace that school textbooks put out by the Ministry of Education include a warning against it.

This issue of what is "sexual" about sex comics is critical, and I return to it later. Before doing so, however, I move to what is on the page itself of specific *ero manga*.

Ero Manga: Texts

The sexual content and male readership of *ero manga* shape what is imaged and imagined on their pages.[26] The primary (if not only) subjects in *ero manga* are thus sexuality and gender,[27] which I examine by asking (1) How does *ero manga* fashion erotics out of the images and narratives it presents? (2) What role does gender have in this presentation? Research for this section is based on the examination of selected cartoons from six issues of *ero manga: Shūkan Manga Times* (July 27, 1980; August 29, 1980), *Manga Erotopia* (August 7, 1981), *Manga Dainamaito* (October 1, 1980); *Manga Erochika* (September 1, 1983), *Manga Jyōji* (vol. 2, no. 17).

Specifically, I focus only on the medium here, questioning how gender and sex are organized, represented, suggested, and evoked through the images and stories of *ero manga*. This is not to say that the text exhausts the meanings of sex and gender[28] or that the text alone is responsible for the meanings, pleasure, play, and ideological work produced by an *ero manga*. In the next section I consider the practice of *ero manga* more broadly: How does the context of reading affect what meanings sex stories hold and what else in a reader's life might be getting read into or out of an *ero manga* tale? For the moment though, my interest is only in what precisely goes into the visual and textual makings of an *ero manga*.

Giving the *manga* just a cursory glance, no more than the few seconds per page that the average Japanese reader purportedly gives it, one notes immediately the preponderance of female bodies; female and flesh are synonymous and dominate the surface of the pages. Each cover, for example, is a cartooned drawing of a woman. In two of the issues I examine, a woman's face alone is drawn to suggest sexual arousal; in the rest there are full-bodied women, naked except for underpants and artificially posed. One is doing gymnastics in such a way as to expose and emphasize her buttocks; another is cupping her breasts while her untied bra straps dangle down and form a swing on which a tiny, odd-looking Japanese man is perched. Although cartoonish, many of these sketches are more realistic than the images inside the comic book itself. They are not photographs, but the covers are made to look more photographic than drawn.

The geometry at work in these images is simple: Female signifies sex, and male, absent from the literal page, is positioned as a sexual player only as a voyeur (the one man who is figured on the cover swings like a child on the enormous playground of a woman's breasts). Beyond the cover, the images shift somewhat. Inserted into most *ero manga* are one to three pages of photos, again only of women in slightly different poses. Some smile sweetly like innocent girls as they frolic in waves with exposed breasts (but not genitalia[29]). Others flirt with the camera but are discreetly dressed in two-piece swimsuits. In other cases, women are more bold; they pull their underpants down around their knees (genitalia and pubic hair are consistently shadowed or hidden throughout), turn their backs to the camera to show a naked behind, or are absorbed in masturbation. Women either pose directly for the camera or act as if the camera is catching them unaware, as with the women who masturbate with eyes closed. In the first they are photographed as mere objects of a sexual gaze; in the second it is their sexual subjectivity that is shot. Such shots position the viewer in two separate ways: as owner of the look (these women are posed for his[30] benefit and it is his right and privilege to look) but also as a Peeping Tom (the masturbating women are looked at as if surreptitiously). The first type of look has been extensively examined by western scholars studying the so-called male gaze in arenas such as *Playboy* magazine.[31] This position is one of dominance for the viewer. What, however, of the second position, which is almost as common (though variously structured) in *ero manga* and would seem to be one of vulnerability, passivity, even impotence (the woman masturbating not only doesn't look at the viewer but also is sexually self-reliant, something the viewer is not)?

Following the photos come the comics. In a *manga* of 350 pages, there are about eight, each twenty to forty pages long. Many are serialized, so they represent only one part of a larger story; in all the visual element is prominent, so much so that the narrative often seems designed to do no more than expose more flesh. The images are overwhelmingly of women who are drawn heavily if not exclusively with their bodies stripped, exposed, displayed, examined, beaten, tied up, held down, decapitated, licked, photographed, painted, viewed, and stabbed (the repeated imagistic trope in "Kaibutsu-sensei" is of a woman tied up and bent down with her body parts, specifically breasts, prominently displayed. This image is conveyed with the bodies of separate but interchangeable women: the woman who is stuck with the popsicle stick, the woman who buys the *manga*, and the women on the pages of the *manga* within the *manga*). Many of these poses are the result of miniplots in which a woman who is in the midst of some activity—a nurse attending patients, a teacher preparing for class, a housewife cleaning her house—is halted by a man who immobilizes her by tying her up, pinning her down, or grabbing her from the back (see Figure 3.2). Kusamori has noted this standard imagery in somewhat different terms. There are standard thematic patterns in *ero manga,* according to him, which involve a woman conventionally categorized as teacher, stewardess, nurse, housewife living in a *danchi* (high-rise apartment building), or high school student (*joshi kōsei*) who is sexually transgressed upon (though not necessarily copulated with) by one or several techniques: She is groped (*chikan*) on the trains, forced into sadomasochism, harassed with obscene phone calls, voyeuristically "peeked" at (*nozoki*), or has her underpants stolen off a clothesline at night (1983:238).

Men appear on the *manga* page, though nowhere to the degree that women do and not as consistently naked. They typically are active in contrast to the passive or passified stance they foist onto women. Overtly driven by sexual desire, some aim to achieve acts of sex (which, for the man, are rarely auto- or homoerotic, although both of these acts are shown for women) by appealing directly to the women. In some cases, then, sex is enacted as a mutually agreed-upon affair, as with the female actress who is spied upon as she washes in a lake after filming a pornographic movie and, after getting angry at her Peeping Tom, willingly beds down with him (even here though, consent follows a transgression). More commonly, however, the male simply takes the female regardless of or against her will, thereby making sex an act of violation and making violation the condition, usually if not always, for sex. Women seem to fare badly, and the words they characteristically speak (especially in sexual encounters) are ones of pain or supplication: "*onegai*" (I beg of you), "*tasukete*" (help me), "*itai*" (it hurts), "*iya*" (this is awful).[32] Sex, typically, is something that is done to them, although women may be shown enjoying sexual acts or fantasies, even ones that, for them, are masochistic, such as the character in "Kaibutsu-sensei" who masturbates to pictures of tied-up women. Some women, as well, become sexual beasts, even predators, often as a result of a horrible rape (Buruma 1984; Kamewada 1981). Standardly, however, whether pleasure is depicted for her or not, the woman experiences some form, often many, of brutalization and humiliation that is visually or textually inscribed as an important element in the coding of the sex itself. A rape victim screams in agony and fear for several frames; an actress ("the number one beautiful woman in Japan") whose brutal rape was filmed and now circulates as a pornographic movie slinks around for pages in visible shame; the woman in "Kaibutsu-sensei" shows outrage and anger with gritted teeth, bulging eyes, effluxes from her nose, and speechlessness.

FIGURE 3.2   This image is taken from an erotic comic book for women and shows a
dominant image: a naked woman tied with her buttocks prominently displayed.
SOURCE: *Scandal I,* vol. 9, 1995 (Tokyo: Ozora Shuppan)

At the end of sexual encounters (which may or may not end the comic, as often there are a number of encounters in a single narrative), women are typically abandoned by their violators. These men have used and abused their bodies and often left them with irreparable scars: a visible stab wound in the abdomen, a searing memory of a terrible rape, a soiled reputation. In one, a teenage girl who was deceived into stripping for a man who pretended to be a professional photographer is tied up by him and endures endless tortures, the last being eggs that are shoved up her vagina. After she "hatches" these like a hen, she regresses to the stage of an infant who needs to be diapered. The man holds her in his arms and murmurs, "Perhaps I went too far, but this too is sexy [*iroppoi*]." The final image is jarring and seemingly at odds with the rest of the text: The man who has been so violent is now holding the young girl much as a parent would a child. He promises to never let her go (uncharacteristic in this genre), but whether he will torment her or take care of her is unclear.

Whereas women as a gender are terrorized and territorialized by *manga* sex, men are warriors and conquistadors, seeing sex as a battle and women as land they must seize (and usually ruin). Not all males, however, fight to win a woman; in the "beautiful woman" story, a heroic male knocks out the pornographers and returns the film to the woman, refusing her offers to reward him with sex. More typically, however, men both act and look like brutes. They are drawn with harsh features—few smiles, gruff expressions, meanness around their eyes—and behave with cruelty and unrestraint. Men laugh at the tears shed by a young woman whose father they've killed and virginity they've just taken. Often males assume the character or caricature of a gangster (*yakuza*), acting outside the bounds of conventional society, or of an outlaw more generally, acting out of narcissistic desire alone and outside the laws of humanity and ethics altogether. Common as well is the trope of disguise; males are literally or figuratively masked when they approach or violate women. Rapists often have masks covering their faces; males who are otherwise trying to approach or deceive a woman frequently assume a disguised personality—photographer, actor, lawyer, doctor. In the cartoon where a man has been surreptitiously watching as an actress washes herself after a pornography shoot, he impresses her with his clothing and sunglasses, which are borrowed, and his motorcycle, which has taken all his savings as a lowly office worker to buy. He thinks to himself both that he looks good and that he is a fake.

The sexual aims that are dominant in *ero manga* and dominantly male are seeing, possessing, penetrating, and hurting. In pursuing these interests, men rely heavily on an arsenal of instruments, weapons, and objects that extend their bodily powers and become interchangeable with them. These include baseball bats, tennis rackets, golf clubs, swords, knives, coke bottles, popsicle sticks, candles, pens, calligraphy brushes, wands, hypodermic needles, periscopes, video cameras, cameras, magnifying glasses, and telescopes (see Figures 3.3, 3.4). Typically sexual

FIGURE 3.3   "Looking machines" (cameras, periscopes, magnifying glasses, video and movie cameras) figure highly in erotic comic books.
SOURCE: *Manga Goraku* (Manga Entertainment), December 9, 1994 (Tokyo: Nihon Bungeisha), p. 43

aims overlap and are pursued with a "tool" that functions polymorphously: A periscope is used to see a woman in her bikini underwater, then penetrates her genitally; after a baseball bat strikes a woman on her buttocks, it enters her anally; a hand slaps a woman on her face, then pinches her breasts possessively; a penis is forced into a woman's mouth and proceeds to almost choke her. Significantly, not only do male body parts act like the objects they utilize but objects are used like human organs before morphing back into inanimate things: A Coke bottle is picked up by a man who uses it to threaten, strike, and penetrate a female victim, after which it is set back on a table and stands alone (as if it were "just" a bottle of Coke) for the final frame.

Notably, male as well as female bodies take on gendered and sexual meanings, and male as well as female bodies are fragmented into specific and separate parts. Yet the fragmentation is not equal but split along gender lines. In the case of males, body parts tend to empower the male and provide the means for realizing his desires: A penis acts as a weapon, a hand as a conqueror, eyes as voyeurs. Further, the everyday landscape is grist for male appropriation; everywhere mundane things can work and play for the man. So just as the male body can become polymorphously perverse, so can the world (poly)morphize into a male tool. By contrast, females are less likely to be given life through dead objects (a golf club is fetishized into a phallus) than to have life taken from them (a live body is objectified by treating it as if it were dead). Not only is more flesh shown on women than men with the connotation of exposure and vulnerability but also nakedness is the result less of nature than power: It is when women are naked that they are subordinated, coerced, and even killed. A naked body is a sign of captivity (hence the importance of

FIGURE 3.4   Bulging eyes and clicking cameras exaggerate the
act of looking here. In the first case, the viewer has lost control;
in the second, the would-be photographer fails to gain control
over what he wants to see and record. Frustrated, he bangs his
hand against the chair, whose seat blocks his view of the
woman's crotch. Once again, the act of looking runs up against a
site/sight that is perpetually incomplete.
SOURCE: *Manga Goraku* (Manga Entertainment), December 9,
1994 (Tokyo: Nihon Bungeisha), p. 52

the women's expressions of fear, pain, and degradation), as in the endless portrayals of women tied with rope that both semiotically marks their bodies into erotogenic zones and sadistically cuts them into pieces. Pushed up breasts, pulled open butts, spread apart vaginas—these are body parts that are not activated into instruments but pacified into specimens much like butterflies pinned to a board. Of course, when women are pinned down, they can be seen. Such is the impulse, Buruma has argued (1984), behind the "special event" common in Japanese strip joints where strippers spread their legs and allow men to gaze at their exposed genitalia. But "seeing" in this case, as Buruma adds, is also an attempt to overcome the fear and insecurity in men generated by what, in much traditional and mythological thought, is considered to be the source of female potency.

Female and male body parts come together commonly in *ero manga* in one of the most standardized and repeated depictions: splayed female buttocks (shown usually in close-up) being penetrated by a male tool, either a penis or phallic stand-in—a candle, a bottle, a bat. When the insertion is made by a penis, orgasm results most often for the male but occasionally for both parties. Yet when an object is substituted, the reaction is more likely to be nonorgasmic and one of pain or humiliation in females and a sense of victory and accomplishment in males (in "Kaibutsu-sensei" the popsicle-pusher laughs with hilarity). Again, naked flesh is shown as a site of male conquest. The singular piece—buttocks naked, turned over, stuck out with underpants yanked off and cheeks pushed open—is exposed to the scrutiny but also rage, force, and desire of someone other than the owner. Exposure here, then, signifies access but also defeat; an exposed butt is the sign of (someone else's) power.

On occasion a woman offers herself anally to a man. Inevitably, however, the offer is either thwarted or rejected. In one case a young virgin is hoping for sexual experience and bends over, offering her nakedness to a man. A dog pushes the man out of the way, however, and humps the disgruntled female. Another comic portrays two women who, wanting sex, expose breasts, genitals, and buttocks to a man who watches them disinterestedly, then runs them down with a surfboard. Female desire or will of any kind, for that matter, often renders the male incapacitated or driven to lash out aggressively toward the woman in acts that will return her, often brutally, to her place. A wife wanting sex with her husband is told he's too tired; women depicted as career women (and decidedly not mothers) are gang raped; a female buying, reading, and masturbating to a *manga* is tied up in a pose she's just seen on the page ("Kaibutsu-sensei"). When women demonstrate not only their own will but also what could be culturally construed as male inclinations—sexual desire, careers, even the consumption of *manga* itself—they are punished, ignored, and subjugated; they are reinstated as females, passive and immobile, by the male.

The male body defines the female gender, and it does so through the body parts that can exert strength and force even if the acts that ensue do not necessarily yield an orgasm (even for the male). Males are also reminded, in the cartoon scenarios, that should they fail to so construct woman—becoming embedded in, rather than taking over, femininity—danger lurks. Referring to women as *"osoroshī,"* or scary, men who are weakened by a female's love, body, or sexuality are threatened, literally, by being engulfed. In one comic, the man who is too tired for his wife engages the comely housewife next door and discovers she's a sex demon who lives off the semen of men. After climaxing thousands of times, he dies. In another, a man who has murdered his lover's husband finds himself imprisoned at the end while she is seen enjoying her husband's inheritance in the arms of another man.[33]

At the much more basic level, males who suck on the breasts of a woman, inflated and full as they consistently are in the *manga,* often turn from this position to one of entering her ass.[34] Embedded in the femininity of maternity, a man must then reestablish himself through the masculinity of his sexuality. Significantly, in order to do so he must turn the woman over.

Cutting the Other, Cutting Off the Self

In her analysis of Japanese *manga,* Sandra Buckley (1991) situates *ero manga* within a wider tradition of sexually explicit art that has catered primarily to a male audience, been marketed alongside other apparatuses and practices for sexual pleasure (manuals, books, aphrodisiacs, sex toys, soaplands), and circulated in forms of popular culture since at least the 1700s. Organized by masculinism, this enterprise has fed and been fed by a sexual orientation (one that Buckley says is phallocentric and is expressed in "phallacies") that "remains intricately bound to penetration, whether it be anal or vaginal, heterosexual, homosexual, or masturbatory" (168). The penis, much like Lacan's phallus, is the signifier par excellence in this sexual construction. It signifies an order of both gender difference and gender hierarchy, clearly differentiating between female and male and privileging phallic penetration of females as *the* sexual act.[35] Further, Buckley adds, although current censorship laws forbid the realistic representation of penises in mass media (for more on the law, see Chapter 7), the phallus assumes this central(izing) role even in absentia. "In the pornographic comic books it [the phallus] is nowhere, and yet it is everywhere. It is always present in its absence" (187).

In this way Buckley interprets the fixation on male conquest in *ero manga.* What is literally not shown on the page is "read into" it by readers well familiar with the codes: Coke bottles and tennis rackets stand for penises; shooting a woman with a camera or banging her with a baseball bat signifies phallic sex and phallocentric sexism. Although Buckley's argument makes obvious sense, I object to the manner in which she finds phallicism to be so monolithic, clear cut, and unproblematic a referent in *ero manga*. I contest as well her willingness to "see" penises where they are not; the reliance males have on the various techniques that assure them dominance (disguises, deception, force, supplemental objects) cannot be so easily dismissed, and the techniques used cannot be reduced to mere devices that ensure circumvention of the law.

Consider the following image from an *ero manga*. A man and woman are in a hotel room. She is sitting on the bed clothed in a two-piece bathing suit; he is standing up, naked except for glasses, holding a baseball bat with which he is practicing his swing. Between the man's legs is a gaping nothingness (see Figure 3.5) and emerging from this space is the bat, which, following Buckley's reasoning, is a phallic substitute. In some simple sense, this is true. But what of the fact that this scene is so patently, even parodically, staged? The bat is so apparently a "thing," and the man's body is so visibly devoid of a penis. And what of the man's need to go from swinging his "bat" to using it in order to attack the woman (see Figure 3.6)? I take up these and other questions in my analysis of *ero manga*, in which I will look at somewhat different aspects of the formal composition of comic texts than does Buckley. Like her, I focus on the trope of male dominance, which is undeniably persistent in erotic comic books. But I also attempt to unravel the various threads of its constructedness—who does precisely what to precisely whom and with what configurations of violence, identity, sex, and gender—without interpreting male force as simply or simplistically about phallic power and sexuality. In this regard, I am guided by the work of Laura Kipnis (1992), who examines the "disgust" oozing from the pages of *Hustler* magazine in terms other than mere sexist chauvinism (in her case, she looks for messages about class and finds a sustained antibourgeois critique). My intention, to be clear, is not to overlook sexism in the constructions of sex and gender in *ero manga* but to problematize it. In order to do this, I also look at the place *ero manga* assumes in a wider culture and economy of labor, family, home, and leisure.

How *ero manga* are consumed is as important to their constructions of meaning, pleasure, and ideology as what is printed graphically on the page. For comic books filled with stories of sexual violence and images of naked bodies, they are marketed and consumed with surprising openness. Such openness is at odds with the way pornography circulates in a country like the United States, where its sale is bounded (by section of town, store, magazine rack, protected cover) and its consumption guided by a notion of privacy (it is read in private space or only in those parts of public space clearly marked for this purpose). *Ero manga*, by contrast, are

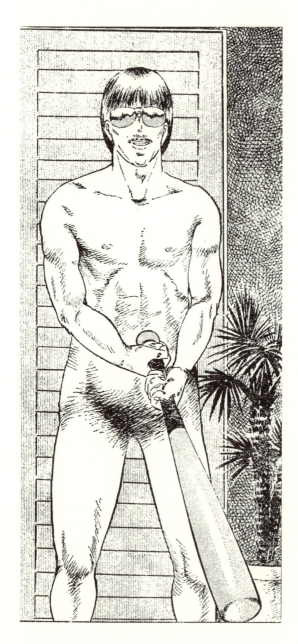

FIGURE 3.5   Censor-
ship laws prohibit the realistic display of penises in
mass media. Here the man's
penis is totally effaced and a
baseball bat substitutes.
Note that there is both a
presence and absence fig-
ured in the image; although
the bat is phallically displayed, the gap between the
man's legs is also clearly revealed. Read against the
grain, so to speak, this
image suggests not only the
man's phallicism but also
his impotency.
SOURCE: *Manga Erotopia*,
August 7, 1980 (Tokyo:
Besutoserazu KK), p. 135

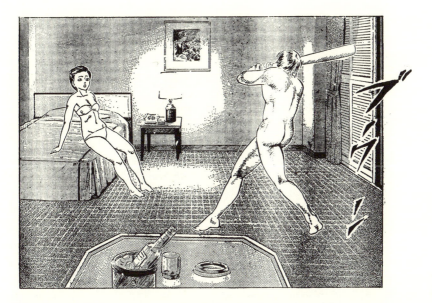

FIGURE 3.6   This man activates his "bat" in a gesture that obviously threatens the woman. Sexuality is heavily imbricated with violence in Japanese comics.
SOURCE: *Manga Erotopia,* August 7, 1980 (Tokyo: Besutoserazu KK), p. 136

positioned in full view in the many establishments in which they are sold. They are placed inside rather than outside the paths their readers will follow in their every-day lives (particularly for those who are most mobile, constantly moving between homes and places of study or labor[36]), and these paths also constitute the circuit within which *ero manga* are normally consumed. Images of naked schoolgirls and stories of their rape or sexual awakenings are thus bought and scanned freely in the domain of open public space.[37]

In this sense, *ero manga* is a very "public" culture. How does this feature interre-late with the content of explicit erotica? Does the public nature of *ero manga* act to tame their sexual or subversive potential (making them "no more" than comics), or do they, in being so publicly acceptable, encourage the acting out of violence against women? Japanese who have addressed this issue say neither is the case. They argue instead that erotic comics have an air of illicit fantasy. They straddle two worlds, and Sato attributes the increased popularity and production of *ero manga* in recent years to this "marginal, guerrilla-like character" (1981). Taking over the air of nonconventionality held earlier by *manga* in general, *ero manga,* he suggests, have become the new "war front," constituting a genre considered pe-ripheral but whose peripherality now generates profits. By adding a line of *ero manga,* for example, some failing publishing houses have managed to survive, and although their publication is still stigmatizing and a risk that is mainly taken on by only small publishing firms, some powerful *ero-gekiga*[38] magazines (e.g., *Alice*, *Erogenika*) have also emerged (Kamewada 1981).

The *ero manga*'s respectable profits are due to a very unrespectable kind of storytelling. Various Japanese commentators, as mentioned earlier, have called the sexual tales in *ero manga* illicit (Sato 1981) and dirty (Kimoto 1983). Yet some consider this to be the characterization given to sex generally in contemporary Japan and argue therefore that *ero manga*, with its explicit dirtiness, is not only not exceptional but paradigmatic of more broad-based sexual codes. Even if such perceptions of sex are more common than the actual practice of reading *ero manga*, Sato argues (speaking here of "porno culture," within which he places *ero manga*) that pornography "do[es] not have a legitimate place in society, and its consumers are made to feel guilty" (1981).[39] Yet feeling guilty does not reduce sales. On the contrary, the transgressive is what consumers seem, in large part, to be buying. And they consume it where it is most imaginable in Japan—in that space where Japanese move from one place to another, temporarily disconnected and released from the contexts and relations that bind them so tightly everywhere else. In a society where one's group and ranking determine not only how one should behave but also the identity one is given (at home a man is husband and father, for example; at work he is X position of Y division in Z company), being outside these groups means one is not bound by their rules and no longer identified by their frames. "He" becomes no one, a social anonymity disengaged from his placements within the spheres and relationships that socially matter. And assuming a mask, as it were, is the stance adopted by not only commuter-consumers but also *manga* males in order to pursue their form of play and of sex.

This structure of disjuncture and facelessness, so seemingly at odds with the principles that dictate social and economic relationships in late capitalist Japan, is key to the images and stories of sex crafted in *ero manga*. What is made ultimately and repeatedly sexual on the page is fleeting encounters and disguised or broken identities. Sex acts are momentary and superficial, engaged as much (if not more) to break someone down than to achieve orgasmic release, and they rarely result in enduring unions. The characteristics of interpersonal relations here—disengagement, distance, and disguise—are virtually the opposite of those ideologized as being essential to the "Japaneseness" of group membership: loyalty, attachment, and mutual self-exposure.[40] The latter is thought of in terms of a stickiness that, like glue, joins workers, for example, to companies not just during work hours but for "24 hours a day" (Aida 1972). By contrast, little is gluelike on the pages of an *ero manga*. Structures of transience, fragmentation, and truncation dominate. The staccato effect is a result not only of the narratival construction—sexual encounters are brief, quickly alternating (between positions, partners, acts), and evanescent (coming out of nowhere and moving, with little transition, into some-thing else)—but also of an emphasis on visuality that tends to displace or under-cut narrative altogether. Still shots continually break into narratives, making the stories pulsate rather than flow as all of one piece.

This is also the case with tempo, which is as hurried for the practice of consum-ing comic texts as for the action taking place within the text. In both, the engage-ment is sharp but also quick: In the stories men violently "get" the woman, then swiftly get out; in reading, consumers become riveted to a comic that they finish in minutes and then dump. The pattern of sex here mimics the pattern of con-sumption—intense, self-absorbed, and instantaneous. Buckley's stress on pene-tration seems only half of the equation; the other (and equally important) part is retreat. In terms of content, this pattern (of union and disrupture) characterizes the construction of sexuality. But what about gender? The configuration of male is certainly built on the motif of disrupture. Male behavior is brutish and narcis-sistic, driven by extreme emotions that find expression in acts of violence and movements that are abrupt, choppy, and rough. Almost everything about males is jagged. Their faces are sharply chiseled and nasty; their bodies are laden (and in-terfused) with machinery and object parts; their language is sparse and incom-plete. And most important, they attack, expressing their desires through aggres-sion more than anything else.

"Woman," of course, is primarily what and who men attack, and the construc-tion of femaleness is based both on this position (one of submission as in the endless shots of women tied up, pinned down, and with naked buttocks exposed) and that of representing the one continuous, smooth, and substantial element in the entire text. For all that they are battered, women continually return, centering the desires of men, the plots of the stories, and the focus of imagery. Their bodies are smooth and "natural," naked, unadorned, and uninterrupted by the sharp edges found on the cyborglike bodies of men. They tend to be gentle and forgiv-ing and speak with few words, softly mingling these with cries, moans, and tears. Their movements are muted and they primarily stay still. Unlike men, they do not, often cannot, run away; and despite being attacked, they typically do nothing to defend themselves, let alone try to fight back. Women stay grounded, or more to the point, they are the ground of the text, sex, and imagery of *ero manga*.

This is the major structure, I propose, to erotic comics as both a practice and text of mass culture. Gender is constructed as a difference between two kinds of identi-ties and ontologies—one impulsive, narcissistic, and machinelike; the other stable, continuous, and naturalistic—and "sex" is the act and relationship of the one trying to break down, break into, and break away from the other. Given such a basic code, there are multiple meanings the text of *ero manga* could inspire and various uses to which the practice of reading *manga* could be put. The most obvious message, of course, would seem to inspire men to misogynistically project and displace onto women their own frustrations caused by home and work. That *manga* are utilized as a diversionary and escapist "play" that "works" to relieve everyday tensions and thereby replenish a person's energy so that he or she can, for example, return to work is a standard functionalist explanation of comic reading in general. Further, the extreme degree of violence and aggression that characterizes *ero manga* (and is found abundantly in other types of *manga* and in other forms of mass media and mass entertainment such as television and cinema) is standardly said to allow the venting of pent-up resentments and desires in a society that is so repressive and controlling so much of the time.

"Woman" in *ero manga*, then, is a polyvalent symbol: She stands both meto-nymically for so-called real women (mainly wives and mothers who manage fam-ilies and homes in which the male's role has become increasingly irrelevant[41]) and metaphorically for other things (such as society in general, the social and eco-nomic expectation to work hard, entrance exams, and the social interrelatedness demanded at work). What is done to this "woman" is expressed, more than by any other gesture in erotic comics, by "sex" constructed variously but dominantly by violence. I want to remind readers of what precisely this violence consists and that it supersedes orgasmic release or genital penetration as *the* constant of sex. In doing so, I will concentrate on one act that is standard, if not necessarily *the* stan-dard, in sexualizing women in cartoon erotica: pulling a woman's pants down and forcibly inserting things into her anus. To complicate and problematize this motif further, I want to mention how prolific a trope it is in the recent genre of sexual comics targeted explicitly to women—ladies' comics. In one comic (also discussed in Chapter 7) in a 1994 issue of *Labien*,[42] for example, a woman who is bound to a man both as his student and lover endures endless forms of dominance at his hands. She is wrapped in tight bandages, ropes, and clothing and has endless ob-jects and liquids shoved into her buttocks: a string of tiny tin cans, a double dildo, and enemas of liquids and narcotics (see Figure 3.7). She agonizes over all of these, and when she asks her master what they are for, he answers (in the case of an enema that precedes the dildo) that he needs to "clean her all out: because other-wise she would be dirty."

Now this is an interesting commentary on action that centers on the butt. One might imagine, in fact, that one of the reasons the buttocks are such a prominent body part in *ero manga* is their association with dirtiness, particularly given that cleanliness is so ardently practiced in Japan and that it stands for cultural and so-cial order (it is literally sacred, a key ritual in Shinto to exorcise pollution). If the sex stories told in *ero manga* are valued in large part for the crudeness and dirti-ness of their depictions, what meaning has this desire for a "clean butt"? Certainly

FIGURE 3.7   From a ladies' comic, this is a common image of a woman being subjected to an enema.
SOURCE: *Labian,* December 1994 (Tokyo: Kasakura shuppansha), p. 16

the "master" does not insert his own penis into this orifice; nor, significantly, does he have any form of genital sex with this woman or show any signs of orgasmic release. Rather, what seems intended by this gesture is to exert another form of control, demonstrated by the fact that as the master "cleans" his submissive, he smiles with a smugness that recurs every time he has asserted dominance. This smile, and the woman's display of pain, follow every bodily interaction in this cartoon between the couple and, in this story at least, are the signs of and for sex (see Figure 3.8).

Although it might be argued that these signs do not denote sex per se but rather dominance, I remind readers that acts in which females are forced into submission are far more common than any other between females and males in the genre of *ero manga* (which are categorized, nonetheless, as comics that are "erotic"). Further, such acts rarely involve genital-genital copulation and even less commonly are shown to result in orgasmic release (in the *manga* I examined, orgasm was shown most often with genital-genital sex, occasionally with oral sex performed on either female or male, and never with anal sex). Of course, a sexuality not

FIGURE 3.8   These facial images differentiated by gender—the male smiles smugly, and the female shows pain and anguish—are used throughout this story of sexual adventure as signifiers for sex acts and sexual relationships.
SOURCE: *Labian,* December 1994 (Tokyo: Kasakura shuppansha), p. 31

dependent on orgasm or even genitals resembles or at least resonates with the conditions under which *ero manga* are often consumed:[43] In public places genital release must be deferred and voyeuristic behavior takes its place. Further, aggression against women for sexual pleasure has proliferated in real life, where acts of Peeping Tomism (*nozoki*), illicit touching on the trains (*chikan*), swiping of women's underwear off their clotheslines at night, and aggressive looking at women have become commonplace. Thus, to return to the question of the fixation on splayed buttocks in *ero manga,* the meaning and pleasure that this body part (in being seen, exposed, hurt, penetrated, possessed) generates is all about power. Power both constitutes and displaces sex, and it is sought not only through reading *ero manga.*

The "power" that is achieved in *ero manga,* however, seems fairly pathetic—a popsicle stick shoved up someone's ass results in no more than a whoop of glee for the perpetrator. Of course, sometimes the attacks are far more gruesome (reports of actual rape are surprisingly few in Japan; here I am speaking of only the comic representations), but the very artifice of the means used (disguises, deceptions, Coke bottles, baseball bats) and the excess of cruelty and force make the scenes appear less awe inspiring than hysterical and unreal. Commentators on *ero manga* often use this dissonance between the "unrealistic" depiction and real life to decry any resemblance between the two and to assert that *manga* are fantasies that no one believes and that have no impact on the behavior of real people. More to the point, perhaps, is the pounding repetitiousness of the attacks; power is so consistently sought on the pages of *ero manga*, yet is it ever achieved, or if so, is it ever sustained? Women are beaten time and time again into submission, but they always return, or if one woman is eliminated, another takes her place. Whatever it is these women stand for, men and their phallicism are fairly powerless in its presence.

Perhaps that is why "she" needs to be so persistently turned over: Thus the attacker can keep her source of resilience and toughness from view[44] and disavow his need for and dependence on her.[45] Of course, attacks continue to break women, to break from them quickly thereafter, and seemingly to break apart bonds of attachment. For all this display of breakage, however, something continues. The real stress in all this might be less on the breakage and more on the display: the show of aggression used as a device to ensure the continuity of a relationship rather than to sever it (what Barthes calls the "antidote" [Barthes 1972]). Such "devices" are found in mother-child relations in Japan, where children are indulged in a degree of aggressiveness (hitting, slapping) against their mothers, and in employer-employee relations, where subordinates are allowed to criticize, bad-mouth, ridicule, and even attack their bosses (usually such aggression is verbal, but I have also heard of instances when it becomes physical) during specially marked occasions (usually during outings where everyone is drinking [see Allison 1994]).

That reading *ero manga* is also used to symbolically express and therefore deflect aggression that builds up in places such as work makes sense. That this activity is therefore ideologically conservative, duplicating rather than remapping a social (corporate, political, educational) order based on the principle of hierarchy to which its subjects, male as well as female, are made to constantly and variously submit (or "take it in the ass," as overturned buttocks so graphically suggest), is confirmed by a number of *manga* commentators. Go (1981), Sato (1981), and Kusamori (1983) all describe readers of *ero manga*, for example, as weakened men—the antithesis of their projected image on the page. In Kusamori's words, "The energy of the readers is a feeling of weakness and debilitation" (241); that is, readers are driven more by the fear of impotency than the swagger of phallic strength, and by rage over being variously beaten down than by desire for sexual companionship or orgasmic release.

How imbricated sex is with power in erotic comics is demonstrated by its absence. In the *Labien* cartoon mentioned earlier, for example, there is one scene in which analism has been suspended and genital copulation takes its place. The partners, not surprisingly, have also changed. Instead of being with the "master," whom she has finally left after his tortures have become excessive, the woman is with a new lover who treats her as an equal. He kisses and caresses her, something she mentions her previous lover never did, and regards sex as something in which dominance has no part. This is interesting yet boring—both to the female character herself and obviously to the *manga* producers. Soon she has left and returned to her old relationship and familiar (dirty, escapist, transgressive, recreational) patterns of sex. On the last page we see her tied up by the master, who stands at a distance with a smug look on his face.

Conclusion

My argument has been that the popularity of dominance in sexual comics has both a generalized and genderized meaning. This dominance encodes, on the one hand, relations of power in which unremitting submission is demanded. Such relations stem from various places and spheres in Japan—school, family, workplace—and they beat down both women and men, as is evident from the commonness with which dominance appears as a sexual preference in erotic comics for both. What is genderized about all this is obvious: Women are the targets for *manga* violence even in comics aimed at women. Women become the scapegoats—the Lacanian "pound of flesh." They are the ones who get pummeled and blamed for institutional practices that were never started by them and that discriminate, typically, against them. These beatings are also not merely comic book fantasy. Sexual harassment is pronounced in Japan; physical violence against mothers and wives by frustrated sons and husbands is also no rarity.

That *ero manga* are misogynistic is undeniable. That they embed and thereby foster an ideology of gender chauvinism and crude masochism is also irrefutable. It is likely that this aspect of erotic comics (as well as of comics and mass culture in general) will change as more women enter the ranks of wage laborers and refuse to enter those of mother and wife. (It will be a comparatively longer time, however, before change will stem from men doing a greater share of domestic labor.) Sexual(ized) dominance is another matter and is a sobering commentary on the demands placed on Japanese people to sustain Japan's corporations, economy, students' high test scores, and the state.

One aspect of *ero manga*, however, strikes me as potentially radical. That is its decentering of sex, gender, and even power from male genitalia (or least naturalized genitalia). Though much of what men do in these stories hurts and degrades women and though the devices that help them are often phalliclike, if not naturalistic, penises, the very fact that there is a disjuncture here—a move away from something that only men could possess and onto things that could become feminized, degendered, or even disclaimed—bears the hint of a different type of social order than that which is hegemonic today. If not only gender but also Japaneseness was no longer moored to a notion of the "natural" body, the construction of national as well as gendered identity might significantly change.

ॐ 4 ॐ

Japanese Mothers and *Obentō*s: The Lunch Box as Ideological State Apparatus

Japanese nursery school children, going off to school for the first time, carry with them a boxed lunch (*obentō*) prepared by their mothers at home. Customarily these *obentō* are highly crafted elaborations: a multitude of miniportions artistically designed and precisely arranged in a container that is sturdy and cute. Mothers tend to expend inordinate time and attention on these *obentō* in efforts both to please their children and to affirm that they are good mothers. Children at nursery school are taught they must consume their entire meal according to school rituals.

Packing food in an *obentō* is an everyday practice of Japanese. *Obentō* are sold at train stations, catered for special meals, carried to work, and sold as fast food. Adoption of the *obentō* at the nursery school level may seem only natural to Japanese and unremarkable to outsiders, but I argue in this chapter that the *obentō* is invested with a gendered state ideology. Overseen by the authorities of the nursery school institution, which is linked to, if not directly monitored by, the state, the practice of the *obentō* situates the producer as a woman and mother and the consumer as a child of a mother and a student of a school. Food in this context is neither casual nor arbitrary. Eaten quickly in its entirety by the student, the *obentō* must be fashioned by the mother so as to expedite this chore for the child. Both mother and child are being watched, judged, and constructed; and it is only through their joint effort that the goal can be accomplished.

I use Louis Althusser's concept of the ideological state apparatuses (1971) to frame my argument, briefly describing how food is coded as a cultural and aesthetic apparatus in Japan and what authority the state holds over schools in Japanese society. Thus situating the parameters within which the *obentō* is regulated and structured in the nursery school setting, I will examine the practice both of making and eating *obentō* within the context of one nursery school in Tokyo. As an anthropologist and mother of a child who attended this school for fifteen months, I base my analysis on my observations; discussions with other mothers; daily conversations and an interview with my son's teacher; examination of *obentō* magazines and cookbooks; participation in school rituals, outings, and Mother's Association meetings; and the multifarious experiences of my son and myself as we faced the *obentō* process every day.

Although *obentō*s as a routine, task, and art form of nursery school culture are embedded with ideological and gendered meanings that the state indirectly manipulates, the manipulation is neither total nor totally coercive. Pleasure and creativity for both mother and child are also products of the *obentō* process.

Cultural Ritual and State Ideology

As anthropologists have long understood, not only are the worlds we inhabit symbolically constructed, but also our cultural symbols are endowed with, or have the potential for, power. How we see reality, in other words, is how we live it. So the conventions by which we recognize our universe are also those by which all of us assume our place and behavior within that universe. Culture is, in this sense, doubly constructive: constructing both the world for people and people for specific worlds.

The fact that culture is not necessarily innocent and power, not necessarily transparent has been revealed by much theoretical work conducted both inside and outside the discipline of anthropology. The scholarship of the neo-Marxist Louis Althusser (1971), for example, has encouraged the conceptualization of power as a force that operates in ways that are subtle, disguised, and accepted as everyday social practice. Althusser differentiated between two major structures of power in modern capitalist societies. The first he called (repressive) state apparatuses (SAs), institutions, such as the law and police, that are sanctioned by a repressive state to wield and manage power through the threat of force (1971:143–145).

Contrasted with this is a second structure of power—the ideological state apparatuses (ISAs). These are institutions that have some overt function other than political or administrative: mass media, education, health and welfare, for example. More numerous, disparate, and functionally polymorphous than the SAs, the ISAs exert power not primarily through repression but through ideology. Designed and accepted as having another purpose—to educate (the school system), entertain (film industry), or inform (news media)—the ISA serve not only their stated objective but also an unstated one, that of indoctrinating people into seeing the world a certain way and accepting certain identities as their own within that world (Althusser 1971:143–147).

Although both structures of power operate simultaneously and in complementarity, the ISAs, according to Althusser, are the more influential of the two in capitalist societies. Disguised and screened by another operation, the power of ideology in an ISA can be both more far reaching and insidious than an SA's power of coercion. Hidden in the movies we watch, the music we hear, the liquor we drink, the textbooks we read, the ISA is overlooked because it is protected, and its protection—or its alibi (Barthes 1972:109–111)—allows the terms and relations of ideology to spill into and infiltrate our everyday lives.

A world of commodities, gender inequalities, and power differentials is seen, therefore, as the natural environment, one that makes sense because it has become our experience to live it and accept it. This commonsense acceptance of a particular world is the work of ideology, and it works by concealing the coercive and repressive elements of our everyday routines but also by making those routines of the everyday familiar, desirable, and simply our own. This is the critical element of Althusser's notion of ideological power: Ideology is so potent because it becomes not only ours but us—the terms and machinery by which we structure ourselves and identify who we are.

Japanese Food as Cultural Myth

The author in one *obentō* magazine, the type of medium-sized publication that, filled with glossy pictures of *obentō* and ideas and recipes for successfully recreating them, sells in the bookstores across Japan, declares: "The making of the *obentō* is the one most worrisome concern facing the mother of a child going off to school for the first time" (Shufunotomo 1980: inside cover).

Another *obentō* journal, this one heftier and packaged in the encyclopedic series of the prolific women's publishing firm Shufunotomo, articulates the same social fact: "First-time *obentōs* are a strain on both parent and child" (*"Hajimete no obentō wa, oya mo ko mo kinchōshimasu"*) (Shufunotomo 1981:55).

Any outside observer might ask, What is the real source of worry over *obentō*? Is it the food itself or the entrance of the young child into school for the first time? Yet as one looks at a typical child's *obentō*—a small box packaged with a five- or six-course miniaturized meal whose pieces and parts are artistically and neatly arranged and perfectly cut (see Figures 4.1, 4.2)—would immediately reveal, no food is "just" food in Japan. What is not so immediately apparent, however, is why a small child with limited appetite and perhaps scant interest in food is the recipient of a meal as elaborate and as elaborately prepared as any made for an entire family or invited guests?

Certainly in Japan, much attention is focused on the *obentō*. It is invested with a significance far beyond that of the merely pragmatic, functional one of sustaining a child with nutritional foodstuffs. Since this investment beyond the pragmatic is

FIGURE 4.1   Example of *obentōs*, signs of maternal love and labor.
SOURCE: *365 nichi no obentō hyakka* (Encyclopedia of lunch box for 365
days), 1981 (Tokyo: Shufunotomosha), p. 83

true of any food prepared in Japan, it is helpful to examine culinary codes for
food preparation that operate generally in the society before focusing on children's *obentō*.

As has been remarked often about Japanese food, the key element is appearance. Food must be organized and reorganized, arranged and rearranged, stylized
and restylized, to appear in a design that is visually attractive. Presentation is critical not to the extent that taste and nutrition are displaced, as has been sometimes
argued, but to the degree that how food looks is at least as important as how it
tastes and how good and sustaining it is for one's body.

As Donald Richie points out in his eloquent and informative book *A Taste of
Japan* (1985), presentational style is the guiding principle by which food is prepared in Japan, and the style is conditioned by a number of codes. One code is for
smallness, separation, and fragmentation. Nothing large is allowed, so all portions
are cut to be bite sized and served in tiny individual dishes.[1] There is no one big
dinner plate with three large portions of vegetable, starch, and meat, as in American cuisine. Consequently, the eye is pulled not toward one totalizing center but
away to a multiplicity of decentered parts.[2]

Visually, food is presented according to a structural principle not only of seg-
mentation but also of opposition. Foods are broken up or cut up to make con-
trasts of color, texture, and shape. Foods are meant to oppose one another and

FIGURE 4.2   An *obentō* cookbook lists suggestions for the month of January.
This lunch is made out of dried salmon flakes, vegetables, fruit, and rice and is
constructed to look like a flower patch.
SOURCE: *365 nichi no obentō hyakka* (Encyclopedia of lunch box for 365 days), 1981
(Tokyo: Shufunotomosha), p. 103

clash: pink against green, roundish foods against angular ones, smooth substances
next to rough ones. This oppositional code operates not only within and between
the foods themselves but also between the food and the containers in which they
are placed: a circular mound in a square dish, a bland-colored food set against a
bright plate, a translucent sweet in a heavily textured bowl (Richie 1985:40–41).

The container is as important as what is contained, but it is really the contain-
ment that is stressed, that is, how food has been (re)constructed and (re)arranged
from nature to appear, in both beauty and freshness, perfectly natural. This styliz-
ing of nature is a third code by which presentation is directed; the injunction is
not only to retain, as much as possible, the innate naturalness of the ingredients—
by shopping daily so food is fresh and leaving much of it either raw or only mini-
mally cooked—but also to recreate in prepared food the promise and appearance
of the "natural." As Richie writes, "The emphasis is on presentation of the natural
rather than the natural itself. It is not what nature has wrought that excites admi-
ration but what man has wrought with what nature has wrought"(1985:11).

This naturalization of food is rendered in primarily two ways. First, nature is
constantly hinted at and appropriated through decorations that serve as sea-
sonal reminders, such as a maple leaf in the fall or a flower in the spring; through

the food itself, such as in-season fruits and vegetables; and through season-coordinated dishes such as glassware in the summer and heavy pottery in the winter. The other device, to some degree the inverse of the first, is to accentuate and perfect the preparation process to such an extent that the food appears not only to be natural but more nearly perfect than nature ever could be. This is nature made artificial. Thus, by naturalization, nature is not only taken in by Japanese cuisine but taken over.

It is this ability both to appropriate "real" nature (the maple leaf on the tray) and to stamp the human reconstruction of that nature as "natural" that lends Japanese food its potential for cultural and ideological manipulation. It is what Barthes calls a second-order myth (1972:114–117). A second-order myth is created when a practice, or "language" in Barthes's terms, is taken over by some interest or agenda in order to serve a different end. For example, people commonly send roses to lovers and consume wine with dinner; a mother makes a practice of cleaning up after her child. These practices serve individual, pragmatic ends. They constitute a "first order of language," or a "language-object," again in Barthes's terms. A second order of language (or a "metalanguage" or "second-order semiological system") is created when the florist who sells roses, the liquor companies who market wine, or conservative politicians who campaign for a gendered division of labor with women kept at home promote such practices for their own ends. Thus what is practical or individual becomes politicized. As Barthes points out, the primary meaning is never lost. Rather, it remains and stands as an alibi, the cover under which the second, politicized meaning can now hide. Roses sell better, for example, when lovers view them as a vehicle to express love rather than as the means by which a company stays in business.

At one level, food is just food in Japan—the medium by which humans sustain their nature and health. Yet Japanese cuisine carries other meanings that in Barthes's terms are mythological. One of these is national identity: Food is appropriated as a sign of the culture. To be Japanese is to eat Japanese food, as so many Japanese confirm when they travel to other countries and cite the greatest problem they encounter as the absence of "real" Japanese food. Stated the other way around, rice is so symbolically central to Japanese culture that many Japanese say they can never feel full until they have consumed their rice at a particular meal or at least once during the day.[3]

Embedded within this insistence on eating Japanese food, thereby reconfirming and reidentifying one as a member of the culture, are the principles by which Japanese food is customarily prepared: perfection, labor, small distinguishable parts, opposing segments, beauty, and the stamp of nature. Overarching all these more detailed codings are two that guide the making and ideological appropriation of the nursery school *obentō* most directly: (1) there is an order to the food, a right way to do things with everything in its place and each place coordinated with every other, and (2) the one who prepares the food takes on the responsibility of producing food to the standards of perfection and exactness that Japanese cuisine demands. Food may not be casual, in other words, and the producer may not be casual in preparing it. In these two rules is a message both about social order and the role gender plays in sustaining and nourishing that order.

School, State, and Subjectivity

In addition to first- and second-order meanings (food as pragmatic and food as culturally coded), the rituals and routines surrounding *obentō*s in Japanese nursery schools present, I suggest, a third order, manipulation. This order is installed by the school system to socialize children as well as their mothers into the gendered roles and subjectivities they are expected to assume in a political order desired and directed by the state.

In modern capitalist societies such as Japan, the school, according to Althusser, assumes the primary role of ideological state apparatus. A greater segment of the population spends longer hours and more years here than in previous historical periods. Also, education has now taken over from other institutions such as religion the pedagogical function of being the major shaper and inculcator of knowledge for the society. Concurrently, as Althusser has pointed out for capitalist modernism (1971:152,156), repression has gradually been replaced by ideology as the prime mechanism for behavior enforcement. We are influenced less by the threat of force and more by the devices that present and inform us of the world we live in and the subjectivities that world demands; thus knowledge and ideology become fused and education emerges as the apparatus for pedagogical and ideological indoctrination.

In practice, as school teaches children how and what to think, it also shapes them for the roles and positions they will later assume as adult members of the society. How the social order is organized according to gender, power, labor, and class, in other words, not only is as important as the basics of reading and writing but is transmitted through and embedded in those classroom lessons. Thus knowledge is not only socially constructed but also differentially acquired according to who one is or will be in the political society one will enter in later years. Precisely what society requires in the way of workers, citizens, and parents will be the condition determining or influencing instruction in the schools.

This latter equation, of course, depends on two factors: (1) the agreement or disagreement among different interests concerning what subject positions are desirable and (2) the power any particular interest, including the state, has in exerting its desires on or through the system of education. In Japan's case, the state wields enormous control over the systematization of education. Through its Ministry of Education (Monbushō), education is centralized and managed by a state bureaucracy that regulates almost every aspect of the educational process. On any given day, for example, what is taught in every public school follows the same curriculum, adheres to the same structure, and is informed by textbooks from the prescribed list. Teachers are nationally screened, school boards uniformly appointed (rather than elected), and students institutionally exhorted to obey teachers given their legal authority (changing in some prefectures these days), for example, to write secret reports (*naishinsho*) that may obstruct a student's entrance into high school.[4]

The role of the state in Japanese education is not limited, however, to the extensive power granted to the Ministry of Education. Even more powerful is the principle of the *gakureki shakai* (literally, academic-record society) by which careers of adults are determined by the schools they attend as youth. A reflection and construction of the new economic order of postwar Japan,[5] school attendance has become the single most important determinant in who will achieve the most desirable positions in industry, government, and the professions. School admission is itself based on a single criterion—a system of entrance exams that determines entrance selection—and it is to the end of preparation for exams that school, even at the nursery school level, is increasingly oriented. Learning to follow directions, doing as one is told, and *ganbaru* (or working hard, never giving up; Asanuma 1987) are social imperatives that are sanctioned by the state and taught in the schools.

Nursery School and Ideological Appropriation of the *Obentō*

The nursery school stands outside the structure of compulsory education in Japan. Most nursery schools are private, and although attendance is not compulsory, a greater proportion of the three- to six-year-old population of Japan attends preschool than in any other industrialized nation (Tobin 1989; Hendry 1986; Boocock 1989).

Differentiated from the *hoikuen*, a preschool institution with longer hours and more like day care than school,[6] the *yōchien* (nursery school) is widely perceived as instructional, not necessarily in a formal curriculum but more in indoctrination to attitudes and structures of Japanese schooling. Children learn less about reading and writing than they do about how to become a Japanese student; and both parts of this formula—Japanese and student—are equally stressed. As Rohlen has written, the "social order is generated" in the nursery school, first and foremost, by a system of routines (1989:10, 21). Educational routines and rituals are therefore of heightened importance in *yōchien*, for whereas these routines and rituals may be the format through which subjects are taught in higher grades, they are both form and subject in the *yōchien*.

Although the state (through Monbushō) has no direct mandate over attendance at nursery schools, its influence at this level is nevertheless significant. First, authority over how the *yōchien* is run is in the hands of the Ministry of Education. Second, most parents and teachers see the *yōchien* as the first step to the system of compulsory education that starts in the first grade and is closely controlled by Monbushō. The principal of the *yōchien* my son attended, for example, stated that he saw his main duty as preparing children to enter more easily the rigors of public education soon to come. Third, the rules and patterns of group living (*shūdan seikatsu*), a Japanese social ideal that is reiterated nationwide by political leaders, corporate management, and educators, is first introduced to the child in nursery school.[7]

The entry into nursery school marks a transition both away from home and into the "real world," which is generally judged to be difficult, even traumatic, for the Japanese child (Peak 1989). The *obentō* is intended to ease a child's discomfiture and to allow a child's mother to manufacture something of herself and the home to accompany the child as she or he moves into the potentially threatening outside world. Japanese use the cultural categories of *soto* and *uchi*: Soto connotes the outside, which in being distanced and other is cold and hostile; and *uchi* identifies as warm and comfortable what is inside and familiar. The school falls initially, and to some degree perpetually, into a category of *soto*. What is ultimately the definition and location of *uchi*, by contrast, is the home, where family and mother reside.[8] By producing something from the home, a mother both girds and goads her child to face what is inevitable in the world that lies beyond. This is the mother's role and her gift; by giving of herself and the home (which she both symbolically represents and in reality manages[9]), she makes the *soto* of the school more bearable.

The *obentō* comes to be filled with the meaning of mother and home in a number of ways. The first is by sheer labor. Women spend what seems to be an inordinate amount of time on the production of this one item. As an experienced *obentō* maker myself, I can attest to the intense attention and energy devoted to this one chore. On the average, mothers spend twenty-five to forty-five minutes every morning cooking, preparing, and assembling the contents of one *obentō* for one nursery school child. In addition, the previous day they have planned, shopped, and often organized a supper meal with leftovers in mind for the next day's *obentō*. Frequently women[10] discuss *obentō* ideas with other mothers, scan *obentō* cookbooks or magazines for recipes, buy or make objects with which to decorate or contain (part of) the *obentō*, and perhaps make small food portions to freeze and retrieve for future *obentō*s.[11]

Of course, effort alone does not necessarily produce a successful *obentō*. But apart from the results, casualness is never indulged, and even mothers with children who would eat anything prepared *obentō*s as elaborate as anyone else's. Such labor is intended for the child but also the mother: It is a sign of a woman's commitment as a mother and her inspiring her child to being similarly committed as a student. The *obentō* is thus a representation of what the mother is and what the child should become. A model for school is inherent to what is a gift and reminder from home.

This equation is spelled out more precisely in a nursery school rule: All of the *obentō* must be eaten. Though on the face of it, this rule is petty and mundane, it is taken very seriously by nursery school teachers and is one not easily conformed to by very small children. The logic is that it is time for the child to meet certain expectations. One of the main agendas of the nursery school, after all, is to introduce and indoctrinate children into the patterns and rigors of Japanese education (Rohlen 1989; Sano 1989; Lewis 1989). And Japanese education, by all accounts, is not about fun (Duke 1986).

Learning is hard work with few choices or pleasures. Even *obentō*s from home stop once the child enters first grade.[12] The meals there are institutional: largely bland, unappealing, and prepared with only nutrition in mind. To ease a youngster into these upcoming (educational, social, disciplinary, culinary) routines, *obentō*s at *yōchien* are designed to be pleasing and personal. The *obentō* is also designed, however, as a test for the child. And the double meaning is not unintentional. A structure already filled with a signification of mother and home is then emptied to provide a new form, one now also written with the ideological demands of being a member of Japanese culture and a viable and successful Japanese in the realms of school and later work.

The exhortation to consume one's entire *obentō*[13] is articulated and enforced by the nursery school teacher. The meal can be made into high drama by, for example, singing a song; collectively thanking Buddha (in the case of Buddhist nursery schools), one's mother for making the *obentō*, and one's father for providing the means to make the *obentō*; having two assigned class helpers pour the tea; and eating together until everyone has finished. Also, the teacher examines the children's *obentō*s, making sure the food is all consumed and encouraging, sometimes scolding, children who are taking too long. Slow eaters do not fare well in this ritual because they hold up the other students, who as a peer group also monitor a child's eating. My son often complained about a child whose slowness over food meant that the others were kept inside (rather than being allowed to play on the playground) for much of the lunch period.

Ultimately and officially it is the teacher, however, whose role and authority it is to surveil food consumption and to judge the person consuming food. Her surveillance covers both the student and the mother, who in the matter of the *obentō* must work together. The child's job is to eat the food and the mother's, to prepare it. Hence, the responsibility and execution of one's task is not only shared but conditioned by the other. My son's teacher would talk with me daily about the progress he was making finishing his *obentō*s. Although the overt subject of discussion was my child, most of what was said was directed to me and entailed what I could do in order to get David to consume his lunch more easily.

The intensity of these talks struck me at the time as curious. We had just settled in Japan and David, a highly verbal child, was attending a foreign school in a foreign language he had not yet mastered; he was the only non-Japanese child in the school. Many of his behaviors during this time were disruptive: For example, he went up and down the line of children during morning exercises, hitting each child on the head. Hamada-sensei, however, chose to discuss the *obentō*s. I thought that surely David's survival in and adjustment to this environment depended much more on other factors, such as learning Japanese. Yet it was the *obentō* that was discussed with such detail ("David ate all his peas today, but not a single carrot until I asked him to do so three times") and seriousness that I assumed her attention was being misplaced. The manifest reference was to box lunches, but wasn't the latent reference to something else?[14]

Of course, there was another message for me and my child. It was an injunction to follow directions, obey rules, and accept the authority structures of the school system. And all of these practices were embedded in and inculcated through certain rituals: In the nursery school (as in any school except such nonconventional ones as Waldorf and Montessori) and practically any social or institutional practice in Japan, activity was so heavily ritualized and ritualistic that the very form of ritual took on a meaning and value in and of itself (Rohlen 1989:21, 27–28). Both the school day and school year of the nursery school were organized by these rituals. The day, apart from two free periods, for example, was broken by definite routines—morning exercises, arts and crafts, gym instruction, singing—most of which were named and scheduled. The school year was also segmented into and marked by three annual events—Sports Day (Undōkai) in fall, the Winter Assembly (Seikatsu Happyōkai) in December, and the Dance Festival (Bon Odori) in summer. Energy was galvanized by these rituals, which demanded a degree of order as well as a discipline and self-control that non-Japanese would find remarkable.

Significantly, David's teacher marked his successful integration into the school system by his mastery not of the language or other cultural skills but of the school's daily routines—walking in line, brushing his teeth after eating, arriving at school early, eagerly participating in greeting and departure ceremonies, and completing all of his *obentō* on time. Not only had he adjusted to the school structure but he had also become accepted by the other children as a member of the

group. Or restated, what once had been externally enforced now became ideologically desirable; the everyday practices had moved from being alien to familiar to
him, that is, from being someone else's to being his own. My American child had
to become, in some sense, Japanese, and where his teacher recognized this Japaneseness was in the daily routines such as finishing his *obentō*. The lesson learned
early, which David learned as well, is that not adhering to routines such as completing one's *obentō* on time leads to not only admonishment from the teacher
but, more importantly, rejection from the other students.

The nursery school system differentiates between the child who does and the
child who does not manage the multifarious and constant rituals of nursery
school. And for those who don't manage, there is a penalty the child learns to either avoid or wish to avoid. Seeking the acceptance of his peers, the student develops the aptitude, willingness, and, in the case of my son—whose outspokenness
and individuality were the characteristics most noted in this culture—even the
desire to conform to the highly ordered and structured practices of nursery
school life. As Althusser (1971) wrote about ideology, the mechanism works when
and because ideas about the world and particular roles in that world that serve
other (social, political, economic, state) agendas become familiar and one's own.

Rohlen makes a similar point, that what is taught and learned in nursery school is
social order. Called *shūdan seikatsu,* or group life, it means organization into a group
where a person's role is determined by group membership and not "the assumption
of choice and rational self-interest" (1989:30). A child learns, in nursery school, to be
with others, think like others, and act in tandem with others. This lesson is taught
primarily through the precision and constancy of basic routines: "Order is shaped
gradually by the repeated practice of selected daily tasks . . . that socialize the children to high degrees of neatness and uniformity" (Rohlen 1989:21). Yet a feeling of
coerciveness is rarely experienced by the child when three principles of nursery
school instruction are in place: (1) school routines are made "desirable and pleasant" (30), (2) the teacher disguises her authority by trying to make the group the
voice and unit of authority, and (3) the regimentation of the school is maintained
through an attitude of "intimacy" with the students on the part of the teachers and
administrators (30). In short, when the desires and routines of the school are made
into the desires and routines of the child, they are made acceptable.

Mothering as Gendered Ideological State Apparatus

The rituals surrounding the *obentō*'s consumption in the school determine what
ideological meanings the *obentō* transmits to the child. The process of production
within the home, by contrast, organizes its somewhat different ideological pack-

age for the mother. The two sets of meanings are intertwined, but the mother is faced with different expectations in the preparation of the *obentō* than the child is in its consumption. At a pragmatic level, the child must simply eat the lunch, whereas the mother's job is far more complicated. The onus for her is getting the child to consume what she has made, and the general attitude is that this is far more the mother's responsibility at this transitional stage than the child's.

Much of what is written, advised, and discussed about the *obentō* has the explicit aim of helping the mother prepare food that the child will eat. One magazine advises: "The first day of taking *obentō* is a worrisome thing for both mother and *boku* [child].[15] Put in easy-to-eat foods that your child likes and is already used to, and prepare this food in small portions" (Shufunotomo 1980:28).

Filled with recipes, pictures, and ideas, the magazine heads each page with "helpful" hints:

- Easy-to-eat is step one.
- Next is being able to consume the *obentō* without leaving anything behind.
- Make it in such a way that the child can become proficient in the use of chopsticks.
- Decorate and fill it with cute dreams (*kawairashī yume*).
- For older classes (*nenchōgumi*), make *obentō* filled with variety.
- Once they've become used to it, balance foods your child likes with those they dislike.
- For kids who hate vegetables . . .
- For kids who hate fish . . .
- For kids who hate meat . . . (Shufunotomo: 28–53).

A number of principles are laced throughout cookbooks and other magazines devoted to *obentō*, the *obentō* guidelines issued by the school and sent home in the school flier every two weeks, and the words of Japanese mothers and teachers discussing *obentō*: (1) food should be cut for easy manipulation with fingers or chopsticks, (child-size) spoons and forks, skewers, or toothpicks; (2) portions should be kept small so the *obentō* can be consumed quickly and without any leftovers; (3) food that a child does not yet like should be eventually added so as to remove fussiness (*sukikirai*) in food habits; (4) the *obentō* should be pretty, cute, and visually changeable by presenting the food attractively and by adding nonfood objects such as silver paper, foil, toothpick flags, paper napkins, cute handkerchiefs, and variously shaped containers for portions and sauces (see Figure 4.3); and (5) *obentō*s should contain related items made as much as possible by the mother's own hands, including the *obentō* bag (*obentōbukuro*) in which the *obentō* is contained.

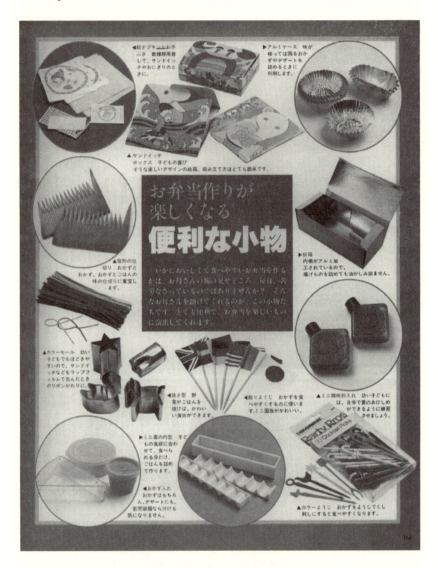

FIGURE 4.3   Stores sell a wide range of *obentō* paraphernalia.
SOURCE: *365 nichi no obentō hyakka* (Encyclopedia of lunch box for 365 days), 1981
(Tokyo: Shufunotomosha), p. 114

The strictures propounded by publications seem to be endless. In practice I found that visual appeal was stressed by the mothers. By contrast, the directive to use *obentō* as a training process—adding new foods and getting older children to use chopsticks and learn to tie the *furoshiki*[16]—was emphasized by those judging the *obentō* at the school. Where these two sets of concerns met was, of course, in the child's success or failure in finishing the *obentō*. In my experience, the *obentō* was ultimately judged based on this outcome and the mother's role in it.

The aestheticization of the *obentō* is by far its most intriguing aspect for a cultural anthropologist. Aesthetic categories and codes that operate generally for Japanese cuisine are applied, though adjusted, to the nursery school format. Substances are many but petite, kept segmented and opposed, and manipulated intensively to achieve an appearance that often changes or disguises the food. As a mother insisted to me, the creation of a bear out of miniature hamburgers and rice or a flower from an apple or peach is meant to sustain a child's interest in the underlying food. Yet my child, at least, rarely noticed or appreciated the art I had so laboriously contrived. As for other children, I observed that even for those who ate with no obvious "fussinesses," mothers' efforts to create food as style continued all year long.

Thus much of a woman's labor over *obentō* stems from some agenda other than that of getting the child to eat an entire lunch. The latter is certainly a consideration, and it is the rationale as well as cover for women being scrutinized by the school's authority figure—the teacher. Yet two other factors are important. One is that the *obentō* is but one aspect of the far more expansive and continuous commitment a mother is expected to make for and to her child. *Kyōiku mama* (education mother) is the term given to a mother who executes her responsibility to oversee and manage the education of her children with excessive vigor. And yet this excess is not only demanded by the state even at the level of the nursery school; it is conventionally practiced by mothers. Mothers who manage the home and children, often in virtual absence of a husband and father, are considered the factor that may make or break a child as she or he advances toward that pivotal point, the entrance examinations.[17]

In this sense, just as the *obentō* is meant as a device to assist a child in the struggles of first adjusting to school, the mother is generally perceived as being the support, goad, and cushion for the child. She will perform endless and multiple tasks to assist in her child's study: sharpen pencils and make midnight snacks as the child studies, study in order to better verse herself in subjects her child is weak in, make inquiries as to what school is most appropriate for her child, and consult with her child's teachers. If the child succeeds, a mother is complimented; if the child fails, a mother feels guilty.

Thus at the nursery school level, the mother starts her own preparation for this upcoming role. Yet the jobs and energies demanded of a nursery school mother are, in themselves, surprisingly consuming. Just as the mother of an entering student is given a book listing all the preentry tasks she must complete—for example, making various bags and containers, affixing labels to all clothes in precisely the right place and with the size exactly right—she will be continually expected thereafter to attend Mother's Association meetings, accompany children on field trips, wash the indoor clothes and shoes of her child every week, add required items to a child's bag on a day's notice, and be generally available. Few mothers at the school my son attended could afford to work even part-time or temporary jobs. Those women who did tended either to keep their outside work a secret or to be reprimanded by a teacher for insufficient devotion to their child. (See Figure 4.4.) Motherhood, in other words, is institutionalized through the child's school and such routines as making the *obentō* as a full-time, stay-at-home job.[18]

The second factor in a woman's devotion to overelaborating her child's lunch-box is that her experience in doing thus becomes a part of her and a statement, in some sense, of who she is. Marx writes that labor is the most "essential" aspect of our species and that we are defined by what we produce (Marx and Engels 1970:71–76). An *obentō*, therefore, is not only a gift or test for a child but a representation and product of the woman herself. Of course, these ideologically converge, as has been stated already, but I would also suggest that there is a potential disjoining. I sensed that the women were laboring for themselves apart from the school agenda regarding the *obentō*. Or stated alternatively, in the role of domestic manager, mother, and wife that females in Japan are highly pressured and encouraged to assume there is, besides the endless and onerous responsibilities, also an opportunity for play. Significantly, women find play and creativity not outside their social roles but within them.

Saying this is not to deny the constraints and surveillance under which Japanese women labor at their *obentō*s. Like their children at school, they are watched by not only the teacher but each other and perfect what they create, partially at least, so as to be confirmed as good and dutiful mothers in the eyes of other mothers. The enthusiasm with which they absorb this task, then, is like my son's acceptance and internalization of the nursery school routines; no longer enforced from outside, the task becomes adopted as one's own.

The making of the *obentō* is, I would thus argue, a double-edged sword for women. By relishing its creation (for all the intense labor expended, only once or twice did I hear a mother voice any complaint about this task), a woman is ensconcing herself in the ritualization and subjectivity (subjection) of being a mother in Japan. She is alienated in the sense that others dictate, surveil, and manage her work. On the flip side, however, it is precisely through this work that the woman expresses, identifies, and constitutes herself. As Althusser pointed out, ideology can never be totally abolished (1971:170), which is true in the elaborations that women work on "natural" food, producing an *obentō* that is creative and, to some degree, a fulfilling and personal statement.

Minami-san, an informant, revealed how both restrictive and pleasurable the daily rituals of motherhood can be. The mother of two children—one aged three and one a nursery school student—Minami-san had been a professional opera

いつも一緒、かわいいキユーピー。

FIGURE 4.4   An ad for Kewpie mayonnaise that reads, "Always together, cute
Kewpie." The image is of a working woman who should be carrying a "cute" child with
her. Thus her role as mother continues even into the workplace. This ideology of the
continuous mother is also expressed in children who "carry" their mothers everywhere,
for example, to school with the mother-prepared *obentō*.
SOURCE: *365 nichi no obentō hyakka* (Encyclopedia of lunch box for 365 days), 1981
(Tokyo: Shufunotomosha), back cover

singer before marrying at the relatively late age of thirty-two. Now her daily schedule was organized by routines associated with her child's nursery school—for example, making the *obentō*, taking her daughter to school and picking her up, attending Mother's Association meetings, arranging daily play dates, and keeping the school uniform clean. Minami-san wished to return to singing if only on a part-time basis, but she said that the demands of motherhood, particularly those imposed by her child's attendance at nursery school, frustrated this desire. Secreting only minutes out of any day to practice, Minami-san missed singing and told me that being a mother in Japan means being a mother to the exclusion of almost anything else.[19]

Despite this frustration, however, Minami-san did not behave like a frustrated woman. Rather she devoted to her mothering an energy, creativity, and intelligence I found to be standard in the Japanese mothers I knew. She planned special outings for her children at least two or three times a week, organized games that she knew they would like and that would teach them cognitive skills, created her own stories and designed costumes for afternoon play, and shopped daily for the meals she prepared with her childrens' favorite foods in mind. Minami-san told me often that she wished she could sing more, but never did she complain about her children, the chores of child-raising, or being a mother. And her attentiveness was exemplified most fully in her *obentōs*. No two were ever alike, each had at least four or five portions, and she kept trying out new ideas for both new foods and new designs. She took pride as well as pleasure in her *obentō* handicraft, but although Minami-san's *obentō* creativity was impressive, it wasn't unusual.

Examples of such *obentō* creations from an *obentō* magazine include (1) donut *obentō*: two donuts, two wieners cut to look like a worm, two cut pieces of apple, two small cheese rolls, one hard-boiled egg made to look like a rabbit with leaf ears and pickle eyes and set in an aluminum muffin tin, cute paper napkin added; (2) wiener doll *obentō*: a bed of rice with two doll creations made out of wiener parts (each doll consists of eight pieces for hat, hair, head, arms, body, legs), a line of pink ginger, a line of green parsley, paper flag of France added; (3) vegetable flower and tulip *obentō*: a bed of rice laced with chopped hard-boiled egg, three tulip flowers made out of cut wieners with spinach precisely arranged as stem and leaves, a fruit salad with two raisins, three cooked peaches, three pieces of cooked apple; (4) sweetheart doll *obentō:* in a two-sectioned *obentō* box there are four rice balls on one side, each with a different center, on the other side are two dolls made of quail's eggs for heads, eyes and mouth added, bodies of cucumber, arranged as if lying down with two raw carrots for the pillow, covers made of one flower—cut cooked carrot, two pieces of ham, pieces of cooked spinach, and with different colored plastic skewers holding the dolls together (Shufunotomo 1980:27, 30). (See Figure 4.5 for more examples of creative *obentōs*.)

FIGURE 4.5   This page from an *obentō* magazine shows four ideas for making *obentō*s that appeal to kids.

SOURCE: *Obentō 500 sen* (500 selections of lunch box), 1987 (Tokyo: Shufunotomosha), p. 63

The impulse to work and rework nature in these *obentō*s is most obvious perhaps in the strategies used to transform, shape, and disguise foods. Every mother I knew came up with her own repertoire of such techniques, and every *obentō* magazine or cookbook I examined offered a special section on these devices (see Figure 4.6). It is important to keep in mind that these are treated as only embellishments added to parts of an *obentō* composed of many parts. The following is a list from one magazine: lemon pieces made into butterflies, hard-boiled eggs made into *daruma* (popular Japanese legendary figure of a monk without his eyes; eyes are added to *daruma* figures when a person reaches her or his goal), sausage cut into flowers, a hard-boiled egg decorated as a baby, an apple piece cut into a leaf, a radish flaked into a flower, a cucumber cut like a flower, *mikan* (nectarine orange) pieces arranged into a basket, a boat with a sail made from a cucumber, skewered sausage, radish shaped like a mushroom, a quail egg flaked into a cherry, twisted *mikan* piece, sausage cut to become a crab, a patterned cucumber, a ribboned carrot, a flowered tomato, cabbage leaf flower, a potato cut to be a worm, a carrot designed as a red shoe, an apple cut to simulate a pineapple (Shufunotomo 1980: 57–60).

Nature is not only transformed but also supplemented by store-bought or mother-made objects that are precisely arranged in the *obentō*. The former come from an entire industry and commodification of the *obentō* process: complete racks or sections in stores selling *obentō* boxes, additional small containers, *obentō* bags, cups, chopstick and utensil containers (all these with various cute characters or designs on the front), cloth and paper napkins, foil, aluminum tins, colored ribbon or string, plastic skewers, toothpicks with paper flags, and paper dividers. Mothers are encouraged and praised for making some of these themselves: *obentō* bags, napkins, and handkerchiefs with appliqued designs or the child's name embroidered. These supplements to the food, the arrangement of the food, and the *obentō* box's dividing walls (removable and adjustable) furnish the order of the *obentō*. Everything appears crisp and neat with each part kept in its own place: two tiny hamburgers set firmly atop a bed of rice, vegetables in a separate compartment in the box, fruit arranged in a muffin tin.

How the specific forms of *obentō* artistry—for example, a wiener cut to look like a worm and set within a muffin tin—are encoded symbolically is a fascinating subject. Limited here by space, however, I will only offer initial suggestions. Arranging food into a scene recognizable by the child was an ideal mentioned by many mothers and cookbooks. Animals, human beings, and other food forms (making a pineapple out of an apple, for example) predominate, perhaps for no other reason than that they are familiar to children and easily produced by mothers. Mothers I knew created animals and faces in supper meals and *obentō* made for other outings, yet their impulse to do this seemed not only heightened in the

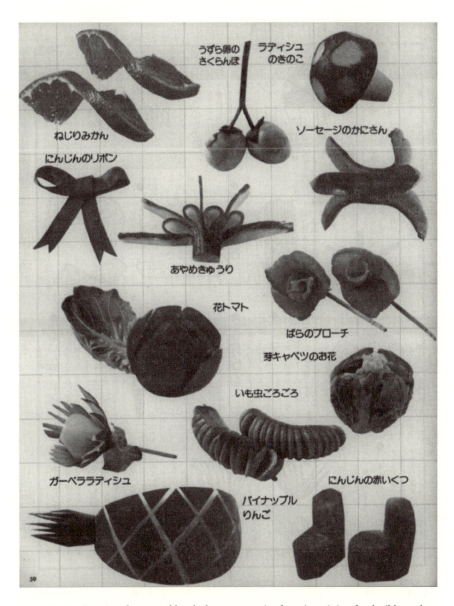

うずら卵の　ラディシュ
さくらんぼ　のきのこ

ねじりみかん

ソーセージのかにさん

にんじんのリボン

あやめきゅうり

花トマト

ばらのブローチ

芽キャベツのお花

いも虫ごろごろ

ガーベララディシュ

パイナップル
りんご

にんじんの赤いくつ

FIGURE 4.6　An *obentō* cookbook shows strategies for reimagining food: ribboned carrots, sausages made into crabs or worms, an apple designed into a pineapple, a flower-tomato, carrots converted into a pair of shoes.
SOURCE: *Obentō 500 sen* (500 selections of lunch box), 1987 (Tokyo: Shufunotomosha), p. 59

obentō that were sent to school but also played down in food prepared for other age groups.

Consistent in Japanese cooking generally, as stated earlier, are the dual principles of manipulation and order. Food is manipulated into some other form than what it assumes either naturally or upon being cooked: Lines are put into mashed potatoes, carrots are flaked, wieners are twisted and sliced. Also, food is ordered by human rather than by natural principles; everything must have neat boundaries and be placed precisely so those boundaries do not merge. These two structures are the ones most important in shaping the nursery school *obentō* as well, and the realistic imagery is primarily a means by which the codes of manipulation and order are learned by and made pleasurable for the child. The simulacrum of a pineapple recreated from an apple is therefore less about seeing the pineapple in an apple (a particular form) and more about reconstructing the apple into something else (the process of transformation).

The intense labor, management, commodification, and attentiveness that goes into the making of an *obentō* lace it, however, with many and various meanings. Overarching all is the potential to aestheticize a certain social order, a social order that is coded (in cultural and culinary terms) as Japanese. Not only is a mother making food more palatable to her nursery school child, she is creating food as a more aesthetic and pleasing social structure. The *obentō*'s message, then, is that the world is constructed very precisely and that the role of any single Japanese in that world must be carried out with the same degree of precision. Production is demanding; and the producer must both keep within the borders of her or his role and work hard.

The message is also that women, not men, both sustain a child through food and constitute the ideological support of the culture that this food embeds. No Japanese man I spoke with had or desired the experience of making a nursery school *obentō* even once, and few were more than peripherally engaged in their children's education. The male is assigned a position in the outside world where he labors at a job for money and is expected to be primarily identified by and committed to his place of work.[20] Helping in the management of the home and in raising children has not become an obvious male concern or interest in Japan, even as more and more women enter what was previously the male domain of work. Females have remained as the center of the home, and this message too is explicitly transmitted in both the production and consumption of entirely female produced *obentō*.

The state accrues benefits from this arrangement. Children depend to a high degree on the labor women devote to their mothering, and women are pressured to perform as well as take pleasure in such routine maternal tasks as making the *obentō*. Both effects are encouraged and promoted by institutional features of the educational system, heavily state run and at least ideologically guided at even the nursery school level. Thus a gendered division of labor is firmly set in place. Labor from males, socialized to be compliant and hard working, is more extractable when they have wives to rely on for almost all domestic and familial management. And females become a source of cheap labor (they are increasingly forced to enter the labor market to pay domestic costs, including those vast sums incurred in educating children) because their domestic duties keep them from taking any but low paying, part-time jobs.

Hence not only do females, as mothers, operate within the ideological state apparatus of Japan's school system that starts semiofficially with the nursery school, they also operate as an ideological state apparatus unto themselves. Motherhood is state ideology working through children at home and school and through mother-imprinted labor, such as the *obentō*, that a child carries from home to school. Hence the post–World War II conception of Japanese education as being egalitarian and democratic with no agenda of gender differentiation does not, in practice, stand up. Concealed within such cultural practices as culinary style and child-focused mothering is a worldview in which what position and behavior an adult will assume has everything to do with the anatomy she or he was born with.

At the end, however, I am left with one question. If motherhood is not only surveiled and manipulated by the state but made by it into a conduit for ideological indoctrination, could not women subvert the political order by redesigning *obentō*? I asked this question of a Japanese friend who, upon reading this chapter, recalled her own experiences. Though her mother had been conventional in most other respects, she had made her children *obentō* that did not conform to the prevailing conventions. Sawa noted that the basic, simple, and rarely artistic lines of these *obentō* resembled the principles by which she was generally raised. She was treated as a person, not "just as a girl," and was allowed a margin to think for herself. Today she is an exceptionally independent woman who has created a life for herself in the United States, away from her homeland and parents. She loves Japanese food, but she is newly appreciative of the plain *obentō* her mother made for her as a child. The *obentō* fed her but did not keep her culturally or ideologically attached. For this, Sawa says today, she is glad.

❧ 5 ❧

Producing Mothers

In early July 1987, my son had just completed his first three months at a Japanese nursery school (*yōchien*). When I picked him up the day before summer vacation his teacher advised me on how to monitor David's behavior during the break: I should make sure he practiced skills he was learning at school, provide opportunities for him to play with children that attended the same school, and keep him from deviating too severely from the routines and schedule of nursery school life. Saitō-sensei also mentioned that he was being sent home with a calendar that we might use to chart some of his summer activities.

The calendar was cute, as such items are for Japanese children: It was brightly colored with anthropomorphized animals brushing their teeth, putting on pajamas, and cleaning up toys. There was also a set of accompanying stickers showing different weather possibilities (cloudy, rainy, sunny) and different activites (playing, swimming, biking, picking up, brushing teeth) so that the events of specific days could be recorded. David and I marked some of his days in this fashion, but we regarded the calendar as more an optional sport than an everyday routine and did not fill it in consistently.

Six weeks later on the first day after summer vacation Saitō-sensei asked me for the calendar. Confused when I told her it was still at home, she asked if I hadn't completed it as had been expected by using the stickers and adding descriptions to mark what David had done every day over break. We discovered in talking that I had missed the first few minutes of a mother's meeting in which these instructions had been explicitly given. I had therefore misread the calendar's meaning, interpreting it as a gift rather than a duty. I offered an apology for my negligence and Saitō-sensei accepted it, but she was implicitly chastising, pointing out how her job would be made more difficult now. Knowing what children did in their hiatus from school helped her to assess the problems they might encounter upon returning.

Even more serious was the implication that I had not kept a rigorous enough schedule or set of routines for my child over vacation, routines that the calendar was intended to not only record but also help instill. If David had spent his break in too loose a fashion, he would find reintegrating into nursery school life problematic. Monitoring their children's lives away from school was the duty of mothers, was the message, and that this duty would be monitored by the school was signaled in the calendar procedure and the authority with which it was given and supervised by my son's teacher.

School, as this incident helped elucidate, is a totalizing (pre)occupation in Japan, an endeavor that isn't delimited to the school building or school day but is expected to infiltrate and shape the child's everyday life. And the mother, as my relations with a Japanese nursery school for fifteen months demonstrated almost daily, is the expected implementor of this extension of school practices into the home, playtime, and everydayness of the child.

Kyōiku Mama: The Everyday Instiller of Everyday Education

In this chapter my aim is to examine the relationship between two institutions, school and motherhood, in terms of how this intersection is shaped by school ideology and practices and how it is experienced by women who are mothers. Broadly I am interested in the *kyōiku mama,* a mother so committed to furthering the education of her child that she does everything from sharpening pencils, making midnight *oya shoku* (snacks), and pouring tea for a studying child to consulting with teachers; investigating the range of schools, tutors, and *juku* (cram schools) available; and boning up on subjects where her child is deficient. Literally *kyōiku mama* means "education mother" and is a term both of respect and reprobation: respect for those mothers who are successful in seeing children through the competitions of the Japanese school system and reprobation for the pressure they consequently must exert on children whose days, nights, and energies are consumed by study. *Mamagon,* or "mother dragon," is a term referring to the condemned aspect of the *kyōiku mama* syndrome.

Here my focus is not on the entirety of the *kyōiku mama* phenomenon, one that has arisen in the post–World War II environment of economic rebuilding, national mobilization of the school system, smaller families, and long commutes to workplaces, all of which have encouraged close mother-child relations in which women often single-handedly supervise the education of their children in the absence of fathers and husbands. My aim is to look at one phase of the *kyōiku mama* life cycle—a mother's role when her child enters nursery school. I will investigate this role in terms of the relationships between school and mothers that produce the behaviors involved in "education motherhood." Specifically, I will pursue two questions: (1) How does the school manage, shape, and monitor a woman's behavior in her role as mother? (2) How do women experience the expectations placed on them by the school system and the educational demands generally of Japan's supercompetitive, schooled society?

I have chosen the nursery school as the site for these investigations despite the arguments made by such scholars of Japanese education as Lois Peak. She has minimized the importance of the mother's role in the socialization of children to school because "Japanese believe that the home and the school are so dissimilar that it is difficult for the family to teach the behavior the child will need in the classroom" (1991:6).

In Peak's view, the school provides the atmosphere for *shūdan seikatsu*—group life—the key structure to such institutions as the Japanese workplace and one that could never be replicated at home. In fact, the children's position as center in a family and the willingness of mothers to indulge them in a relation of spoiled dependent (this behavior of acting spoiled is called *amae* in Japanese) is inimical to the behavior expected of students. Therefore, according to Peak, home and specifically the child-mother relationship not only are not consistent with the interpersonal dynamics of school but must be actively transcended and displaced in the school environment. Emphasizing that nursery school is oriented far less to academics in Japan and far more toward the adoption of group dynamics that will be the foundation of all future educational and social endeavors for the child, Peak further discounts the mother's role. Her implicit assumption is that the energies of *kyōiku mama*–hood are activated primarily at the time of entrance exams, which she notes occur for less than 1 percent of nursery school children upon entering elementary school and for only about 6 percent of children when entering junior high school. She writes that since the vast majority of Japanese youth do not sit for entrance exams before the age of fifteen, the importance of these exams is far less central in the educational lives of Japanese children than is often assumed. And accordingly, the role of mothers is far less central in socializing children to the routines and practices of school life than the institution of the school itself (Peak 1991:3).

Norma Field, in a 1995 paper on the infiltration of school life into the sphere of what should, or once did, constitute play for children in Japan, has argued a different position. She presents statistics on the high rates of stress-induced diseases in even elementary school–aged children: According to a 1992 survey of grammar school children, 63.2 percent suffer from high levels of blood cholesterol, 36.2 percent from ulcers, 22.1 percent from high blood pressure, and 21.4 percent from diabetes (Arita and Yamaoka 1992, quoted in Field 1995:53). Field also notes that 50 percent of fourth- through sixth-graders living in Tokyo attend cram school, which often lasts until nine o'clock at night (54); she depicts the rigors of a study regime that begins long before the age of fifteen, the time that most Japanese children encounter their first entrance exam. Field emphasizes that even young children are habituated to test-taking in preparation for the major tests they will take upon entrance to high school and college.[1] Every skill and subject is taught, and every child is subsequently judged, in terms of retinues of tests that routinize the child in an "atomized, mechanistic mode" (61) of acquiring knowledge through test performance. The effect, writes Field, is to inscribe a purpose and regimen into every activity. Even play is organized into a lesson or structure that will mold the child into a good student.

In contrast to Peak, Field believes that it is the anticipation of entrance exams that dictates how Japanese children are treated, instructed, and managed at even the early stages of their educational careers. And unlike Peak, Field argues that this test orientation structures the child in a mode of performance that starts as early as "age zero" (she cites the popular books of Ibuka Masaru, who urges mothers to educate children even in utero [Field 1995:55]) and seeps into all domains, even those of play, home, and vacation. Concluding that there is a "disappearance of childhood in contemporary Japan," Field stresses the evaporation of any activity, relationship, or domain that offers a reprieve to the child from the constant stress-inducing pressures to study and perform. This includes, of course, the realm of mother and home, which become not an antidote to school, as Peak suggests for every stage except that of taking entrance exams, but rather the very mechanism for extending study management into realms outside the institution of school itself.

Making performance continuous and insinuated into the everydayness of the child's life is an effect of Japan's *gakureki shakai* (academic-pedigree society), the principle that adult careers depend almost entirely on the schools children attend, which in turn depend almost entirely on the passing of entrance exams at the stage of high school and college.[2] No matter how one assesses this principle—as the foundation of Japan's economic prowess built up from the ashes of world war defeat or the great price extracted from Japanese citizens for living in an economically secure but competitive society—few dispute its dominance or the consequences for those who are unwilling or unable to meet its demands. Children pick up early the connection between their success as students in the routines of study and their future success as adults in the networks of work and social status. The argument I will make here is that mothers play a pivotal role in both embedding the child into the continuousness of the study and performance patterns of a *gakureki shakai* and also offer the child a measure of emotional security and intimacy with which to survive these demands.

My position, in short, takes something from both the theses made by Lois Peak and Norma Field: from Peak, the notion that mothers and home give children a special attention that schools can and will not and from Field, the notion that it is the everydayness of study routines that exceed the dimension of school (and the culminating entrance exam) proper that really mobilizes children into the regime of a *gakureki shakai*. The position of mothers vis-à-vis the educational imperatives aimed at their children is, in my view, therefore contradictory: They impose a behavioral regimen on the child consistent with that of school but outside its parameters; yet they also cushion the child from this regimentation with nurturance and comfort. Mothers, as I will point out, are not unaware of these contradictions. They often express anxiety and resentment at being compelled (by the school, society, often other members of the family such as husbands or mothers-in-law) to push their children into habits of study and performance, and they often try to make their children's lives easier with treats, indulgences, and creative pleasures. One effect of this pattern is that what is obligatory is made desirable: Tasks of learning and performing are encased in acts of love and play so pleasant that they disguise and thereby instill the tasks at hand.

The Discipline of Summer Vacation

In 1987 an article by Yoshimura Takashi entitled "Strategies for Summer Discipline That Facilitate the Independence of Children" appeared in a popular mothers' magazine (*Okāsan Benkyōshitsu,* or *Mother's Studyroom,* published by NHK[3]). Strategic advice for mothers on how to cultivate behaviors in children that are, by implication, desirable is found across diverse media (newspaper columns, special television programs, books, mothers' magazines, articles in children's magazines and comics, handouts from school with directives or hints for mothers). Such messages display a high degree of ideological consistency. For example, one of the most basic premises of all this mother-focused discourse is that mothers need to direct the energies of their children in ways that will make their learning at school easier and more productive, and this premise applies no matter what the age or level of the child. Given this premise, most advice for mothers focuses on specific strategies for attaining specific behavioral goals.

In the case of "Strategies for Summer Discipline," the desired behavior is independence (*jiritsu*), which means not the ability or inclination to chart one's own course in life and act in isolation from others but the aptitude to internalize certain habits of self-maintenance that are expected of students in the school environment. My reading of this article coincided with the end of summer vacation and the reprimand I received from David's teacher for the incompletion of his summer calendar. Interested, I found its discussion consistent with the emphasis Saitō-sensei had placed on maintaining the "flow" of school life over vacation and not disrupting a "rhythm" of patterns and routines needed while school is in session (Yoshimura 1987:26). Curious that this very consistency with school was encoded in the word "independence," I began to understand that the meaning of this concept is heavily shaped by the demands and constraints of Japan's schooled society and addresses those behaviors needed in order to survive and succeed in it. In short, "independence," so often advocated in discussions about child-raising and child-training in Japan, comes to mean the development of patterns, skills, and attitudes that enable the child to adapt to and be successful at the labors of school (and later, work).

Significantly, the word "discipline" (*shitsuke*) in the article refers both to the discipline a mother is supposed to instill in her child and to the discipline she is expected to exhibit as a role model for the child. Significant as well is the fact that the authority giving advice in "Strategies for Summer Discipline" is a nursery school teacher, Ms. Ariga,[4] precisely the figure who monitors the child's relationship to school and mediates this relationship with the mother on an everyday basis when school is in session. It is not surprising, then, that the tone of the teacher's voice in this text is as subtly reprimanding as was that of Saitō-sensei when she spoke to me of the calendar.

Ariga makes the point that "the independence of life rhythms begins by gaining strength in breakfast"(Yoshimura 1987:26). Acknowledging that it is easy to slip into a more relaxed pattern over vacation, Ariga emphatically warns against this tendency:

> There are many cases of children losing the rhythm of nursery school life over summer vacation. The children will ask if they can stay up later because it is vacation and the mothers will permit a new bedtime. But doesn't this cut a new pattern? If children stay up late they'll also sleep in later . . . Pretty soon a chain has set in and the life rhythm has been broken. And if this continues for forty days, once September comes these children will be drowsy all morning long. (26)

Her solution is to establish "fun" routines in the morning: Mother and child should participate in morning exercises transmitted on a local radio station and later linger and communicate over a hearty breakfast, as they rarely have time to do on a school morning.

Again, Ariga warns against laxness. Recognizing that mothers welcome summer vacation partially because they are liberated from making the elaborate lunches (*obentō*) for their children in nursery school, she says: "This feeling of liberation has a connection to being neglectful and careless"(Yoshimura 1987:29). Criticizing mothers who make big dinners but scant breakfasts or who combine breakfast and lunch, she reminds women that breakfast is "the source of children's energy and if a mother neglects this she is taking something from her child's energy level" (29). "Give breakfast meaning by communicating with your child," Ariga urges. She then provides a list of other techniques for routinizing the days of both mother and child over summer vacation. The two most important guidelines are establishing an order and schedule for vacation time and trying to maintain a consistency between these summer routines and those of school. Accordingly, she urges mothers to keep up friendships established at school and to arrange playdates with these friends so as to avoid their disrupture. Again, she acknowledges that mothers may be seeking a "liberation" from such activities. Arranging playdates, for example, can take place almost daily during the school year and consume endless energy and time. But a woman must think of what's good for her child rather than what's relaxing for her, writes Ariga. Children take pleasure in their friendships with others and further, these interpersonal ties are what constitute the *ningenkankei*, or human relationships, of any social group in Japan, including the *shūdan seikatsu* first introduced at nursery school. Consequently, maintaining play connections among nursery school students during vacation is of critical importance for the child and is a mother's responsibility.

Other behaviors that are addressed in "Strategies for Summer Discipline" as desirable for establishing a child's "independence" include picking up toys after play, washing hands after being outside, gargling, making friends, keeping clean, and eating nutritious food. For each of these desired goals, the teacher offers strategies for their inculcation, such as getting a child who has poor food habits to help out in selecting and preparing the ingredients for healthy meals. The suggestions are often ingenious but also elaborate; for example, Ariga used a "trick" with a son who liked trucks but hated washing his hands. She made a path out of masking tape from the door of their house to the bathroom so that he could drive his trucks from outside to the sink, thus coupling the chore of handwashing with play. Ariga points out that this technique worked far better than simply ordering the child to clean his hands.

Along the same vein, she encourages mothers to do whatever is necessary to make a particular chore or routine pleasurable and fun for the child. If gargling is to be started the next day, for example, she suggests that mothers go out and buy a cute new cup with which to begin and associate the process. Again, such a technique is preferable to that of merely ordering a child, because making a routine "feel good" is more effective (Yoshimura 1987:34). What is desirable to the mother can also be made more desirable to the child simply by articulating the "feel good" aspect of the chore to the child: "When you wash your hands, it feels good, doesn't it?" (34). Finally, Ariga speaks of transforming one's house so that it mimics important features of the classroom. The rationale is that spatial and physical consistency will facilitate habituating the child to certain routines. "There is a way to make the habits followed at nursery school continue into the home. In short, let's make the conditions the same in the bathroom [for example] as at school. Even if you use different towels, put them at the same height. This makes a big difference. Children who see this will follow the same habits as at school" (34).

By the end of this article I felt exhausted by the mere mental imaginings of the various strategies recommended and encouraged by Ariga. To what degree were such suggestions taken seriously by Japanese mothers? I wondered. How fully might they be implemented on a daily basis, and how much were they (in)formed by expectations on the part of nursery school officials? As I had already encountered in any number of ways, nursery schools (as somewhat distinct from day-care centers)[5] do expect a very extensive involvement from mothers at the level of assisting children in the adoption of and adaptation to the routines of nursery school life. Making habitual such routines as eating one's lunch, cooperating with others, following a teacher's rules, and keeping clean and making this habituation desirable *are* precisely the roles implicitly assigned to mothers by nursery school policy and so explicitly and clearly articulated by Ariga in the article. The agenda is to make the integration into school easier for children, and it is an agenda in which the place, space, authority, and practices of school life are given a prior and superordinate position. Mothers are to make this agenda realizable and assimilatable for children, and in doing so they are expected to act as "mothers" culturally constructed as self-sacrificing managers of home, family, and children.[6] An ideology of motherhood, in other words, becomes linked to and adopted by an ideology of education and productive performance instituted through a school system. How a nursery school itself issues both recommended strategies and compulsory directives that presuppose as well as construct this mother-school link is the subject to which I now turn.

Productive Mergences: Mother's Love and School's Discipline

In April 1987, my family moved to a middle-class neighborhood thirty minutes from downtown Tokyo. I would be conducting a postdoctoral research project in this setting on the interrelationships of domesticity and motherhood. Given the state of Japan's gendered division of labor,[7] which has meant that the domestic sphere has continued to be feminized in this stage of industrialization and late capitalism in Japan, I was interested in how this domestic feminization is both shaped by institutional (economic, political, social, educational) relations and managed and experienced by a class of woman who is positioned most clearly within it: married women with children who (at the present) are not working outside the home.

Putting my son in a local nursery school proved to be a fortuitous move in terms of my research. I made contacts that developed into interviewee groups,[8] but equally important, I became involved myself as a mother in the institutional environment of a nursery school. From this position I could observe and participate in the routines of motherhood. What I learned was both how crucial the school system is in determining and organizing mothers' lives and how creative and tireless women typically are in carrying out this school-ordered labor in the home. I will use the data and experience I acquired as mother-anthropologist in 1987–1988 in the context of Yamaguchi Yōchien[9] to discuss what I perceive to be a dialectical relationship between home (mother) and school.

I must specify at the outset that I intend to be neither totalistic nor exhaustive in my (re)presentation. Yamaguchi Yōchien is a private school in a middle-class neighborhood that caters to families with stay-at-home mothers. These factors affect the mother-school-child dynamics that would be realized differently in, for example, day-care centers, which are organized for mothers who work outside the home. Although my remarks are more specific than general, my aim has been to examine the mother's role in Yamaguchi Yōchien in terms of ideological behaviors that are duplicated in principle, if not exactly in the same forms, elsewhere in Japan.

Before being accepted into Yamaguchi Yōchien, every child, and the parents, must undergo an interview.[10] On the day of our interview, the principal (*enchō-sensei*) greeted us, briefly spoke about the school, and then called David's teacher (Saitō-sensei) into the room. Almost immediately she turned to me, rather than my husband, and pointed to the booklet entitled *Guidebook to Entering School* (*Nyūen no Shiori*), which was at the top of a huge pile of entering materials. Skipping the first page ("Goals to aim for before entering school," a list of skills and behaviors a child should have mastered before entering school[11]), Saitō-sensei turned to page 2 and the heading "Things to prepare at home." Included here were four categories: (1) things used in transit from home to school, such as shoes, boots, overcoats, raincoats; (2) meal-related items, which included not only the *bentō* box and a cup, napkin, and chopsticks but the *bentō* bag (in which to put the box);[12] (3) classroom-oriented items such as hand towel, bag to carry back and forth from school, bag for inside shoes, bag for gym clothes, and smock to wear inside school; and (4) dusting cloths. The focus in our interview with Saitō-sensei was on two subjects: the things I needed to make for David before he started school and where I should attach his name labels (listed on page 6 under the heading "Method of attaching badges"). Saitō-sensei was animated as she spoke—friendly, welcoming, and engaged. The matters of which she spoke, however, were almost exclusively ones of regimentation: how the child's clothing and belongings must conform to school standards and how (implicitly) the mother must effect this conformity.

Once at home, I reopened the "Guidebook" to the pages that Saitō-sensei had so insistently pointed out and realized the enormity of the tasks at hand. Not only were there a number of specific items to purchase, make, or affix labels to, but many of these were specified further in terms of dimensions or materials. For example, we were advised to make the hand towel (*otefuki*) from towel material but in the size of a handkerchief: thirty centimeters from tip to tip. Further, we needed to attach a hoop at one end for hanging and make four of these: two for everyday use and two for reserve. I bought two towels and remade them into the school *otefuki* because I could find no such item with the required details in the shops. Other mothers later advised me that some of the nursery school paraphernalia are available for purchase but that a "good" mother will still make as much as she can on her own.

Another item, the *tesage,* or the bag used to "carry all those things that the school-dispensed satchel (*kaban*)[13] cannot" ("Guidebook," p. 2) proved to be the most complicated object and an arduous task for me. I had no sewing machine and as yet no fellow mothers to advise me on how closely to heed the specifications in the guidebook: thirty centimeters high, forty centimeters long, five centimeters deep (so that it can stand upright) with a handle and made out of a thick piece of cloth. Mothers were advised to "please make an easy-to-use thing with your own hands." Similarly, the bag for gym clothes (*taisōgibukuro*) was to be thirty centimeters long, twenty-five centimeters wide, with a drawstring that pulled to one side. The bag for indoor shoes (*uwabakibukuro*), by contrast, was simply requested but without specific dimensions, as were the meal items and the two dusters. Smocks,[14] as I fortunately learned in time, could be purchased at the school, though for those making them, the design and positioning (and number) of pockets were designated. On all these items labels needed to be attached or, in the case of the indoor shoes, names written. What should be written (class and name in some cases, just name in others), where precisely the label should be affixed (lower left corner on bags, lower right corner on any piece of clothing, in the middle on the towels and indoor shoes), and what size it should be (for example, eight by four and a half centimeters for gym clothes) were clearly spelled out.

As is already apparent to the reader, a mother's involvement at just this preliminary stage of readying the child for school is extensive and heavily prescribed. Further, the elaborate and precise instructions can be explained in part by the school's desire to homogenize the children (make them uniform in dress and personal belongings) and in part by the school's desire to impose order, any order, on the children as they enter into a new disciplinary regime. That this initial regimentation takes place in the arena of the basic and personal—things worn on bodies and things that accompany bodies from home into school—is not accidental. As Foucault has written (1980) about social order being inscribed at the site of the person's body, so too is the new order of an educational regime written into the very things that come into closest bodily contact with the child. And it is these things that are both other than and more than the time and place of school per se that render a transformation of the child into student, a transformation that is expected to be full-scale and continuous. As Aida Yuji has written about the Japanese worker, "Certainly, looked at from the outsider's perspective, work doesn't remain within the finely demarcated hours of worktime. When actual worktime is over, people [in the west] become private persons. But in Japan work is not compressed into the eight hours of actual worktime as it is in America. For the whole 24 hours a day a worker cannot forget that he is a worker" (1972:67).

The ideology of identity merging with work that Aida articulates for the adult Japanese male is similar and thus continuous to, I would argue, that of a child's identity being merged with schooling that begins at the stage of nursery school education. And although this mergence is authorized by the school,[15] it is the mother who makes it possible.[16] She works in the domestic sphere "with her own hands" to supplement and encourage the school order. It is not surprising, then, that transitional objects, things that move back and forth between home and school, figure highly in the instructions in the guidebook. It is also not surprising that some of these transitional objects are also transportational ones: the plethora of bags that contain those essentials of nursery school life that move continuously between home and school. The *tesage* (large school bag), for example, is not only the most complicated and major production (unless a smock is made) but is also a container that must be filled and emptied on an everyday basis. Every afternoon one is instructed to look into these and the *kaban* (school-issued yellow bag) for memos and any dirty clothes that must be laundered overnight. Every morning a mother refills the bags with any essentials for the day's schooling. And at the week's end on Saturday,[17] smocks, handtowels, and the indoor shoes are returned for cleaning. The indoor shoes (*uwabaki*) must be scrubbed clean with brushes before Monday.

In addition to seeing to the *tesage,* there are two other domestic jobs that the mother must perform on a daily basis. The first is sending the child off in a clean and ironed uniform,[18] which usually means ironing a jacket and pants or skirt and laundering and ironing a clean white shirt every day. The second is the making of the *obentō,* that highly elaborate, five to six minicourse meal that mothers spend as much as forty-five minutes preparing on the four lunch days of the week (see Chapter 4).

Interfacing home and school in such media as the finely tuned *obentō* and the carefully shaped *tesage*—things that bring home into school as much as they bring school into home—is a relationship and behavior that schools expect mothers to enact in other less materially based ways as well. At Yamaguchi Yōchien we were asked to participate both at school and at home.[19] Mother's meetings were held at the school about every six weeks, and meetings with the principal were held three times a year. We were asked to participate in the daily "farewell ritual," when children, teachers, and parents all line up to say good-bye to each other, and become involved in the three big annual events of the school.[20] At home we were expected, as mentioned in Chapter 4, to make our children sociable by arranging playdates with other (Yamaguchi Yōchien) children as often as possible and maintaining certain schedules, routines, and activities consistent with those at school and instructional for cultivating specific skills. At the time of summer vacation, for example, Yamaguchi Yōchien's version of "Strategies for Summer Discipline" came in the shape of various verbal suggestions given by the teacher both personally and in the last mother's meeting before break as well as in a set of summer directives: one in child-oriented language with accompanying pictures for the children ("Promises for Summer Vacation") and one directed to the mothers ("The Way to Spend Summer Vacation"). In the child's guideline (printed on heavy paper and intended obviously to be hung on a wall) there was a series of "let's" suggestions: "let's get up early (the clock reads 7:00), let's go to bed early (the clock reads 8:00), let's not forget our greetings, let's brush our teeth after eating, let's not overeat or overdrink cold things, let's take a nap, let's return home at 5:00,[21] let's pick up, let's wear a hat in the sun, let's not run out in front of cars, and let's play outside." In the handout to mothers, sixteen specific behaviors were listed, including keeping an early bedtime, watching in-between meals, participating in radio exercises, brushing teeth after eating, following traffic rules, picking up one's belongings, and joining hands before and after meals. The phrase used under the subheading for behaviors concerned with health was "let's live according to regular rules" (*kisoku tadashī seisaktsu o shimashō*), "regular" being a concept the school obviously did not want to leave to chance or individual interpretation.

Women's Experiences in Their Roles as Education Mothers

To my western sensibilities, Yamaguchi Yōchien was engaging in overkill. Too much of our lives was being surveiled by the school system, and how "regularly" my son was adjusting and conforming to the nursery school regimen had become too dominant a concern in my life and in my relationship with David. Like the hypothetical westerner referred to by Aida in a previous quote, I come from a social order where there is some sense of separate realms and a notion that not all of what we consider personal (home, dress, vacation time, personal belongings) can or should be penetrated by an institutional force such as the school system. How,

I wondered, do Japanese mothers experience the same expectations, demands, and regulations of a school institution and to what degree do they heed them? These are the questions I address in this section.

The data I use here are preliminary: selected passages from only a few of the thirty-five women I interviewed extensively over fifteen months and that will form the basis of a much longer manuscript on Japanese mothers. Few of the Japanese women I encountered expressed any overt criticism of the various directives put out by Yamaguchi Yōchien in terms of the labor involved for them. Some welcomed a nonlunch day because of the respite from making the *obentō*, and some complained occasionally of constant laundering and scrubbing of their child's dirty white shirts or (white) indoor shoes. Most of the women in interviews spoke of their daily schedules as "full," "busy," and "active" and mentioned having little "free time" to do anything not child or domestic related. Their bedtimes usually coincided with those of their children (typically 9:00) because they were too exhausted to stay up later.[22] This busyness, incurred in part by the demands and routines of a child's nursery school life, was rarely bemoaned, however, or thought to be an excessive price to pay for having a child attend nursery school. As a general principle, these women thought that they should be involved in their children's education, that this was their role and not their husbands',[23] and that the school had the authority to dictate and monitor quite specific behaviors for both them and their children.

Again, the women with whom I spoke generally found staying at home to be a decided advantage for their child for two reasons. It made going to school easier and happier for the child, but it also made the child's school experience as valuable as possible in terms of future education. These women viewed nursery school, in other words, as a first step to the academics of later learning even though nursery school is not significantly academic itself. And because nursery school is important for the child's educational development, a mother's love, support, and energies in the school domain were deemed important. In these discussions, women revealed what I have called earlier a split or contradiction in the role of the so-called education mother; that is, a mother must both ensure that children conform to educational rigors and routines and also offer a cushion or prop to help children survive them. At this level of talk, no woman articulated her position as contradictory or dialectical. A few, however, did specify events, practices, or behaviors at Yamaguchi Yōchien that concerned them and brought into question how they, as mothers, should appropriately respond.

Noguchi-san, for example, told me that her son was experiencing stress over the upcoming Sports Day event. He was practicing daily at school to master the skills needed, but his deficiency had been pointed out by the teacher. As a result, the child was asking to stay home from school. Noguchi-san had allowed him one day at home but did not want to continue letting him skip school. She finally gave him the option of dropping out of school (since he was still four and only at the first-year level), but the child chose not to because he didn't want to stop seeing his school friends. Given that the boy would be remaining at school, Noguchi-san saw no solution to his problem over Sports Day except for him to endure it the best he could. The notion of consulting with the teacher over the pressure she was exerting and the criticism she was giving was unthinkable to Noguchi-san because the teacher might receive these comments as implicit criticism of her and as an effect be even more stern with the child.

Other mothers reacted similarly to specific policies and teachers at Yamaguchi Yōchien. One day, at Noguchi-san's house, for example, four other mothers with children in David's class were gathered. All except one expressed similar concerns about the upcoming Sports Day and the role Saitō-sensei was playing in it (see Figure 5.1). Two other children were experiencing stress, and the interpretation was that Saitō-sensei was working all the children too hard and was being particularly hard on those children who were not mastering the required skills quickly enough. Some of these children were being criticized in front of the other children, which is harsh punishment in a school system where the peer group is so central. Noguchi-san recounted, at this point, another story about Saitō-sensei, who had been the teacher of her first son, now aged ten. He too had been deficient in a Sports Day activity and in the weeks of training leading up to the event had been routinely criticized both in front of the other children and to the mother. On

FIGURE 5.1   Undōkai (Sports Day) at the nursery school my son attended in Tokyo. The mothers joined in on a special event where they were pitted against their husbands. In the yearbook photos of Undōkai, however, the photo showed only the mothers.
SOURCE: *Sotsuen Kinen* (Graduation Album), 1989 (Tokyo: Enyuji Yōchien)

the day itself, Noguchi-san tried to greet Saitō-sensei and, hearing again of her son's failings, bowed deeply, along with her husband, for all the grief they had caused the teacher. Although the Noguchis were angry, they felt they could take no action because any complaint to the principal would be reported back to Saitō-sensei and be likely to make her more, rather than less, harsh on the boy. As for the boy, the event deeply scarred him. Convinced that he had no aptitude whatsoever, for years he refused to participate in any sports or physical education classes.[24]

Other mothers mentioned other behaviors, policies, or attitudes on the part of teachers that concerned them. These included the schoolwide tendency to let children work out their own problems even if this meant that certain children were getting pushed around or hit by others as well as Saitō-sensei's tendency, reported by a handful of mothers, to play favorites. Three mothers in particular said that she was too harsh on their children: too critical and demanding and not as overtly nice and friendly as she was to other children. None of the mothers citing specific problems with Yamaguchi Yōchien, however, indicated that they would take the matter up with either the teacher or the principal. Their preference was to endure the situation as well as possible by giving the child extra love at home or, in one case, considering transferring the child to a different school upon graduation of the grade she was in. Implicitly the common attitude was that problems, hurdles, and difficulties in school are to be expected and, to some degree, endured and coped with by the child as a kind of challenge. Hence, although these women were troubled by certain aspects of the school situation and concerned about their child's well-being, not one was willing to either confront the school authorities or let her child stay home from school. The bottom line seemed to be not whether their children were always having a good or easy time at school but rather whether school was adequately preparing them for later life (specifically later school life). And on this score the mothers seemed in general agreement that Yamaguchi Yōchien was a good school.

On the issue of school authority, no mother explicitly complained of the school being too extensive or assertive in its monitoring of a mother's role in her child's education. Occasionally, however, a woman would tell of being criticized for some failing. One woman who worked in her mother-in-law's rice store, for example, was reprimanded for not spending enough time with her child, a criticism given in the context of reporting a child's problems in learning to jump-rope at school.[25] Other women were similarly urged or encouraged to exert greater efforts in getting their child to perform some behavior. Often women simply reported these conversations with their child's teacher, conversations that could occur almost daily after picking children up at school. They expressed worry or concern that their child wasn't mastering some skill, seemingly agreeing with the teacher's assessment both of the child's progress and the mother's duty in working outside of school to help a child develop such school-related skills as jumping rope, eating one's lunch, washing hands, gargling, paying attention, and chinning on the uneven bars. Sometimes mothers appeared tense and nervous about continuing negative reports from teachers. Many mothers worried as well about the parent-teacher conferences (held about one month prior to the end of school) and about the home visitation—a visit the teacher makes to the home of each student in part to assess the home environment.

A number of my friends received rather negative reports of their children during the parent-teacher conferences held after the first academic year we were in Japan. One mother was told that her daughter was incompetent in every task, skill, and behavior expected of children her age. One example given was that she failed to draw triangles the "correct" way. When this woman (Tanaka-san) pointed out that Sachiko-chan drew triangles at home all the time, she was told that her drawing order was incorrect. Privately my friend laughed, telling me that she found the teacher's worldview too rigid and her assessment of the girl ridiculous. Yet she did not complain to the teacher; neither did another friend whose son received a similarly bleak report that the mother also, in private, did not accept. For her part, Tanaka-san was concerned enough about the disjuncture between her pedagogical values and those of the teacher and school that she was considering placing Sachiko-chan in a university "feeder" school for first grade. This system, called an "escalator" system, ensures that children, after completing the initial entrance exam to get in, will be passed until they graduate from high school. In such an atmosphere Tanaka-san hoped that pedagogy would be less rigid and a student's progress, less rigidly assessed.

Some women expressed grave reservations about the general structure of education and its effect—competition—in contemporary Japan. Īde-san said that she didn't think Japanese mothers had a choice: "Even if we have worries, we need to make our children study." She admitted that her husband's view was different, that he didn't care if their children attended university as long as they were happy and managing to make a living. Īde-san disagreed: "We have no choice (*shikata ga nai*). All mothers in Japan need to "hang in there" (*ganbaru*) and make their children do the same."

Another woman (Mori-san) in the same interview group expressed a different position.

Even if we get our children to study hard, well, that's the image of us Japanese, right? A home where men are absent because they are working and mothers and children who only concentrate on studying. . . . My worry is that we are just producing kids who fit into the mold. In school it is stressed that there is one right way to do things.

So we and the school keep enforcing this idea: the one-pattern idea. Plus we have to keep teaching our children to follow authority and be subordinate to their superiors. They must learn how to agree with what others say and do: to go around saying '*hai hai*' [yes, yes] all the time.

Mori-san stated that she would not send her children to cram school in the future and simply wanted education to be a process that enabled her children to live healthy, self-reliant lives. "In this society, since one can't go very far without education, I hope they do okay in school. [But] I just want them to be average and able to face anything because they are boys. Even if they don't make it into a company, they can become bakers. As long as they work hard (*ganbaru*) and have a good nature."

The other three women in Mori-san's group were sympathetic to her position, and many other women I spoke with were similarly worried, distraught, or anxious about the school system their children were in and the future challenges ahead of them. Most, however, expressed that they had no choice and were resigned in the face of a system that they were sure would determine their children's futures whether they liked it or not. Given this situation, most also spoke of how they tried to make the chores of learning and adjusting to the school regimen as pleasurable and endurable as possible. In this context they referred to "skinship" (as a westernized word), the idea that it is important to spend as much time with children as possible because school is an ordeal for a child. A mother's love and labors are thus connected to the difficulties a child faces in entering and attending school. Such caregiving is seen as a type of compensation, as well as an incentive, for the latter. Importantly, I came to see, school is not expected to be, or criticized for not being, a particularly happy time for kids. School is about hard work, learning to adjust, and entering a system of hurdles that is often unkind but inevitable—thus the highly elaborate *obentō*, the beautiful *tesage*, the constant efforts to arrange and host playdates, and the endless devices used to get children to learn and perform.

Although some women, as I have noted, could articulate concerns and doubts about the school system, few women did the same about the role they were playing and being expected to play in encouraging their children to perform in it. Only one woman clearly expressed personal doubts about the energies she expended that effectively sutured her children ever closer to the performative circuit of school. She knew she was acting "right" as a mother, she said, but these motherly acts of sitting next to her older boy as he studied, for example, and making sure her younger son learned how to adjust to nursery school were only putting these boys deeper into a school system she was not as sure was so "right." This woman, a model of the type of peppy and resourceful mother who completes every domestic chore with elaboration and turns every learning task into a game or adventure, had fallen, she confessed, into the throes of a deep depression.

Conclusion

My aim in this chapter has been to dislodge the genericism of the "education mother" syndrome and to question how real mothers, in the context of a Buddhist nursery school in a middle-class Tokyo neighborhhod in the late 1980s, are expected and compelled to assist their children in adapting to school. Unlike those scholars who argue that the educational role played by mothers comes at a much later stage in their children's schooling (for example, at the point of preparing for entrance exams [Peak 1991]), I have shown how the institution of school itself demands a much earlier involvement from mothers. It is at this level of everydayness that children are situated into a structure and ethos of performance that complements and thereby extends that learned at school. The implementer of this continuous education into the vacations, playtime, and home of the child is the mother, and she is often burdened with feelings of anxiety, doubt, and concern. Being a *kyōiku mama,* by this assessment, involves neither a simple behavior nor one that is generated solely or even primarily by mothers themselves. Rather *kyōiku mama* denotes a relationship among mothers, children, and a school system that has been situated within the political and economic relations of Japan's postindustrial labor market. As Norma Field (1995) suggests, children are being programmed at ever earlier ages to assume a posture of productivity that will continue into later life. Mothers, I would suggest, are being programmed into and by the same model.

❧ 6 ❧

Transgressions of the Everyday:
Stories of Mother-Son Incest
in Japanese Popular Culture

In the 1980s a number of stories about mother-son incest were reported in the popular press in Japan. The elements of each were remarkably consistent: An adolescent male entering the period of intense study leading up to entrance exams is distracted by sexual desire. His mother, who has assumed the role of a *kyōiku mama*, notices the distraction and worries that it will obstruct the boy's work. To prevent this, she offers to become her son's lover and thereby satisfy his pressing need. The boy complies and the two commence an affair. The sexual relationship, found deeply pleasurable by both partners, quickly turns the boy into a model student. In the end the boy typically passes his exams and is appreciative to his mother for her help. The incest, however, does not end. Rather, the confusing relationship between man-woman and mother-son is left unresolved at the story's close.

Circulating in the mass media of low- to relatively high-brow publications (magazines for young women such as *Josei Jishin*, for adult women such as *Fujin Kōron*, and for mixed adult audiences such as *Gendai no Me*), the tale of mother-son incest knits together two plots. The first narrative is entrance-exam preparation. Referred to as *jukenbenkyō* (literally, exam preparation) or "exam hell" (*shiken jigoku*), it typically lasts from one to two years, can cost families vast sums of money, is a time when students are expected to sacrifice friends and hobbies to spend long hours in study, and characteristically involves incredible efforts on the parts of mothers (Amano 1989). Exams determine acceptance into high school and university and thus into Japan's "school-record society" (*gakureki shakai*), where the schools one attends are the single most important factor deciding employment and career. Exam results largely determine adult identity, social status, and job security, at least for males.

Coupled to this story is one about the transgressive union of mother and son in sexual passion. The articles describe these unions as "fearful," "shocking," "surprising," "upsetting," and "scary," descriptors marking the acts as deviant and illicit. Though the actual frequency of incest is impossible to assess,[1] those who speak publicly about it generally agree that the competitiveness of the educational system and a gendered division of labor that mitigates against the presence of adult men in the home encourage what is often called an overpresence of the mother in the lives of children. Matricentric Japanese families are often described in terms of excesses,[2] but few actually claim that incestuous sex is anything more than a rare occurrence. The Japanese I spoke to about incest, mainly middle-class housewives, all claimed to find the idea shocking. Many, nonetheless, also added a story they knew of someone, someplace who had supposedly been involved in just such a relationship.

Why did these two stories—of transgressive, incestuous sex and normal exam preparation—fuse as they did, and why were they faddishly cycled within Japan's popular culture of the late 1970s and early 1980s? Of what and to whom did they speak?

I approach these stories less in terms of realistic probability and more in terms of desires and fantasies. To develop my analysis, I adopt notions of desire and fantasy inspired by Freud and Lacan and expanded in the feminist scholarship by figures such as Kaja Silverman. As I will be borrowing so heavily on this literature, I would like to briefly lay out those concepts and theories that are most central to my argument. Desire, as psychoanalytic theorists point out (Freud 1975; Grosz 1990; Rose 1982; Mitchell 1982; Lacan 1977), is conditioned and structured by the very impossibility of attaining what one wishes for. Desire is the longing for precisely what is denied by the rules and exigencies of social life, and consequently, it becomes repressed. As explained by Lacan, desire is the product of a child's entry into what he calls the symbolic, the order of language that marks the stage beyond the imaginary where self and identity occur within the primary dyadic relationship between mother and child. In the symbolic the mother-child dyad is broken by a third term, the phallic father, whose authority mobilizes rules, taboos, and principles under which the child is repositioned, depriving her or him of the narcissism once indulged by the mother. Desire emerges at this point as a loss, as what the child must necessarily accept of the rules of membership in a community in order to achieve the status and identity of an adult. Thus, for instance, when the child addresses her or his demands to the mother, the mother must respond by addressing particular needs, and desire is what is constituted as the difference (as that which exceeds need and is not satisfied).

When I use the term "fantasy," I am drawing on the work of psychoanalytic scholars such as Jean Laplanche and J. B. Pontalis (1968) and feminists such as Kaja Silverman (1992) and Judith Butler (1990, 1993) who use it to mean the form and articulation given to desire. I underscore in my use of "fantasy" the

Freudian-Lacanian conceptualization of desire as that which is not only frustrated but also organized by social conditions. As such, fantasies express what is normally and normatively repressed and what is realistically or socially denied. Fantasy is not mere or random escapist fancy, as the term is often used colloquially, but rather is constituted in relationship to the specific milieus in which people live and to which they refer even when constructing imaginary worlds. This reference to lived experience is obvious in the incest stories, where the scenarios, for the most part, are strikingly realistic. Yet where these narratives depart from realism is striking as well: A tale that is familiar is transformed into one that is extraordinary and phantasmic. This condition of impossibility is what characterizes these stories as fantasies in my mind, but the repressed desire given expression here is not simply for incestuous sex but also, and simultaneously, for success at normative role expectations (good mother and hard-working, productive male).

Lacan's concept of *petit objet à* and Freud's of the fetish both refer to objects or substitutes that are used to fill in for that which is desired and imagined but realistically impossible (Freud 1961; Rose 1982). Laplanche and Pontalis speak similarly of constructions that are "propped up" onto lived experience ("anaclisis") and that fantasize what is unavailable or contingent, such as the mother's breast when the mother is absent or sexual satisfaction within the assumption of a subject position that denies it, for example, the fantasy in Japanese mother-son incest stories. It is fantasy itself that constitutes the origins of sexuality, according to Laplanche and Pontalis (1968), providing the fantasizer with an image both of the (m)other who is available and a self whose desires can be constantly fulfilled. For this reason fantasy is masturbatory in that it relieves the subject from depending on conditions outside the self for pleasure and is formed through stories, images, and objects (as for the fetishist) over which the fantasizer has far more control than in interpersonal relations.

Freud has argued (1961) that the person who structures pleasure through fetishes instead of relations with others is stalled at a stage of narcissism prior to differentiating from the (m)other and recognizing and accepting the gender difference so critical to the Freudian schema of becoming an adult. In the mother-son incest stories, this is one aspect of the narrative: a relationship between a mother and son halted at the undifferentiated stage of the imaginary. This plot unfolds within the domestic space of a home constituted by a dyadic family of mother and son. There is a third term, however, hovering throughout the text. It is the school system; but more broadly it is the gendered relations of labor that in the 1970s retained an ideology of differentiating between males as productive workers and females as reproductive mothers. In the era of the appearance of mother-son incest stories, Japan's recovery from its defeat during World War II was well established and officially attributed to the labors of its hard-working population, in turn attributed to the high performance of its students. The role of mothers in ensuring the success of children at school was given recognition and encouragement in these terms—as a Japanese cultural response to the demands facing Japan as a nation competing with other economies in a global market of late capitalism. In the incest stories the tensions of this solution, I will argue, are being expressed. Women denied entry themselves into a symbolic of male workers and political rights are preparing their sons to assume their place as adults in the social order. They both do and do not want their sons to become differentiated from them. Boys too desire both identity as successful adults and the narcissistic mergence with mothers that such identity will cut off.

For this reason, what is compelling about the Japanese mother-son incest stories of the 1970s is their repetition of the same, fetishized scenario. All of the stories bracket the relationship between mother and male child as it enters the pivotal stage of exam preparation, which signals a boy's maturation into adulthood, a mother's test of her skills as a good mother, and the eventual separation between mother and child as the son moves on to school and a job. Sexual desire intrudes on this scene usually from the direction of the maturing boy and threatens the socially appropriate completion of the mother-son relation. Mother fears the sexualized boy will abandon his studies, fail to achieve success on his exams, and compromise his future. Her son's failure would also mark her own failure as a mother. As the woman wards off this threat by offering to be her son's sexual companion, she achieves sexual gratification for herself but also fulfills satisfactorally her job of maternal social reproduction and thereby papers over with fantasy a gap in her own life. Rarely do the stories of mother-son incest go beyond this point. The scenario thus stalls and repeats on just two interactions, sex between mother and son and cooperation on exam preparation.

This strange combination of the normative and transgressive has many implications, from simple fulfillment of repressed desire to signs of frustrations in Japanese family life and gendered relations. Each of these revolves around the same ideological facts, however: the competitive exam system, matricentric family life, the primary role of mothers in child socialization, and the gendered division of labor that makes salaried work more a male than a female occupation. My main point throughout is that the fantasy of incest is grounded in an ideological order yet is not reducible to it. This fantasy, like others, exceeds and reimagines the real precisely in the form of a desire. In these narratives the desire specifically is for a sexuality that even in 1994 was held by many to be antithetical to family and home (Nohara 1994). It would appear that those most delimited to the domestic sphere—wives and mothers who do not work at wage labor and children before they leave the home—are the consumers of this desiring narrative. The incest story also inverts a popular myth of gendered and sexual relations in Japan by mocking the story about the macho and phallic man who is permitted to philander while his submissive wife waits patiently at home. In so doing it challenges gendered stereotypes and produces a set of scary counternarratives about women and mothers who wield control and men who perform satisfactorily sexually and socially only when they are sons. Finally, the popular incest story reconceives the family not as the site for the suppression of sex but as the stage for its enactment (see Figure 6.1). This shift plays at the borders of the symbolic, the realm of gendered hierarchy and masculinist privilege, into which the boy's entry is both engineered and stalled by a mother whose own access to the symbolic is obstructed.

Evils of Incest

The stories of mother-son incest that appeared between the end of the 1970s and the early 1980s range in tone from condemnatory to sympathetic and almost celebratory. Many read like firsthand accounts in a confessional mode. Others adopt a more third person, reportage motif, using data culled from other sources, such as the Daiyaru Hinin Sōdanshitsu, a telephone counseling agency that started publicizing in 1979 that it was receiving calls reporting mother-son incest.[3] The director of this agency in the early 1980s, Arakawa Yasuko, told me that virtually all of the incest callers were boys, most of whom she figured were using the incest as fantasy to masturbate while talking on the phone to an older, female counselor. Still she found the stories disturbing. They indicated, in her view, unhealthy strains in Japanese family life and society. Arakawa's reaction, like those of many status quo media commentators, stressed the tragedy of incest. In the stories that assume a similar position, the boy is characterized as the victim of a selfish and transgressive mother whose deviance rests entirely and solely in her sexuality but who, in every other respect, conforms to the standards of good motherhood. This is certainly the case in an article by Kakinuma Miyuki (a reporter and editorial member of the feminist journal *Feministo*) that appeared in the respectable journal *Gendai no Me* under the title "The Truth and Falsehood of the Fantasy of Mother-Son Incest" (1980).

Kakinuma's explicit aim in the essay was to challenge the reality of mother-son incest, which she says burgeoned as a new fad and cultural fantasy in the mid-1970s. She disputes the reports of its frequency, arguing (on the basis of data from Hinin Sōdanshitsu) that it occurs no more often in Japan than in countries such as the United States, and she lambasts the press as well as the public for circulating a sensationalist myth. Still, she admits some truth to the stories, finding them to be crystallizations of gendered domestic relations that reproduce dependent, childish men, a situation Kakinuma blames on mothers. Kakinuma begins her essay by

FIGURE 6.1   Rarely is the sexual woman portrayed as a mother. In this interesting exception, a mother feeds her oddly adult-looking baby. The image plays with the theme of mother-son incest.
SOURCE: *Manga Goraku* (Manga Entertainment), December 9, 1994 (Tokyo: Nihon Bungeisha), p. 171

recounting a story taken from the casebook of a counselor at Hinin Sōdanshitsu. A boy is in an incestual relation that Kakinuma presents as an unmediated reflection of true events, a curious presentation given her position on the phantasmic nature of incest in the mass media.[4]

In Kakinuma's reiteration of the case, the boy appears weak and unsure: He states that he is seventeen, but the counselor hears the tone of a child. He admits to feeling troubled, but the counselor must prod him to speak further. "You're not well, are you? You're a male, right? Speak up, please."[5] The boy says the problem is his mother; she caught him masturbating and told him to stop. He couldn't give it up, however, and she caught him at it again. She cried and scolded the boy, making him feel bad. At this point the counselor intercedes to say that masturbation for boys is normal, but the boy seems not to hear. He proceeds to tell how his mother offered herself as his sexual partner and that their sexual relationship has intensifed in recent weeks. Now the mother approaches him even in his sleep. The counselor asks whether he enjoys it. The boy answers yes, but he also calls the incest his "handicap for being a male" and describes his mother, otherwise giving and helpful in her assistance in his studies, as "hellish" when it comes to sex.

Under questioning, the boy explains that his father died a number of years ago and his mother, thirty-nine, enforces a six o'clock curfew even on nights when he has no school. In the name of study, his mother has also forced him to give up a girlfriend, so the boy spends almost all his time away from school at home with his mother. He is constantly tired, the boy complains, the result presumably of the heavy demands placed on him by his mother to both study and engage in nightly sex. Hearing this, the counselor suggests that he urge his mother to remarry, since she is, after all, still young, and that he try to talk about this with someone close. Talking with someone else would only cause a big stir, the boy fears, but he agrees with the counselor's opinion that separation from his mother is necessary and voices the hope that it will come to pass when he enters university.

Of course, he must first pass his entrance exams. Grateful to his mother for making it possible for him to rise to the top of his class, he is nonetheless resentful of her sexual manipulation. When it comes to considering action, however, the boy seems reluctant to act precipitously to end the present situation. It is as though he feels he must pay any price, including that of incest, to ensure that he pass his entrance exams. The counselor warns that such a relationship will have long-term effects even if and when he physically leaves home. Yet the boy appears resigned to merely speak about his situation rather than seek a way out. At the end of the forty-minute conversation he states, "Somehow I will cope," and he hangs up.

This is a story about maternal excess and the victimization of a child. The child is in the impossible situation of needing his mother's academic assistance and fearing that her rape will destroy his relations with other women in the future. It is important to note that the intensification of the mother-child interrelatedness that sets the scene for incest here is, in fact, conditioned by a number of Japanese institutions and cultural practices outside any adult's control, to say nothing of children's, that affect both mother and son. These include horrendous competition in the exam system, a gendered division of labor that makes women primary caregivers and minimizes the caregiving role of fathers, and a cultural model of family in which the marital bond is subordinated to that of parent-child. None of these factors figure, however, in the previously cited incident, where the incest is attributed entirely to the woman's sexual urges, unsatisfied since her husband's death and misdirected onto her son rather than onto a new husband. A situation shared by millions of Japanese every year, then, managing exam preparation for children, is displaced onto the character of the bad mother and her story of incestuous desire.

Another example of an incest narrative where the mother is portrayed as explicitly evil appeared in the women's journal *Fujin Kōron* in the first of a two-part series entitled "Mother-Child Incest: Drowning in Forbidden Happiness." Under the title "The Night I Went Crazy on Account of My Son's Cuteness" (Shinoyama 1980), the first story is authored by a forty-one-year-old Tokyo housewife who describes a domestic situation similar to the case in Kakinuma's account. A housewife with a largely absent husband is raising an adolescent boy who, though a good student, is increasingly distracted by sexual interests. Now in high school, this boy gets drunk after he learns that a girl he likes has fallen for another boy. Violently ripping open his mother's blouse and sucking on her breasts, as in his infancy, the boy then rapes his mother, who though initially resisting, rises eventually into sexual ecstasy.

The incest ends with this one event, and since the father-husband was out of the house when it happened, the mother is assured that no one will ever know what transpired. Yet something "terrible" has happened. Her son has become quiet and now returns home late from school. Soon he is hanging out with a delinquent crowd in the neighborhood and smoking marijuana with them in a *kissaten* (coffee shop). Because he is not studying and his academic record has deteriorated, the mother confronts her son. The boy answers defiantly, "What qualifications do you have to lecture me about university? I hate dirty women like you, Mother. As soon as I graduate from high school I intend to leave home. Next time you try lecturing me, I will tell father everything!"

The rest of the story is mainly concerned with the mother's musings about the incestuous episode as a mistake that she has made, "a terrible thing between mother and child." Her action is perhaps unforgivable, yet she finds an explanation for it in how "cute" her son was on the night they had sex and how attached she has been to him as her only child. Admittedly, she overprotected him; yet she wonders whether she could have done otherwise. He had no siblings, after all, and all her maternal love has devolved upon him alone. In the end she states that should her son change his mind and want to enter university, she will do whatever she can to help him. Her last sentence reads paradoxically: "Having thrust my son aside, if I would be given another chance to start afresh and live my life over again, I would kill myself."

In this tale, told from the woman's perspective, the incest is more a regrettable accident than a calculated seduction, and the mother's role is more one of weak abettor than active agent. And yet, as in Kakinuma's account, the woman is assigned the blame despite the fact that, in this case, the boy was clearly the aggressor. This account makes the woman's sexual nature the "cause" of the event. Because she had not had sexual relations with her husband for a year and a half she was, in her words, particularly "receptive" to the advances of her son. Incest has dramatic effects in this account too, but they are more visible and social, since the boy loses his academic goals and becomes a delinquent all as a consequence of the rupturing of trust between mother and son. The mother, too, is a victim in the sense that she has lost her intimacy with her child and her hope for his future. Meant to be tragic, then, this narrative could be read as a reminder about what good mothering entails: sacrifice to children and the suppression of personal, particularly sexual, desires.

In both narratives, incest is an act of sexual transgression that has destructive effects. It leads to loss that in some way is a loss of identity prompted by the rupture of (a normatively correct) mother-son bond. The boy in the first version fears that he will lose (or form) his own identity unless he can break physically and sexually from his mother; in the second, the boy has lost his social identity by becoming a delinquent. Also, the woman in the *Fujin Kōron* account has lost her identification as mother both because her son refuses to recognize her as such and because the loss of his own future reflects the failure of her mothering.

Incestuous Pleasures

In the incest stories mentioned thus far, the role assigned sexuality is almost totally negative. Not all the stories of mother-son incest, however, take this shape. In some, the sexual urges of the woman are given a more sympathetic reading. In others, incest is treated as the almost perfect solution for balancing duty and desire for both mother and child. In the latter case, it is always the mother who claims that incest is as beneficial for her child as it is for her, and the plot always stars a child who has become a "model student."

One such story by a thirty-eight-year-old female office worker appeared as the second part of the *Fujin Kōron* series "Mother-Child Incest: Drowning in Forbidden Happiness" under the title "Fearing the Happiness of Man and Woman Although We're Mother and Child" (Yamauchi 1981). The setting is the familiar one of the mother, an absent husband-father (divorced in this case), and a son on the brink of entrance exams. Discovering a note in the pocket of her son's pants from a neighborhood girl she has heard is a shoplifter, the mother asks her son (Masao) about their relation and is led to believe it is sexual. Mother forbids Masao from seeing the girl again but imagines he will do so anyway. Then one night as she is sleeping, as always next to Masao, he touches her and makes love with her. Sexual feelings suppressed in the woman since her divorce ten years earlier are reawakened, and as the woman is also resolved to curtail the relationship between her son and the "delinquent" girl, she starts to have intercourse with her son every night.

Immediately the boy is transformed into a model student and doting son (the two behaviors are conflated in the text). He returns home from school promptly, studies hard, helps his mother with a part-time job during the summer, and is commended for being a dutiful son. Early in the narrative he passes entrance exams into a reputable high school, after which the story reads as if it is a romance between two lovers. Their sex life is described in graphic detail, what positions they engage in, where and when sex takes place, how aroused the woman becomes, who does what and to what body part. The mother speaks of her own sexual transformation in terms of physical changes such as the luster she now sees in her skin, the disappearance of headaches and stomach pains that have nagged her for years, and the regularization of her menstrual cycle. Even her coworkers have commented on how youthful she has been become and wonder if there isn't a new man in her life.

Still, interwoven into the sexual text is a moralizing subtext in the form of an internal debate over the rightness and wrongness of incest. In her mind the woman calls the incest a "sin," asks for her son's forgiveness, and says she will commit suicide if anyone discovers the "disgusting" secret she and her child share. Yet the narrative also makes excuses for the relationship, pointing out that it has made the boy into a model student and prevented him from becoming a delinquent. Masao himself is said to have written in his diary that in this age of high sexual activity among Japanese adolescents and high abortion rates for junior and senior high school girls, his mother is using their sexual relationship as a "safeguard" to protect him. Similarly, the mother notes, he never would have passed the entrance exams into a good high school without her intervention. This is her "self-justification." But she admits that she also loves the sex, which is unmatched by anything she ever experienced with her husband.

At the admission of sexual pleasure, her writing resembles that of a lover rather than a mother, for it focuses on the connection between her own transformation into sexual womanhood and his into academic manhood. The maturing of her son as a student justifies not only the incestualizing of the mother-son bond but also the sexualizing of the woman-mother. Since she fears more than anything that one day her son may think she is "lewd," the mother makes a point of telling him that she never slept with another man in the ten years since divorcing his father. She uses this evidence to prove that she has been a "good" (that is, nonsexual) mother and then implies that if she is to become sexual, incest is certainly better because it is more consistent with her maternal role than an affair or remarriage.

More than in the earlier stories, incest is presented sympathetically in this narrative, and the portrayal of the mother particularly takes an overridingly positive shape. But other stories more definitely legitimate and even celebrate incest, such as the account published in the book *Hikisakareta Sei* (put out in 1980 by *Gendai no Me*, the publishers of the journal by the same name) and attributed to a forty-year-old housewife. In this narrative the author declares that she does not find her incestuous relationship to be a "bad thing" at all and questions rhetorically in the end whether the bond with her son isn't a "new form of love" rather than a "disgrace." The details of the case are true to form. A boy preparing to take entrance exams to Tokyo University arrives in Tokyo weeks in advance, accompanied by his mother. They check into their hotel and on the very first night the mother approaches her son, who is sleeping naked on his bed. She fellates him while allowing the towel to slip from her naked body. Because she washes his laundry, she knows that her son masturbates, and she is not surprised when he responds to her initiation.

The boy studies diligently during the day and at night becomes his mother's lover. He takes the exams and does well, but not well enough to pass into Tokyo University. Disappointed but not defeated, he returns home with his mother and recommits to studying for the exams, which he will take again in another year. His mother, of course, will assist him in his studies and in the meantime maintain her relationship with him in bed, now reduced to once a week so as to avoid the eyes of the husband-father. The narrative ends as the mother notes that the recent flurry of articles on mother-son incest in the press, some of which speak of a "sexual revolution" going on in Japan, make her feel that what she is doing with her son has "legitimacy."

This account resembles the others but for one major detail. Whereas in most incest stories the role of the father-husband is effaced at the beginning of the text (he is dead, divorced, busy at work or with his mistress), here effacement continues throughout the text. Throughout the story the narrator weaves accounts of both the men in her life, husband and son, but always to the detriment of the husband. She compares her son's prospects (entering the Law Department of Tokyo University to become a high-ranking public official) to her husband's career. The latter, she feels, became a lower-level public official because he graduated from law school at a second-rank university and has consequently spent his work life bowing and scraping to superiors, a "wretched" situation for the entire family. But there are more profound differences. The boy's body is athletic, much stronger than her husband's; the boy has a penis much more "majestic" than her husband's; and the boy knows how to give pleasure, unlike her unimaginative husband.

Obviously, the woman imagines her son to be far more attractive than her husband. But she also differs from the girl she was twenty years before when she married a thirty-eight-year-old widower with a twelve-year-old daughter. Then her husband, a newly appointed city administrator, appeared "dazzling" in his status and promise. She married for reasons more of security, it seems, than anything else, and the same need for security will keep her with him on a retirement salary that will allow her a "comfortable" lifestyle. Yet the dull, pragmatic marriage is far different from the bliss, intimacy, and sexual passion the narrator describes with her son. The story of incest turns out to be a story about the frustrations and disappointments of married life.

In fact, the narrator directly attributes her incestuous behavior to sexual frustration. When her husband became impotent she was a woman in her sexual prime, and she has been abnormally "nervous" ever since. Stated so frankly, the woman's sexual frustration is given more sympathetic recognition and significance here than in any of the previous incest accounts. When she saw her son sleeping naked she therefore found him irresistably "cute" (an odd but revealing description for the male whose penis she then sucks) and initiated an incestuous relation on the basis far more of a woman's sexual desires than a mother's instincts to protect and assist a studying child. Of course, in the narrative, these two feminine positions and desires merge: The woman is a mother whose son "needs" her, as she states, in his work. But the mother is also a woman whose own needs for sexual and emotional intimacy are satisfied by her son as an attractive and sensitive man. The two sets of needs—a son for a mother and a woman for a man—are so well accommodated by the mother-son incest, in fact, that the relevance of the husband-father and the role of woman as wife effectively drop out by the end of the text. Sex reconfigures the family, in other words: The marital bond is effaced and the son takes over the father's place in the bed, heart, and even social ambitions of the mother.

Incest, Taboos, and Two Myths: Oedipus and Ajase

The belief that the incest taboo is not only universal but also the grounding principle of sociality itself has been axiomatic in fields such as anthropology. As argued by the structuralist scholar Claude Lévi-Strauss (1975), for example, the incest taboo is what differentiates humans from nonhumans and is the rule that, by forbidding sexual relations between certain categories of persons, establishes kinship, which in turn generates social exchange. Men, not allowed to reproduce with their own sisters, will marry them out as wives to men of other kinship groups whose own women will, in turn, be married in. In the Lévi-Straussian view, then, women are the medium of an exchange conducted in terms of male authority and desire and are constitutive of kinship and social viability.

Such a position has been challenged on two grounds: First, its construction of kinship is based on western categories that inflate the importance of sexuality and sexual taboos such as incest;[6] second, it describes a political system in which males dominate as universal and socially essential.[7] I concur with these critiques and build my own analysis of Japanese mother-son incest stories on the basis not of a universalist assumption that incest (defined as a sexual transgression of kinship categories) is always and necessarily the greatest threat to social integrity but rather on its meaning within the context (cultural, historical, and political) of these specific stories and the moment of their circulation. It is here, within the narratives themselves, that the incestuous relationship of mother and son is referred to as evil, illicit, and sinful. Yet the incest is also spoken of as a technique used to ensure the boy's success as an adult male, which will reconfirm the woman's identity as a good mother. The reference seems contradictory: Incest both transgresses and supports social norms, and the stories end with the ambiguity unresolved.

What interests me about these mother-son incest stories is the confusion of normativity and transgressiveness in the mother-son relation as it pertains specifically to the course of the boy's maturation into a man, for this latter theme certainly supplies the narrative's overarching structure. And within the structuring story of a boy's maturation, I will focus on the role attributed to the mother. Her special mothering is considered beneficial to her son's progression into socially respectable and successful manhood yet as also (possibly or absolutely) detrimental to his sexual and emotional maturation into a man who can separate from mother and home and form interpersonal relationships on his own. In other words, the requirements for manhood are fundamentally split. But there is an important implication linked to this splitting. If and when the boy leaves the side of his mother, she loses control over his life and he then proceeds into a domain that denies her (equal) entry. As feminists such as Chodorow (1978), Dinnerstein (1976), Benjamin (1988), Kristeva (1980), Flax (1990), and Rubin (1973) have pointed out for western societies characterized by gender inequity, differentiation from the mother at the age of adolescence becomes a factor in a boy's development of a worldview that devalues women and inflates the importance of men.

Further, as the feminist scholarship of MacKinnon and others has shown, male dominance of political and economic realms in a society like the United States is reinforced by a habit of sexualizing male power and female subordination (MacKinnon 1979). In the mother-son incest stories I consider here, quite to the contrary, the sexual encounters, rooted to home and enacted in the relationship between mother and son, encode a power dynamic and a worldview in which the labor of the woman as mother is valued, not despised. The consequent role incest plays in advancing or inhibiting the boy's transition to normative manhood in a specifically Japanese economic-political context of male chauvinism is an obvious concern that I pursue here as well.

My critique relies heavily on two narratives, the Oedipus myth as formulated by Freud (1964b) and western psychoanalytic scholars and the Ajase myth, a theory advanced by Japan's founding psychoanalyst, Kosawa Heisaku, in 1932 (Okonogi 1978, 1979). However, the originators used myth to explain social maturation into human manhood, in the case of Freud, and in Kosawa's case, the formula for becoming Japanese. I retain the mythic stories and believe them to be significant, but I consider myths to be paradigmatic fantasies: stories that articulate hegemonic identities, norms, values, and power relations through narratives about boy children becoming adults and the desires they must learn to contain in order to achieve social maturity. The Oedipus myth encodes a formulation of gendered relations in which adult males exert social power, adult females lack social authority and sexual subjectivity, and boys are encouraged to turn away from their mothers at the age of adolescence and establish an individualistic identity consistent with the gendered patterns of adults. Such a model, I believe, accurately describes a phallicism that is still the dominant norm in the United States and one that hovers, to some degree, over the mythic formulations of gender, sexuality, and the symbolic in the Japanese mother-son incest stories of the 1970s. The Ajase myth, in contrast to the oedipal model that originally motivated Kosawa's proposal, is a crystallization of Japanese values, norms, and socialization patterns based on what Kosawa argued was a matricentric rather than the patricentric principle Freud had assumed to be universal. Whereas Kosawa spoke of a matricentrism rooted in the essence of a Japanese timeless traditional culture, mother centeredness in contemporary middle-class families is, I would argue, best explained with references to specific demographic, political, and economic conditions that have arisen in the postwar period (Yuzawa 1982; Kanō 1986; Shields 1989).

Along with the school system, the mother-centered family has been assigned the ideological task of reproducing a workforce nationally and culturally identified as Japanese. Norms for mother-child interaction encoded in the Ajase myth remain dominant in official and public discourse today and ground the plot of exam preparation in the mother-son incest stories that I examine here. Added to the incest plot, however, are elements of sexuality and sexual transgressiveness not included in the Ajase myth. This complicates the story in ways that I attempt to unravel and interpret by borrowing from models of phallicism and matricentricism suggested in turn by Oedipus and Ajase myths.

As I have laid out the Oedipus and Ajase myths in great detail already (Chapter 1, and the Oedipus myth also in Chapter 2), I will give only a brief recounting here. *Oedipus* was originally a Greek tragedy written by Sophocles; the Ajase myth is a Buddhist (originally, a Sanskrit) story from India. Both were adopted by psychoanalysts in other cultures as paradigmatic models of how a boy becomes a man (Freud used *Oedipus* as he wrote from Vienna at the turn of the century, and Kosawa used the Ajase myth to write about Japan in the early 1930s). In both stories the key characters share familial relations, and in both, these relations are threatened by nonkinlike behavior. In *Oedipus*, a son kills his father and marries his mother, acts committed while Oedipus is in a state of self-ignorance (he does not know who he is, i.e., that his mother is his mother and his father, his father). In the Freudian adaptation, the Oedipus myth dramatizes, through the violation of taboos, the path of becoming a man. A man must achieve self-awareness through recognizing his father as an authority, his mother as a tabooed object of desire, and himself as a person who must go outside his family to mate. That Oedipus so abysmally failed in this recognition is marked by the blindness he inflicts upon himself.

In the Ajase myth, it is the mother who first commits a dubious act. Desiring to keep the affections of her husband, she impregnates herself with the reincarnated spirit of a sage she has selfishly killed. Fearful of the hex the sage may put on her, she tries to kill her child. Failing, she becomes a dutiful and loving mother, but Ajase, her son, learns of her misdeeds when he becomes a youth perched on the threshold of manhood. Furious, Ajase tries to kill his mother. He, too, fails, and the upshot is that mother and son forgive one another and remain forever entwined in a bond of mutual forgiveness. In this story, as adapted by Kosawa, the recognition a child must acquire in order to become a man is that his mother is human rather than an ideal and he must learn to cultivate give-and-take with others rather than narcissistically demand full attention.

The differences between the two models are basically four: (1) The role played by the oedipal mother is primarily passive (as the object of [male] desire), whereas the role of the Ajasean mother is active, not limited to or even focused upon (sexual) desire, and pivotal to the plot. (2) The father's role is central in the oedipal model, and patricide leads to the boy's inability to assume manhood. In the Ajasean myth, by contrast, the father barely figures at all and has no primary role in the son's development to manhood.[8] (3) The oedipal model is based on a clear-cut set of rules that operate on the threat of violence (the boy's mutilation of himself at the end is the sign of his transgressions and failures). The Ajasean model is organized more along the lines of interpersonal relations that depend on mutual forgiveness and empathy. (4) In order to achieve manhood, the oedipal boy must accept the exclusiveness of his parents' sexual bond and separate from both to establish himself as an individual, whereas the Ajasean boy needs to remain bonded with his parents, particularly his mother, but with the newly mature attitude of mutual respect.

Foucault has written (1980) that sexuality became the site of the "truth" of the individual in western bourgeois societies. This connection between sexuality and identity formation lies at the core of western psychoanalytic theory and presumes a construction of self that is individuated from others. Such a notion of self differs quite remarkably from the interactive self proposed in the Ajasean model, where sexuality is also not the pivotal factor triggering the boy's transition into manhood. In the Japanese mother-son incest stories of the late 1970s, by contrast, genital sex plays the central role in the plot and is connected, in ambivalent fashion, to the boy's future; he must distinguish and differentiate himself as a successful member of the white-collar middle class in order eventually to become a man. It is in the context of social performance that intercourse occurs, both the performance of the woman as a good mother and the performance of the boy as an industrious student; but only the boy is in the process of transition, and for him the incestuous sex will condition his adult identity.

For this reason it is significant, I would say, that the construction of genitalia and intercourse in the incest stories involves both the mutuality of pleasure between female and male and the one-sidedness of the mother, who uses sex to ensure her son's place in the same phallic order that restricts her own position. In the last story I described (*Hikisakareta Sei*), for example, the affair commences when the mother sees the naked body of her son and shows him hers; the pleasure they enjoy is spoken of repeatedly as mutual. Yet the mother also associates her son's penis with the phallicism she hopes he will achieve; in the same passage where she speaks of his penis as "majestic," she also describes her ambitions for him in terms of a better school, better job, and more prestigious career than her husband ever managed. The same is true in "Fearing the Happiness of Man and Woman Although We're Mother and Child," where the mutuality of sexual pleasure is coupled to the study agenda of the boy, who becomes a model student through his mother's double role (sexual partner and academic coach). The sexual integration of the incest (problematic, of course, particularly for the boys)—the boy recognizes that his mother is not just a mother but also a woman, and the mother recognizes her son is not just a son but also a man—resembles the mutuality that developed between Ajase and Idaike. Yet joined to this matricentric dynamic is the mother's study regimen, forced onto a child who is always and only a boy in these stories. She trains him to perform adequately in a realm that operates here arguably as the Lacanian third term; it is a symbolic of schools, exams, and eventually a labor market in which positionality is conditioned and differentiated by discrete factors (gender, class, age, nationality, race) and behavior must be adjusted away from an imaginary of narcissisitic bliss and dyadic harmony with mother and toward a grammar of norms, rules, and repressed desires.

The symbolic in terms such as wages earned, political positions gained, four-year universities attended, managerial jobs attained, and public careers achieved remains a male domain in Japan (Iwao 1993). However, the labor of women as mothers and wives is critical to the maintenance and reproduction of the symbolic. Males are expected to prioritize the job, and that is only possible when wives manage all domestic responsibilities.[9] Children who are scholastically competitive are often heavily dependent on mothers, and this is more true the higher the child aims his ambitions. In the incest stories, ideologically normative identities defined and differentiated by gender—females are mothers, and males are workers—get reproduced, and although the sexual interactions may be mutually pleasurable and interactive in a way that resembles an imaginary dyadism of mother and child, they are also structured with a teleology (aimed at intercourse and focused on genitalia) that feeds into a social teleology (performance of a boy on exams) complementary to the symbolic.

Yet there is also a contradiction here. The sex of incest is overdetermined by the absence of the husband, but it is also unsustainable; once the boy succeeds, he will leave the home and bed he shares with mother. This is one of the reasons, of course, that the stories repeat and fetishize the same two interactions (studying and sex) and end inconclusively with lovers still entwined. Given that such a scenario is not realistic, however, the fantasy does not simply reproduce an ideology of gendered normativity. Nor, of course, given its emphasis on good mothers and dutiful sons, does it produce a story that stands completely outside the realm of norms. What then *is* the relationship between normativity and desire as constructed for both mother and son in these narratives?

Three factors always motivate women's actions with sons in these narratives: sexual frustration in their married lives, the desire to be good mothers, and attraction for their sons. They are never driven, in these stories, by lust alone, which could be satisfied, of course, by any number of fantasy characters. Rather, they want to be both sexually satisfied *and* good mothers, the very objective that is impossible in real life. For as enumerable studies, articles in women's magazines, home dramas on television, and divorce statistics point out, home is a domain where sexuality is denied and suppressed because, as one woman reported her husband commenting recently about their postmarital sexual abstinence, sex doesn't work after marriage because then "it is family" (Nohara 1994). Women suffer this loss more drastically than do men simply because males are given another alternative, the realm beyond the home where they work and establish their social identity. Here they also "play," sometimes on company expense, at clubs, bars, and cabarets where extramarital liaisons with women are socially allowed (Allison 1994). Such recreation is seen, in part, as the reward men achieve for working hard, and those who work the hardest and are most successful have the money and power to acquire the most desirable mistresses. In the stories of incest, wives desire similar pleasure and rewards, and as men seek it in the (public) realm where they labor, women seek it in the realm where they labor. The finite scope leaves only one object of desire, the child, and were it a girl child, perhaps the fantasies would be more subversive.

Significantly, incestuous mothers do not express craving to enter a world of work itself or to leave the ranks of motherhood. They are thus worlds away from the position of a feminist like Kakinuma, mentioned earlier, whose corrective to incest fantasy is for women to create work lives for themselves outside the home (Kakinuma 1980). Incestuous mothers want what their husbands have, but they do not want it with them. They want, that is, to assuage a sexual desire motivated in part, I would argue, by feelings not of oppression but of pride in their roles as mothers. As women I interviewed for a postdoctoral project on mothering repeatedly stated, work gave their husbands a financial base that they lacked, but in every other respect they regarded their own work to be more satisfying and more important to their children (Yuzawa 1982). In their minds, then, the phallicism of the symbolic was something they neither envied nor completely respected; and because the stressfulness, pettinesses, demands, and humiliations of salaried jobs wore out their husbands, mothers also expressed ambivalence about working so hard to ensure that sons would follow in their fathers' footsteps. This may be another reason that incest stories tend to stall at the point of a son's departure from home. But the equation is clear: If men are rewarded with sexual pleasure for work that women do not entirely respect, why shouldn't women, who labor equally hard to rear children, be similarly rewarded? Incest not only rewards mothering, it also extends it. The separation of child from home, signaling the end of her job, is delayed by the incestuous attachment.

These mother-son incest scenarios frame the relation of motherhood and desire in a way that invites interpretation. At one extreme the lustful mother is a powerful, loving, and justified woman whose sexual impulse is overdetermined by two conditions within her family: an absent or impotent husband and dependent children poised on the brink of success or delinquency. In this reading, the incest story suggests that mothers should not abandon desire and that mothers can be "good" even when satisfying sexual urges. A good-mother interpretation might point to how absurd and pitiful it is that mothers are limited in their object choices to their own sons, rather than new husbands or lovers, and how regrettable it is that the path of normative femininity (within marriage and toward motherhood) is sexually so stultifying. At the other extreme lies the evil, bad, and castrating mother, a woman who fails as a mother and jeopardizes the emotional, sexual, and perhaps even social life of her son. Desire is posed as that which mothers should forsake and that whose pursuit is more appropriate for nonmaternal categories of women such as unmarried working women and women servicing men in sexual entertainment. Yet a third way of considering these stories would rely on both characterizations. When the goodness of mother is stretched to the extreme of incestuous badness, the spectacle is transformed into a laughing in the face of all the endless injunctions and expectations placed on women in Japan to be good mothers.[10] A response to the excessiveness of normative maternity, incest exceeds the norms of motherhood so dramatically, yet also so narrowly (only in sex), that it makes the very institution of motherhood appear phantasmic and absurd in itself.

The relationship between normativity and desire for boys in these stories is configured quite differently. There is a structural sameness in the sense that being a dutiful student excludes enjoyment of sex, along with other pleasures. The very site of sexual satisfaction for the incestuous boy (i.e., within the context of his studies) exemplifies the primacy of norms. Yet the intimacy he phantasmically enjoys with his mother is a model of the desire that researchers of Japanese sexuality believe Japanese men spend their adult years searching to replicate (Nakatani and Kinjō 1982; Wagatsuma and Fukuda 1983). In this regard, the fantasy seems to combine both imaginary and symbolic constructions by dangling the possibility that one might remain close to one's mother and still proceed into the work world via good examination scores. Yet there is also another factor at work for the boy. As a male he knows that even if his desires must be deferred for the moment, once he enters the world of work, he will be allowed to play in the sphere of adult male pleasure. In this regard he will follow in the steps of his father, whose very absence in the text signifies his presence at a place other than his wife's side—with a mistress, for example. In much the same fashion as the oedipal scenario, then, Ajasean boys who must repress a desire in order to enter the symbolic do so with the promise of future satisfaction. They grow up and become like their fathers. And on this score, of course, the path for females is significantly different. The oedipal girl must confront her static castrated state, unchanging through time, and the Ajasean mother recognizes her son, whose departure from home is imminent, as the only lover available to her.

In a sense, then, boys give up a little more in the incestuous scenarios than do their mothers. The danger to the son is also greater. Clinging too closely to mother even when the agenda is to ensure his social success later in life threatens to keep the boy forever home, if not literally, then emotionally, sexually, and symbolically. Japanese men with so-called mother complexes are said to typically suffer sexual dysfunction with adult women (Narabayashi 1983). More tricky is the specter of impotency that haunts the white-collar worker (*sararīman*) in popular culture generally and specifically characterizes some husbands in the incest stories (Allison 1994). Research into the rise of impotency in recent years in Japan tends to attribute it to both stressful working conditions and family dramas where fathers and boys are managed by overpowering mothers. Narabayashi brings these factors together (1983 and personal communication) to argue that impotency is most common in males who follow the "elite course" of intense studying to perform at the most august rank of school competition, who subsequently achieve the most prestigious jobs, and who attribute their successful performances to the years spent locked in close proximity to their devoted "education mothers." That impotency and success both mark the masculinity of adult Japanese is characterized in opposing imagery—the phallic man who succeeds at both working and playing hard and the impotent man who, still tied to his mother, has a penis that cannot rise phallically at all—and signals the very danger and underlying tension of being a man in Japan today. Let me stress this point again. The fantasy of incest articulates the normative as being phantasmic itself. Here adult masculinity depends upon yet is threatened by hard work and by the support a son must receive from his mother to become such a successful worker.

The ambivalence between what is simultaneously requisite and dangerous for Japanese males is recapitulated in the inconclusive incest plot, where repetition can be read in terms that are both empowering and masochistic. Boys fulfill not only the wish to succeed at school and to be sexually satisfied but are assured of their potency, a fate not at all verifiable in the case of their disempowered fathers. Further, incestuous sons remain attached to their mothers and therefore sustain the bond of intimacy that many adult men have claimed is more compelling than any other. Viewed more negatively, the incestuous mother cannibalizes and castrates the male; she feeds off his body and dictates his study regimen regardless of whether her son desires sex or success.[11] She is a parasite who lives on the pleasure and success he provides her (all women are parasites in a society where only men have access to pleasure and fame). Having thus devoured him, the mother leaves the boy emotionally and sexually impotent, as unable to realize pleasure as an ordinary woman. In this sense, the gender roles are switched: The incestuous mother becomes the phallic player, and her incestuous son is transformed into her dephallicized object. Boys who imagine or experience incest may find such a scenario frightful, as did the boy in Kakinuma's (1980) article.

Such a fantasy may, however, give pleasure if it allows the boy to imagine himself in the structural position of the feminine rather than the masculine: If femininity is conceptualized in passive terms, he may take pleasure in disavowing responsibility, being submissive, and being engulfed by a figure larger in every sense than himself. That this is a fantasy of some boys has been confirmed. That it is also the fantasy of some men is suggested by certain themes in erotic comic books; by clubs for men that cater to the desire to be diapered, spanked, or dominated; and by the work I have done on Japanese nightlife (Allison 1994).

Conclusion: Timing and Nationalism

Fantasies of mother-son incest became faddish at a moment in Japanese history thirty-five years after Japan's humiliating defeat in World War II and a decade following the first signs of its remarkable recovery, the economic growth spurt of the late 1960s. The nationalistic self-confidence that has emerged more fully in recent years was quite tentative then and had been preceded by postwar debates regarding Japan's reconfiguration. The ensuing reconstruction was based both on the democratic constitution installed by the United States during occupation and on the Japanese traditional values of hard work and loyalty to the group and family.[12] The family and the school system were social institutions that had been restructured by the occupying forces after the war. The traditional lineage system of the *ie* was dismantled because it harbored undemocratic values (hierarchy by gender and age, primogeniture, a corporate unit operating under the authority of one head), and the schools were remodeled to instill the notions of individualism, gender equality, and separation of church and state. Despite such mandated restructurations, however, Japanese elites directed much energy toward rebuilding Japan on the basis of what they held to be a distinctly Japanese function of school, that is, to preserve and reproduce Japanese integrity (Horio 1988; Shields 1989; Lock 1990; Kanō 1986).

The pivotal juncture between school and family became the mother, or rather the mother who upheld the tradition of maternal sacrifice to family and applied this value to her children's peak performance at school. Husbands and fathers had to work hard in the realm outside the home. Their main contribution to family was their paycheck, so work became their primary duty. In the 1970s and 1980s, however, not only single women but married women with children began to move into this realm of the labor force in increasing numbers (Takahashi 1989). Simultaneously, the mean size of families dropped to a new low, triggering fear that the commitment of women to motherhood was weakening or being abandoned altogether

(Lock 1990). In this era, just a few years before the mass mediazation of incest, a series of imagined and real stories appeared about newly born babies abandoned by their mothers in coin lockers at public places such as train stations. Sixty-eight cases were reported between 1969 and 1975 (Murakami 1994). As narrativized by Murakami Ryū in his novel *Koin Rōka Bēbi* (Coin Locker Babies), the scenario of child abandonment came to signify a mother who was so consumed by her own desires that she literally killed her baby. The desires of these mothers were conceived then to be virtually life (nation) threatening. Stated differently, women who forsake motherhood are murderers.

The theme of desire proved pivotal in the sensationalism that accompanied the "coin locker baby" syndrome. Murakami's fictional protagonist, for example, went shopping and fussed over her appearance immediately after she killed her infant. Such behavior might conceivably typify any society that, like Japan, is at a stage of late capitalism where commodity fetishism, consumption, and immediate gratification are the individual's primary aims. In the coin-locker incidents the murderous women's desires came to signify a selfishness that was individualistic and implicitly western, totally at odds with the selfless stance of Japanese mothers. By the time of the mother-son incest fad a few years later, the threat to motherhood was similarly configured in terms of desire, but the desire had become explicitly sexual and its fulfillment was sought by women not outside but within their roles as mother. This realignment of the mother-desire relation signaled new concerns, I would argue. I find far less fear that women will abandon the home for jobs and far more anxiety over the control handed to mothers in their pivotal roles of reproducing the children who later compose the workforce and thus of upholding the Japanese state. Interpretations given to mother-son incest at both ends of the spectrum (i.e., the mother who feeds or, alternatively, consumes her child) reflect a relationship in which mothers control their sons. Women who entered the labor market during the time of the incest stories and who experienced gender inequities that far exceeded current barriers might have chosen to reclaim their roles and labors at home and reimagine themselves in the one domain where they exercised real authority. I am not suggesting that the fantasies of mother-son incest were, in and of themselves, subversive of the dominant order, where women were and still are to a great degree excluded or marginalized on the basis of gender. Rather, I suggest that such media myths speak of mothers' critical roles in the lives of their sons and how decisive this role has proven to be in the lives of adult men. The symbolic as a male-dominated, -ordered, and -privileged domain can be rethought in light of such a story. Without a mother a boy will not even enter the symbolic, and how the mother interacts with the boy, sexually as well as academically, is a major factor in how he will perform later and variously as a man.

The stories speak as well, as I have attempted to show, to fears of excess stemming from women's control of the mother-son relationship. Women should be kept in their place is the dictum of any patriarchy, yet in the home women are so emboldened they not only act out sexually and in the position of aggressor rather than compliant object but they also do so with (and against) a son—the same son who embodies the future on which Japan as a nation depends ideologically. To put it simply, the threat is that women will become phallic not in the workforce, which restricts their entry, but in the home, where their place is overdetermined. And if mothers come to occupy the phallus, men's occupation of it is endangered—precisely the fear commonly expressed in images of the socially respected white-collar man becoming impotent. This is an interesting commentary on the path Japan chose to reassert the power of its state apparatus: a social order in which women mother, men work gruelingly hard, and children are driven through a school and exam system that applies increasingly intense increments of pressure. Considered in this way, the scenarios of mother-son incest resonate with the oedipal fear that the child who is not separated from mother by the phallus risks ever being able to assume that phallus himself, a consequence obviously more fearsome to boys than to mothers.

Mother-son incest stories are no longer so popular, and studies indicate that married women, although still sexually frustrated in marriage, are increasingly likely to seek out an extramarital affair;[13] but the dual specter of the overpowering mother and endangered male is crafted in other arenas such as the highly violent and misogynistic sexual imagery that proliferates in such popular media as television, animated films, and comic books. Here too, as with the incest scenario, the contradictions and tensions of Japan's socially engineered postwar identity are finding expression.

There is nothing simple about the fantasy of mother-son incest. It is neither totally far-fetched nor totally realistic, neither pure escapism nor something that captures or subverts the dominant order. Rather the stories repeat the lived experiences of real people with one alteration regarded as both transgressive and imaginable. Within these stories, the normative is phantasmic and the fantasy is simply normal.

❧ 7 ❧

Pubic Veilings and Public Surveillance: Obscenity Laws and Obscene Fantasies in Japan

On the cover of the book stands a woman. She looks out from behind a set of wooden doors that are geometrically cut with latticed openings. Her body, which is naked, is framed and partitioned by these borders. Her face peeks out but the neck and shoulders are hidden; the stomach is fully shown, but there is barely a hint of breasts; hands are visible but only the lower part of one arm; and whereas her pubic area is concealed, the upper thighs are amply exposed. The sun is reflected on this image in a manner that is similarly disjointed. Breaking unevenly onto the surfaces, it shines brightly in some places while retreating, in others, into shade. The woman's stomach basks in sunlight. By contrast, shadow engulfs her hands, legs, and face.

This photo of flesh and sunlight plays with borders. A naked woman is its center, but her body is as much shielded as yielded by the artifice of the pose. The density of the doors and the unevenness of the light fragment what is seen of the woman and are as critical to the composition of the photo as the body itself. Nakedness here is both presented and absented, drawing the viewer's gaze but eluding it as well. As such, the erotics of the pose come from what is suggested rather than actually shown. This portrayal also satisfies Japanese obscenity laws, which dictate that bodies, in order to be publicly displayed, must be arranged or altered in such a way that the pubis and genitalia are hidden. In the photo, the doors accomplish this effect. They obstruct from sight censored body parts; they also eroticize this obstruction, making that which cannot be seen an object for desire (see Figure 7.1).

❧   ❧   ❧

The book for which this photo serves as cover is entitled *Santa Fe*. It is ironic, given the discretion of its cover, that *Santa Fe* has been embroiled in a controversy

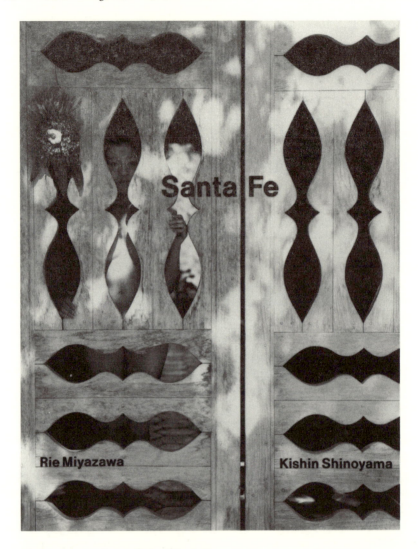

FIGURE 7.1   Cover photo of *Santa Fe*.
SOURCE: Shinoyama Kishin, *Santa Fe* (Tokyo: Asahi Shuppansha, 1991)

about indecent exposures. A collection of photos all of singer-actress Miyazawa
Rie by photographer Shinoyama Kishin, *Santa Fe* was one of several Japanese
publications in 1991 that not only showed pubic hair on female models but also,
and more noteworthy, were not censored by the officials for doing so. Circum-
venting the obscenity laws that, enacted at the turn of the century, had prohibited
the visibility of pubic hair in public media, these photos[1] were passed by the cen-

sors on the grounds that their display of pubic hair was artistic rather than obscene. In the case of *Santa Fe*, only a handful of the photos even showed hair, and in all but one, it was so buried in shadows as to be barely visible. One shot, however, where Miyazawa is sitting on her knees in a field of grass, was taken in full sunlight, and her pubic hair glistens brightly and fully at the center of the photograph. For this *aidoru tarento*—a teen idol popularized on the basis of her wholesome good looks and pure character—the crotch shot destabilized her place of cuteness and propriety within the public imaginary (Schilling 1992). Even more disruptive of the pubic/public border was the advertisement of *Santa Fe*, accompanied by photos, in two of Japan's most respectable newspapers, the *Asahi Shinbun* and the *Yomiuri Shinbun*.

An explosion of public discourse called the "hair controversy" (*hea ronsō*)[2] ensued in the wake of these events. Conducted in such media as newspapers, magazines, radio talk shows, and television, it was an outpouring of Japanese opinions, both offered and solicited, from social commentators and pornographers to housewives and businessmen on the issue of obscenity. Some found the liberalization of the law to be refreshing given that sexuality and nudity are already such staples in public culture in Japan. Others, however, found the exposure of pubic hair to be truly transgressive, the point at which the imagery of bodies becomes excessive and obscene.[3] No matter what the position taken, however, there was a shared recognition of change. Until 1991, the authorities monitoring obscenity had been rigid about certain conventions defining it. These were basically the realistic depiction of pubic hair and genitalia. The law itself is far vaguer on its definition of obscenity: that which produces a sense of shame in a "normal" Japanese person who encounters, in public, an image or text whose primary intention or effect is to stimulate sexual desire (Beer 1984). Legislators had adopted for years the public representation of pubic hair and genitalia as its standard for interpreting the law's notion of the obscene. On what basis this selection was made, however, and whether it was targeted at the pubis itself as the most real part of the sexual body or at a particular realistic representation of it was never clearly explicated by those who ruled on obscenity cases, such as the one against the movie director Ōshima Nagisa heard by the Supreme Court (Ōshima 1988).

In this chapter I ask, Why, how, and with what effects has the state in postwar Japan (after the end of occupation in 1952 and prior to the softening of censorship laws in 1991) policed obscenity according to a principle of the exposure in public media of pubic realism? My inquiry revolves around the particular question of why such vigilance has been upheld at this border when the entry into the public arena of other bodily and sexual displays has been so willingly tolerated. Pictures of seminaked women appear in news magazines, naked breasts are shown in advertisements posted at such public places as train stations, scenes of rape and nudity are transmitted on prime-time television, sadomasochistic scenarios are printed in comic books sold as openly as they are read, panty shots of girls are sketched into television shows and magazines targeted to children, and naked women are pictured on cards for call girls that are deposited in the mailboxes of private residences. In the realm of printed and visual media alone, Japan is well known for the openness and pervasiveness with which sex is referred to and nakedness displayed. In fact, the packaging of bodily exposure that decenters or obscures genitalia and alludes to a form of sexuality that downplays or defers genital copulation is big business. It sells products and is productive itself of a construction of leisure that is sold to Japanese consumers as escapist recreation.

It is the nature of this packaging that drives my interest here: what the state sanctions as well as condemns as the means by which nakedness, sex acts, and erotic desire are represented within the ever-widening circuits of public culture. Significantly, the government has not outlawed the representation of bodies and sexuality altogether. Rather, following Foucault's insight, I will argue that the state has in fact endorsed and encouraged a sexual economy of a particular order, one that evades the state surveillance of pubic realism and therefore constructs the stimulation and simulation of sexuality as a fantasy nondependent on the graphic or visual display of genitalia. What results is a public culture in which the conjuring of sex depends on body imagery that either decenters the genitals or alludes to them indirectly (see Figure 7.2). Thus there is tolerance for the preponderance in Japanese media of peepshots up the skirts of girls and women at the ever-present white underpants (see Figure 7.3); the fetishization of body parts other than genitals, such as buttocks and breasts; the infantilization of females, who are (or are made to appear) prepubescent and lacking pubic hair; and acts of sadomasochism in which there is no genital copulation, stimulation, or exposure. These images all avoid the realism of genitalia, which centers the state's definition of both sexuality and obscenity. Thus such mass sexual tropes as voyeurism, infantilization, and sadomasochism are something other than "obscene" and other than "real." They are fantasies that can penetrate the public only by covering, effacing, or decentering the pubis.

Given the depth and extent of such penetration, it might seem that obscenity laws are strangely misplaced in Japan. By proscribing genital mimesis, they allow (as not legally obscene or even sexual) the "phantasmic" reproduction of the body in practically any other form—nipple and panty shots of young girls, for example, in adult magazines and children's cartoons. Thus by restricting one bodily sight/ site, the state permits and stimulates the mass production of a host of others. Restrictive laws are actually a boost to the big business of sexual fantasy-making in Japan, which, in the format of "fantasy," can be marketed to children as well as adults.

FIGURE 7.2   Although the law permits scenes of child sex in mass media, it has forbidden the explicit representation of genitalia. What results is sex acts involving undeveloped—both literally (by making the characters prepubescent) and figuratively (by keeping the image graphically simple)—genitalia.
SOURCE: "Media de Yokujōsuru Hon" (A Book for Sexual Arousal by the Media), *Bessatsu Takarajima*, vol. 196, 1994 (Tokyo: Takarajimasha), p. 27

But if obscenity laws effectively feed rather than curb the mass culture of fantasy sex in Japan, they also do something else. In banning genitals from public images, the law also protects as "real" one region of the social body from the sexualization of mass culture. This region, I will argue, is family and home, and the center of this region is the Japanese mother. She rarely appears in the market of sex fantasies (see Figure 6.1). Young girls, whose very lack of pubic hair signifies their feminine immaturity, are featured instead, as well as sex acts that have no chance of leading to reproduction—voyeurism, sadism, anal penetration, fellatio. What is prohibited as "obscene" by the state, then, is also that which is most sacred and central to the state's ideology of national identity—stable families, reproductive mothers, and orderly homes.

Travel and Borders

In the urban landscape of postwar Japan, travel between work and home has come to consume an ever larger proportion of the everyday lives of working Japanese. In large part, this is due to skyrocketing land prices, which have increasingly distanced affordable housing from the business and service centers of cities. Commuting can constitute as much as two or three hours one way, or five or six hours total in one day, heavily reducing the time one can spend at home. Some stay close to work during the week and commute back to home only on weekends.

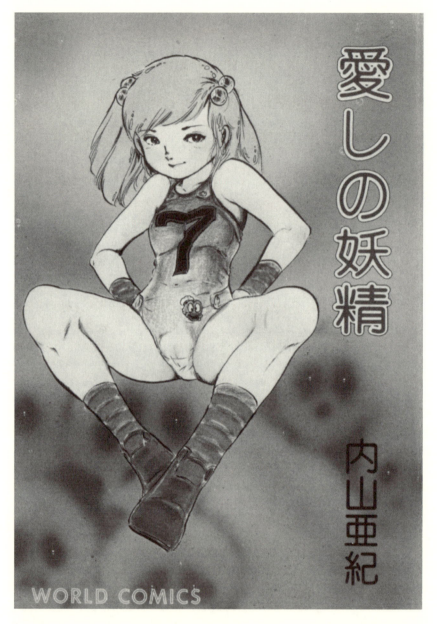

152

WORLD COMICS

愛しの妖精

内山亜紀

FIGURE 7.3   The crotch shot of a young girl is a dominant trope in comic imagery. Eroticization is infantilized here; the girl has girlish socks and hairdo and Donald Duck insignia yet poses provocatively with legs wide open. Note how the focus is drawn to her crotch, which remains hidden from full view.

SOURCE: Uchiyama Aki, *Itoshino Yōsei* (Lovely Fairy), 1980 (Tokyo: Kubo Shoten), cover

Such a calibration of space and time is broadly consistent with the ideology of work that has been supported by political institutions and economic forces since the early 1950s.

Targeted mainly at middle-class, white-collar males,[4] this ideology has propagated a strong view of work as the main vessel for energy, identity, duty, and responsibility. Implicitly, home and its management are left to women, who as wives and mothers have been directed to work hard reproducing future generations of Japanese workers and subjects largely in the absence of men. Implicitly as well, these ideological and physical conditions of work, particularly for those adhering to middle-class standards (and particularly since the urban buildup following World War II, when family size dropped and commuting distance between home and work increased), have made the home peripheral not only to where time is spent and labor engaged in but also to where leisure, as work's antidote, is pursued.

It is in this space that is configured, literally or figuratively, away from home that a business of mass-marketed leisure has built up in the years of postwar recovery, particularly those following the economic growth spurt in the late 1960s. Not surprisingly, the routes of commuter travel have been heavily exploited by this business. Not only do increasing numbers of Japanese spend increasing portions of their days commuting but also for those with frenetic schedules, the time spent traveling may constitute the only unscheduled, and in this sense "free," time in their day. For such commuters, the consumption of printed media offers the promise of both a temporary diversion to ease the length and monotony of daily travels and a momentary escape into other worlds, whether these be created by romance novels and sex comics or history texts and newsmagazines. Dispensaries for media entertainment line the heavily used train and bus routes of urban transportation. Train kiosks and newsstands, stalls, convenience stores, and bookshops are ubiquitous. One can, cheaply and conveniently, purchase a vast array of printed media—newspapers, comic books, weekly and monthly magazines, journals, travel guides, and paperback books—that offer diverse categories of information and entertainment along a spectrum of styles and tastes and targeted to multiple audiences.

That 60 percent of mass-circulation magazines (including newspapers and comic books) are currently sold at train stations indicates the close imbrication of commuter travel and media consumption in Japan today (Beer 1984). That the same stations are also dotted with garbage bins that are filled with the reading material that commuters are prone to throw away at the end of their commutes suggests how bracketed this time and space of urban passage is. Moving from one place to another and temporarily displaced from the identities and duties pinned down at either end, commuters have an open terrain for diversionary fantasizing.

In a society that remains heavily ruled by codings of identities fixed to such definite contexts as work, home, and school, to be suspended in a terrain that is betwixt and between, if only momentarily, is to become socially dislodged and therefore anonymous. For this reason, the prosaic commute can be imbued with the aura of illicitness and danger, or at least escape and release. It is in the interests of those who market media culture, of course, to feed these associations. Hence the idiom of travel as crossing or dislodging borders is used to build allusions to otherness. Ordinary Japanese can imagine temporary displacements from the everydayness in which they labor, study, and reproduce.

This territory of public space, transected by the circuits through which people, goods, information, and images pass with such increasing frequency and urgency in Japan's postwar years, has been targeted by the state for its monitoring of obscenity. The choice is obvious on two accounts. First, the domain of the public is the site of concentrated business and traffic: It is where people work, spend money, seek entertainment, and intermingle. All nation-states have some notion of this shared and communal space in which the behavior of citizens is surveiled and monitored by the law. Second, the public is where a form of sexuality has become mass-marketed as a booming industry. This development also is hardly unique to the conditions of postwar Japan. As scholars of late capitalism have argued, the allure of sexual pleasure is cultivated in economies increasingly dependent on consumerism as a means of selling products through allusions rather than the guarantee of value. As theorists in the tradition of the Frankfurt School go on to argue (Marcuse 1966; Haug 1986; Horkheimer and Adorno 1991), sexuality in advanced capitalism is not only borrowed to sell things but also constructed and contained to the shape of a commodity itself. Thus, since desire stimulates buying only when it remains perpetually deferred, sexuality must be dangled in front of consumers in such a way that it promises an excitement that can never be fully realized; that is, to commodify sexuality requires that it be shaped into a form that is both capable of exciting and unable to definitively satisfy. Such a form also meets the psychoanalytic definition of fantasy.

Needless to say, it is in the interests of a government such as Japan's to endorse corporate success, which is furthered by marketing products with sexuality. In Japan's case, I would add that the government has been additionally compelled to support sexual industries because recreative sexuality, in various forms, is used so frequently to sustain work relations (as when companies foster camaraderie by entertaining workers in hostess clubs [Allison 1994]), release and relieve work-induced stress (the well-known sex tours of Japanese men to places such as Thailand and sex quarters such as Shinjuku in Tokyo), and endure the long commutes. Yet the indulgence of a public sex culture must also, of course, have limits. After all, the hedonistic pursuit of pleasure is antithetical to both home and work, the mainstays of both productivity and reproductivity in Japan. The government is faced, then, with a dilemma. The marketing of a sexuality that promises something unrealizable has both benefits and dangers to the political status quo. It adds a patina to lives otherwise routine and frustrating. Yet its very suggestion of otherworldliness and dislocatedness from the norms and expectations of hegemonic identity also bears a subversive potential. To wander outside limits, after all, may feed a desire for a longer and more permanent stay.

What Is Dirty, and What Is Clean?

The state's regulation of sexual expression in public media seems, on the surface, to be contradictory. On the one hand, there is incredible indulgence. On the other, the state has, until recently, rigorously and consistently outlawed realistic depictions of genitalia, including pubic hair. The vigilance concerning these sites/sights has been declared by many commentators (such as Kimoto Itaru and Okudaira Yasuhiro[5]) and accused violators (such as Ōshima Nagisa and Suei Shoji [Ōshima 1983, 1981, 1988; Suei quoted in Bornhoff 1991]) to be arbitrary and characteristic of a state that needs to assert its authority over the public in ways that can be visibly inserted into everyday culture. Such signs of censorship are indeed ubiquitous. They are almost as apparent, in fact, as the constructions of sexuality they seemingly monitor.

Here is a post-1991 example: In the December 1994 issue of *Labien*, a magazine in the new genre of women's comic book erotica generically referred to as "ladies' comics" (targeted to working women who are the new consumers of sexual leisure), the pages are filled with stories and images of sadomasochism, forced enemas, anal insertion of various objects and substances, fellatio, pedophilia, bondage, homosexuality, masturbation, arousal, kissing, and nakedness. Throughout as well there are obvious markers of censorship, all the more obvious because each is purposely drawn in rather than merely added over a preexisting photograph (see Figures 7.4, 7.5, 7.6, 7.7).[6] These consist of an assortment of whitened, blackened, and shadowed shapes—mainly boxes, rectangles, dots, and ovals—that cover over or obscure genitals and pubises. So, for example, a black dot is affixed to what would otherwise be the outline of a woman's labia or a white box stands in place of a man's penis. In some cases the effacement is partial; in one frame a woman's pubic hair is shown half exposed with a white box intruding partway up. In, to me, the most interesting concoction, a man's penis is sheathed in a black condom that disguises the color but not the shape of his realistically drawn erection.

Kimoto Itaru, a legal scholar, has argued that it is the law and its regulation of obscenity that has made the visual and textual representation of sex in Japan

FIGURE 7.4   Genitalia are displayed as a fading blackness.
SOURCE: *Scandal I*, vol. 8, August 1995 (Tokyo: Ozora Shuppan), p. 13

"smutty" and "lewd." He states that contemporary representations contrast with the "principle of pleasure" (*kairakushugi*) in earlier representational forms such as *ukiyoe* (woodblock prints that were popular during the Tokugawa era, 1603–1868) that visualized both bodily nakedness and sexual engagement (Kimoto 1983).

Kimoto is correct with his point (which is Foucauldian) that the compulsiveness with which the state has regulated obscenity in postwar Japan has in itself been a stimulus to the industrializing of sex marketed along the lines of dirtiness. To Kimoto this dirtying of sex is lamentable and distracts from the "pleasure" sex could otherwise produce. Yet this smuttification is precisely the aesthetic distinction being created, Kimoto's own tastes notwithstanding. As Yoda Akira, a commentator writing more generally about the pleasure industries in Japan and their appeal from a male perspective, has put it, to enter into a world constructed on

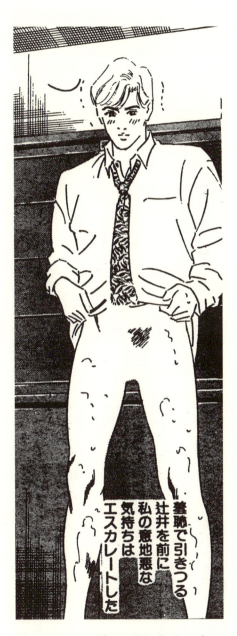

基聴で引きつる辻井を前に私の意地悪な気持ちはエスカレートした

FIGURE 7.5   The penis is eliminated,
but the man is still drawn in as naked.
SOURCE: *Scandal I,* vol. 8, August 1995
(Tokyo: Ozora Shuppan), p. 14

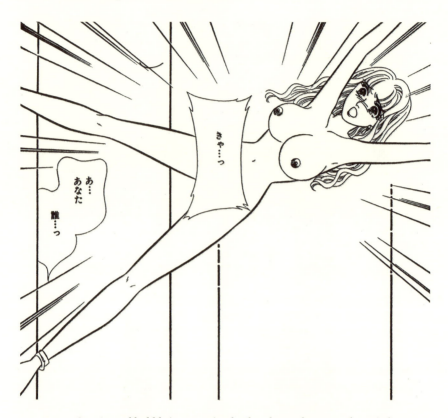

FIGURE 7.6   A word bubble is conveniently placed over the woman's genitals.
SOURCE: *Belle Rose,* vol. 3, November 1994 (Tokyo: Shōnengahōsha), p. 234

the sole principle of sexual titillation is to leave one's everyday world of work, troubles, and responsibilities behind. For him, the scenarios laid out in pornography are fantasies that are as improbable as they are deviant—"a world of sexual stimulation and abnormalcy, . . . sado-masochism, . . . animalistic sex, and sex with young girls" (Yoda 1981:22). The crudeness of sex is what he values, not because it is mimetic of the sex life he has or has much chance of realizing but because it symbolically disassembles the everydayness in which he lives. The very immediacy and inconsequentiality of women stripping, for example, allows a man to disengage from "worries at home and matters that are troublesome at work" (Yoda 1981:21) and become immersed in nothing but the presence of female flesh, which is continuous despite the changes of women on the stage.

For Yoda, the element of visuality is also important. Looking is critical to male sexuality, he claims. So is the craving for "noneveryday" sex (*hinichijōteki na sei*).

FIGURE 7.7   Fuzzed out to avoid realism, this pubic area is still eroticized despite, or perhaps because of, the artifice rendered on it. SOURCE: "Media de Yokujōsuru Hon" (A Book for Sexual Arousal by the Media), *Bessatsu Takarajima*, vol. 196, 1994 (Tokyo: Takarajimasha), p. 26

Writing here as a confessed participant in the pleasure trades rather than as an intellectual observer and deconstructivist, Yoda assumes a linkage between sexual looking and deviance, which he naturalizes as emanating from, rather than being constructed for, male desire. That working women too, however, are now being targeted by the industries that mass market sexual leisure, including visual fantasies of deviant sex, indicates how generalized rather than gendered these desires have currently become. This point can be illustrated with an example from the ladies' comic *Labien*, entitled "Aigan Daisan wa Maia" (Maia, the Third Story of a Pet) and authored (or, at least, signed) by a woman. The lead character ("heroine" seems the wrong characterization here), Maia, is a young, pretty woman who, infatuated with her male teacher, allows him to control her in a sadomasochistic relationship of ritualistic abuse. Sketched as to be perpetually in pain, Maia is forced to endure enemas, anal penetration by a variety of objects and substances, bandages and ropes tied tightly over her entire body, and clothing that severely cinches her waist and exposes her breasts and buttocks to strangers. In these scenes, Maia is referred to as a "doll" and the type of sex she engages in as "abnormal." Only at one point, after she has left her lover and been befriended by a man she calls "nice" are there any frames of kissing or genital sex. These take up only two out of thirty-seven pages, however, and in the end Maia has returned to her master, who is shown tying her up again in the final frame with her speaking at last. "Tie me tighter, tie me tighter," she implores.

What pleasure a female viewer would extract from such scenarios is not the immediate issue I wish to address here. Rather, it is a construction of sex with a narrative about desires and activities that are identified in the text as "noneveryday"; that are visualized with images graphically and repetitively showing nakedness (though little of genitals and no pubic hair) as well as dominance, anal penetration, fellatio, and bondage; and that are found in a magazine sold openly in public. Japanese authorities do not judge this publication to be obscene. They have banned, by contrast, a recent photographic magazine in which one photo showed the details of a woman's labia too clearly.[7] There is a certain, but officially different, construction of dirtiness operating in both cases. In the first, it is self-installed by the publishers of a magazine whose other stories in this particular issue include a wife who whips her husband, a man who masturbates while watching videos of his daughter when she was a child, a woman who solicits two men to engage in sex while she photographs them, and a woman who is gagged and bound while forced to shit on a toilet. In the second case, the photographer who publishes the magazine and who has asserted in an interview that his intention is "to give erections," which he finds to be "only natural," has been accused by the police of producing obscene material.[8]

Modernizing the Public, Fetishizing the Pubic

On what grounds has the state fixated on only one body part and made its exposure in public media the sign of obscenity? As the law reads today, it is the context of the public that is determinant in rendering pubic realism obscene. Implicitly, what is offensive about genitalia is not the fact that they exist but showing them (and drawing attention to them) in public—not the site per se of the pubis but its public sighting. The Supreme Court judges who wrote a brief explaining their decision to ban twelve passages from the Japanese translation of D. H. Lawrence's *Lady Chatterley's Lover* in 1958 were clear about this distinction. Sexual desire is not an evil in and of itself, they stated, but humans are different from animals in experiencing these "innate feelings" as shameful, a sense of shame that increases as people acquire "spiritual soundness, emotional maturity, and social development. . . . For instance, even in an uncivilized community, the custom of completely exposing the sex organ is rarely found, and there is no society in which sex acts are performed openly in public. Thus, it must be stated that so far as it relates to mankind, the non-public nature of the sex act is only a natural manifestation of a sense of shame deeply rooted in human nature" (Saikō Saibansho 1958:4).

A connection is made not only between civilization and the covering up of bodies and sex in public but also between sexuality and body parts: The "sex organ" stands metonymically for "sex acts" in general. Genitalia stand, then, for the whole, for both a kind of sexuality (reproductive) and a kind of state (civilization that is indexed by the degree to which bodies and sex acts are covered in public) (see Figure 7.8). This means that the sex organ in the context of the law is a marker of the body's entrance into a state of civilization; it is not a place or a thing but a border that serves to mark territories on the map of social and civilized space. Foucault has noted the power and meaningfulness of such borders. Of significance is not the "what" on either side of borders—wearing clothes as opposed to exposing genitalia, acting in public as opposed to nonpublic space, participating in shameful as opposed to nonshameful sexuality—but rather the imposition of distinction altogether (Foucault 1980). The same can be said about the legislation of obscenity; what is critical in Japan is not the fact that covered or uncovered sex organs are prohibited but the territorialization of national and public space according to body zones and how they relate to different forms of sexuality. Normalcy is invoked in forbidding the literal entrance of pubises into public terrain. And even as a prohibited shame (= obscenity), the public pubis connects bodily genitals with public space.

In his theories on the phallus, Lacan has argued similarly that its social meaning is not as an organ per se but as a relationship: It is the master signifier that signifies signification itself and, as the third term, signals the disruption of the imaginary stage of blissful and narcissistic dyadicism between mother and child and compels the child's entry into the symbolic of norms, rules, and signs. Standing for power and morality, this "law of the father" establishes the terrain of the sociopolitical order, which determines identity and consigns desire to the side of outlawry, disorder, and repression. Because the phallus represents the law and is meaningful only within the law, the phallus should not be confused with or reduced to any single body part such as a penis, Lacan has argued (1977:281–291). Yet as feminists including myself have pointed out, the penis *is* the shape by which phallic power is most often configured in a phallocentric society. Further, this conflation of phenomenal penises and philosophical phallicism is neither arbitrary nor innocent.[9] Rather, when gender organizes social, political, and economic relations in a community based on a principle of hierarchy that privileges men, males have rights and authorities that females do not and maleness is given a symbolic capital that femaleness lacks. It is this difference, both real and imaginary, that is encoded in a phallic system grafted onto penises rather than female body parts. The phallus, in other words, signifies not only meaning but also power, and as master signifier, it is signifier for the master as well.

Specific relations of history and power are at work in the case of Japanese obscenity laws as well. Although the obscenity laws operate in part independently of the particular definition given obscenity, the fact that obscenity has been defined as

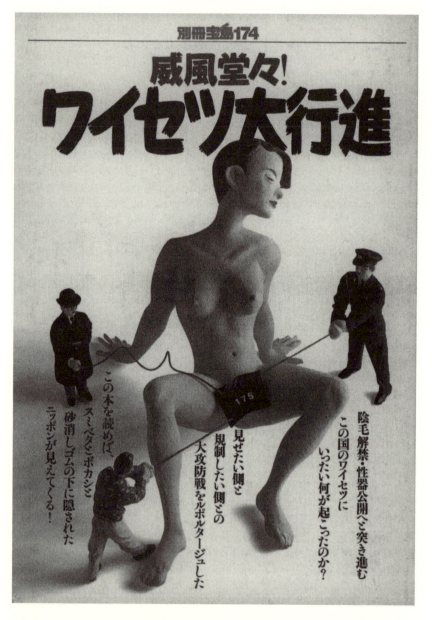

FIGURE 7.8   Cover design for a special issue on pornography in the journal *Takarajima*. Various authorities are pulling on the strings of Article 175, the penal code barring realistic display of genitalia in mass media. The article covers the pubic area of the naked woman.

SOURCE: "Waisetsu Daikōshin" (Indecency Marching), *Bessatsu Takarajima*, vol. 174, 1993 (Tokyo: JICC Suppankyoku), cover public realism for almost a century in Japan is significant. Critically, contemporary laws on obscenity originated during Japan's period of modernization with Article 175 of the Criminal Code in 1907 and Article 21 of the Customs Tariffs Law in 1910. During this period, having been forced out of its isolationalism (the Tokugawa era, 1603–1868) in the mid-1800s and propelled into trade relations with the United States and Western Europe, Japan rapidly and radically developed the infrastructure—industrialization, military buildup, imperialism, parliamentary government—of a modern nation. Mimicking the west, Japan was the first nonwestern state to achieve modernization. Its recognition as a global power, however, was handicapped by the presence of cultural and racial differences: customary behavior such as mixed bathing and nursing in public, for example, which western travelers to Japan perceived as indications of Japanese heathenism.

It was as a corrective to this western perception of Japanese "primitiveness" that the modern laws against obscenity were first imposed: They were a means of covering the national body from charges that it was obscene. To Japanese at the time, it must be noted, exposing one's body to bathe or to nurse was considered neither dirty nor sexual. Further, sexuality itself lacked the connotation of dirtiness. Rather, under a Shinto rather than Judeo-Christian religious ideology, these are bodily functions that, along with burping, excretion, and picking one's nose, are viewed as matters more of nature than of shame. In fact, shrines still display fertility gods and images with exaggerated genitalia, sexual characteristics, and breasts. In mythology (Kawai 1988) and other artistic, religious, and dramatic traditions, the reference to and representation of sex is tolerated, even indulged. What to the Japanese was a part of the everyday, however, led others to dismiss their country as a land of "nudity, rudity, and crudity" (Dore 1958:159).

To cleanse itself of this primitivist image and acquire the identity and credibility of a modern nation, the Japanese state outlawed bodily exposures (i.e., nursing in public, mixed public bathing). In part, acquiring such an identity meant adopting western standards for corporeal deportment. In part as well, it meant developing a notion of the public as a terrain that is monitored and administered by the state. Thus the behavior of the Japanese, as state subjects, in this terrain is regulated and surveiled. Stemming from both these impulses, a concept of "public morals" was formulated, and based on such rulings as that in 1900 banning any subject matter considered "injurious to public morals" regardless of the intent of the artist or author (Rubin 1984), censorship cases increased. Bodies and sex, in particular any references or representations that were construed as too realistic, too direct, or of a sexuality too approving of nonfamilial norms, became a primary focus. Significantly, the western stereotype of Japan as a body excessively exposed was taken almost literally by the Japanese state, but the state's response to this perception was, as Homi Bhabha has applied the Freudian concept to colonialism, one of ambivalence (Bhabha 1992). On the one hand, the attempt was made to re-form Japan by eliminating the differences that it posed to, and that were dispar-aged by, western culture. On the other hand, censorship was invoked in order to protect Japan's own social body from being infiltrated and de-formed by western influence. The graphic genitalia on western nudes, for example, were banned in magazines, covered by maroon curtains at art exhibitions, or, in the case of at least one penis on a sculpture displayed in public, literally sawed off. Targeted as well for state surveillance was literature, journalism, and intellectualism characterized as part of the school of naturalism, which, popular around 1910, was identified as western influenced with its trope of realism and its associations with socialism, individualism, and free sex (Rubin 1984; Mitchell 1983).

A line was drawn around genitalia that was codified by law in 1918, when the courts ruled that in public media the "pubic area need not be hidden but there should be no anatomical details to draw the viewer's attention" (Rubin 1984:44). Pubic details were prohibited not only in works of literature and art entering the country but in those from Japan's past. For example, the ban on the public sale and display of erotic woodblock-print scrolls (*shunga*) from the Tokugawa era, in which genitalia and sexual positions are graphically detailed, continued until the 1990s. The ban has cut both ways, censoring the same body part—Lacan's "pound of flesh" as it were—on the self as well as the other. And a desire for banned goods (flesh) has been generated on both fronts, as much for bootleg *shunga* as for un-censored copies of *Playboy*. Pubic realism has operated as a fetish, in other words, in the Freudian sense. It stands for that whose sight generates anxiety in the viewer—a boy, when viewing female genitalia, sees the threat of castration—and the site of otherness is covered with an alternate site in which difference has been erased (Freud 1961:149). Banning public realism serves to appease the fear of cas-tration (or impotency), that is, Japan's fear both that it will be denied recognition as a global power by the west and that, by accommodating itself to western stan-dards (and the west's own fear of impotency in the face of rising Japanese strength), it will lose its cultural core of Japaneseness. The fetish of pubic obscen-ity is consequently ambivalent, generated both from feelings of insecurity and protectionism around the self and from hostility as well as receptiveness toward the other. The pubic zone stands for an identity, body part, and sexuality and is covered so as not to offend with its dirtiness but also to protect what is "real" from outside contamination.

Covering Territories: State and Border Control

Pubic prohibition operates as a Marxian fetish as well in that what is actually a network of historical, transnational, and political relations gets reified and obscured by a focus on the object of the ban alone. And for many of those most affected by the law, this choice and fixation seems enigmatic. Most describe it as simply irrational or arbitrary, as the means, as Ōshima Nagisa has stated it, for the state to exert its authority over the fantasies and pleasures of common people. Ōshima is the director and producer of several films, including the sexually explicit *Ai no Korīda* (In the Realm of the Senses), which was filmed in Japan, edited in Paris, and banned from reentry into Japan according to Article 21 of the Fixed Tariffs Law. He was accused of obscenity on the basis of a book produced by the publishing firm San'ichi Shobō, in which still photographs from the movie were reproduced. Twelve photographs were deemed to be obscene for depicting "poses of male-female sexual intercourse and sexual play" and nine passages in the script for their "frank description" of male-female sexual intercourse (Ōshima 1988:269, 273). Ōshima, outraged that he was charged even after following the conventions for obscenity and deleting references to and images of genitalia and pubic hair, attempted to force the officials into a clearer explication of their position on obscenity. Demanding to know the grounds on which genitalia, sex, and the representations of either are found to be obscene, he also questioned Japan's right to retain a concept of public morals that, so critical to the fascistic state of prewar and wartime Japan, was supposedly dismantled in the democratic reorganization after the war. Although Ōshima eventually won the case after years of struggle in court, he failed to educe the clarity he had sought.[10]

Many who have been charged with obscenity in Japan, including Ōshima, have challenged the state for failing to guarantee the freedom of expression it instituted in Article 21 of the so-called democratic constitution imposed in 1947 by the occupying forces. The first test case was in 1969, when the importation of an art book of nudes (*Sun-Warmed Nude*) was denied permission. The Supreme Court retried the case and upheld the decision in 1981, arguing that Article 21 does not ban all forms of censorship, that it excludes restraints on obscene and defamatory expression (Beer 1984). This ruling contradicts the interpretation given to Article 21 during the years of Japan's occupation, when under the ruling command of SCAP (Supreme Command Allied Powers), the censorship of sexual media was eased. With the end of occupation in 1952, however, the laws regulating obscenity, which had remained on the books since prewar times, were reactivated by the Finance Ministry. Today it continues to police obscenity according to a concept of the infringement upon public morals of the (public) stimulation of sexual desire.

Contemporary producers of sexual materials such as Suei Shoji, a writer, commentator on Japanese sexual mores, and head of the publishing house Byakuyosha, find contemporary obscenity laws anachronistic and out of sync with contemporary views on bodies and sexuality. A veteran of many police bans himself, Suei has attempted various methods to evade the literal proscriptions of the law: attaching fake hair from a woman's navel to her ankles, shaving the pubic hair off models, and drawing over the pubic area with magic markers. Although his methods constitute a game of sorts, the police always have the upper hand, and Suei has begun to tire of the money and time he must expend just to stay afloat (Bornhoff 1991:400, 407). Further, like other producers of sexual materials, he also publishes more mainstream media and fears the stigma of obscenity charges.

The threat of a warning or ban is in fact the real enforcer of obscenity legislation today, many argue (for example, Kimoto 1983; Maeda 1980). Because obscenity is regulated by a plethora of laws beyond those of the Criminal Code and Fixed Tariff Law—including the Entertainment Facilities Law, the Broadcast Law, the Prison law, the Law Regulating Business Affecting Public Morals, the Child Welfare Law, and thirty-nine local youth-protection ordinances—many businesses that may engage in the marketing or sale of sexual media wind up instituting their own agencies for self-surveillance (Beer 1984; Kimoto 1983). These include the Eirin (the Film Ethics Sustaining Committee, Eirin Iji Īnkai), which is a private self-regulatory body for movies,[11] the Tetsudō Kōsaikai (the Railroad Benefit Association, or RBA), which monitors the sale of mass publications in train stations,[12] and review panels by every television station including NHK.[13] Further, parents and other concerned citizen groups such as women's groups and PTAs can appeal to local politicians or file a complaint using a youth-protection ordinance (or the National Child Welfare Consultative Committee, which, under the Child Welfare Law, can issue warnings) to compel publishers or sellers of media to withdraw or ban particular publications on the grounds of charged obscenity.[14] At a different level, self-surveillance comes from artists, authors, and publishers incorporating their own forms of censorship into their work. Called *fuseji*, these marks are a visual sign of the attempt made to censor and thereby evade official bans and seizures. Another effect of such censoring is its incorporation into a popular aesthetic, as mentioned already, evidenced by such staples in mass culture as voyeurism, where what is hidden does not prevent looking as much as inspire looking of a particular kind.

Surveillance of the obscene, coming from both above and below in Japan, is overdetermined and made visible in the act of making invisible such sights as pubic hair and genitalia in media from comic books to TV. The circuits of this policing pervade public culture in Japan. Not surprisingly, censorship is also rigorously enforced at the borders demarcating Japanese territory. A committee of experts with "learning and experience" is appointed by the Customs Bureau to set the obscenity standards for all goods entering Japan. All visitors and returnees to Japan have their belongings inspected at ports of entry; these inspections are noteworthy not only for their rigor but also for what is found: The Customs Bureau reports that attempts to smuggle pornography (until recently, constituted as anything with visible genitalia and pubic hair) into the country in suitcases have skyrocketed (from 12,400 such cases in 1977 to 30,200 in 1979, for example; Beer 1984). For materials that are being imported by publishers and distributors, inspection occurs at designated customs areas such as the port at Yokohama, where cadres of workers scrutinize incoming materials according to a scientific method for measuring and counting the visibility of exposed hair or genitalia. Scrutinized are, first, such likely offenders as men's magazines—for example, *Playboy*, *Hustler*, and *Penthouse*—and next, artistic, fashion, and photographic publications including films. When obscenity is found, it is removed—blotted, scratched, airbrushed, obscured—often at considerable cost to the importer (Bornhoff 1991; Maeda 1980).

The rigors of this process and the marks it characteristically leaves on imported media signify both the danger implicit in material emanating from outside the borders of Japan and the compulsiveness of the Japanese state in asserting its standards of propriety over anything moving into Japan. Said to be as protective of its national borders on the issue of obscenity as it is on trade, Japan has been highly criticized on both scores for its provincialism and hostility. In recent years there has been a string of protests from foreign artists, filmmakers, and publishers (often delivered from the offices of their governments) whose work has been censored by Japanese customs. In 1985 nude photos taken by the French surrealist photographer Man Ray were impounded by the Customs and Tariff Bureau, which refused to release them until the obscene portions were blacked out to comply with local standards. In this case the French government protested and the Foreign Ministry stepped in, so the Man Ray show was allowed to proceed uncensored. In the same year, at the first Tokyo International Film Festival, two foreign directors—Hector Babenco from Brazil and Michael Radford from Britain—threatened to withdraw their entries (*Kiss of the Spider Woman* and *1984*, respectively) if a single frame was censored. After intense debate, the films were shown untouched, but warnings were given that the films would have to be adjusted in compliance with local standards for commercial release (Bornhoff 1991). Such "adjustment" befalls all imported media circulating in the market of popular culture. With marks of excision often crudely disfiguring the text, foreign media are identified as both alien and obscene, a conflation of othernesses authorized by the state to the stated end of protecting what are identified as Japanese mores. Consistent with such an ideology of obscene foreignness, AIDS has been represented in the mass media as a germ that entered Japan on the body of a Filipina prostitute (from an encounter she supposedly had with a Greek man)(Treat 1995:651). Signs are posted at border points such as airports, warning Japanese of the danger of AIDS as they leave and reenter Japan.

One effect of monitoring all incoming visual and printed media is that the meanings intended by their foreign producers are altered and at times mutilated.

The fixation on airbrushing out, patching over, and clouding the genitalia can make a particular scene in a movie, for example, appear simply ridiculous. Viewers of *Woodstock* in Japan (both Japanese and foreigners) remember it for its disfigurements: an endless decrotching that became far more memorable than the story. Likewise, exposed genitalia are found where they otherwise might go unnoticed, as happened in the movie *Amadeus*, in which a distant sight of pubic hair was less concealed than revealed by airbrushing (Bornhoff 1991). Scenes not intended to be sexual are consequently made both erotic and obscene by the very authorities whose job it is to patrol against obscenity. And meaning can be not only altered but lost by such a literal and rigid enforcement of censorship boundaries. Despite pleas from the British director and Japanese distributor of *The Crying Game*, the pivotal scene was shown with its exposed penis clouded over (Regelman 1993:1, 68). As an example of how incomprehensible the movie thereby becomes, Donald Richie reports overhearing two women discussing the film after watching it in Tokyo. Bewildered and unsure of what on the body of the "woman" her male friend had found so disturbing, one offered her opinion that it was leprosy.[15]

Lacking Parts

In Japanese mythology, the exposure of hidden body parts can have radical effects. In one myth, the sun goddess, Amaterasu, shuts herself in a cave out of anger at her brother, Susanō. Trying to lure her out in order to restore sunlight to the earth, a group of gods and goddesses begin to party and one raises her skirt, thereby exposing her genitalia to the others. The hilarity that ensues piques Amaterasu's curiosity, forcing her to leave the cave. In other myths, viewers are stunned, awed, impressed, amused, startled, and transfixed by the sight of a woman's genitalia. Alternatively, there are folktales in which one's body is seen against one's wishes. Usually this person is a woman who forbids a man, often a husband, from looking at her in a particular context of time or space (e.g., childbirth). Transgressing the taboo, the voyeur sees what is usually hidden: a body or body part, referred to as "shameful," that reveals a disguised identity—crane, snake, demon, monster. A loss of some type always ensues; the man may be punished or die, but more frequently, the woman simply leaves, breaking up the marriage and home.

These stories evoke a sense of power at the site/sight of revealed body parts, whether this leads to a disruption or solution to a particular set of circumstances and whether what is seen is viewed as shameful or awesome. As part of Shinto mythology in Japan, the stories also suggest that the fetish of pubic exposure, which has so marked Japanese obscenity laws since the turn of the century, cannot be entirely attributed to the events in the mid-to-late nineteenth century of modernization and western contact. Rather, there were cultural practices connected to forbidden looking and partitioned body zones already in existence that, to use Barthes's term, provided the form by which the state could fashion a new "myth" of public cover.[16] This historical connection is an example of what Ernesto Laclau and Chantal Mouffe (1990), Jean and John Comaroff (1991), and others have pointed out about ideological formations: Their effectiveness relies on reworking rather than removing cultural traditions. Thus, "native" and "other" are always deeply intertwined and sedimented in social behavior, and it is important to historicize our studies of culture while bearing in mind the continuities of cultural ideas as much as the ruptures caused by historical events.

I now return to my original focus: How does the myth or fetish of veiled pubises work today, situated as it is at the crossroads of law and desire? In this environment of state censorship, how do producers and publishers of mass media make their images of bodies and sex appealing to consumers?

In response to the dual conditions of avoiding pubic realism and generating sales, various conventions are used in images and texts that allude to, display, and otherwise represent sexualized bodies and tales. One is to deemphasize the prohibited pubis, thereby eroticizing other body parts such as the buttocks and breasts, both of which are highly fetishized in the mass media (the fact that buttocks are often shown without the model's face also suggests various gendered and sexual possibilities). Another is to configure sex acts as nondependent on genitalia. As mentioned earlier, such activities include insertion of various objects and substances into other bodily orifices, mainly the anus; bondage; urination and excretion; kissing; and various acts (pinching, sucking, kissing) done to breasts. A third convention is to use models who are or are made to appear prepubescent and therefore lacking in "nature" what by law they are prohibited to show. In the case of females, this has meant using ever younger models whose pubises are shown without hair. Whereas females are therefore infantilized, the trend for males is to provide substitutes for rather than deprive them of mature genitalia. Augmented by phallic weaponry, males are shown with baseball bats, tennis rackets, guns, swords, sticks, and golf clubs, which they often use to conquer or violate women whose vulnerability has been exaggerated as well by anatomic underdevelopment. A fourth strategy for not showing the pubic zone is to show it with the marks of censorship clearly inscribed. Examples have already been discussed: They include using models with clean-shaven pubises; covering genitalia with sheaths (for penises) or high-cut underpants (for women); blocking the view with partial obstructions; and employing voyeurism to excite a gaze that can never fully see the desired site.

In the efforts employed to circumvent genital realism, there is an incitement not to hide sex but rather to show it in a particular form. This form has a curious resemblance, in almost every way, to the characteristics of perversions as the anti-model to normalcy as laid out by Freud in his *Three Essays on the Theory of Sexuality* (written, coincidentally, at the same time that Japan installed obscenity laws) (Freud 1975). If we use the Freudian measure of sexual maturity as the organization of sexuality by genitals, copulation, and heterosexual coupling, what is popularized in Japanese mass culture (and even in the work of Nobel Prize winner Ōe Kenzaburō[17])—analism, scopophilia, female infantilization, the deferral or avoidance of copulation, nongenital-based aggression—is strikingly "perverse." Of course, Freud's model of sexuality is western rather than Japanese, but perhaps this is the very point. If the legal concept of obscenity in Japan was inspired by a western notion of bodily propriety based on what Deleuze and Guattari have called an oedipal norm (Deleuze and Guattari 1983), the perverse tendency today in mass sexuality could be seen to subvert this norm by decentering the genital core of oedipality. Are the would-be colonized of western imperialism speaking back, enforcing a law that compels transgression?

Perhaps, as John Treat has argued recently for the "schizophrenic" characterizations in Yoshimoto Banana's book *Kitchen*, whose popularity is transnational, "anti-oedipality" is the predominant form of mass entertainment and pleasure in Japan's late-capitalist economy and dislodges the idea of a genital center to any notion of self, family, gender, and the nation (Treat 1995). But I take a position different from his. At least in the case of sexual culture, genitals have been not erased as much as reinforced by the legal prohibition against showing them. Such prohibition inspires a voyeuristic economy, one in which desire is stimulated by simulating something that can never be entirely had. Proximity to a woman's genitalia, whose possession or sight is still somehow obstructed, is a titillation with big market value in Japan: It is behind the fad in the 1980s of the *nōpan kissa* (clubs where the waitresses wore clothes but no underpants and customers could look but not touch), the *nōpan* karaoke (karaoke service with *nōpan* waitresses), *nozoki* clubs (Peeping Tom clubs where customers look up through the glassed ceiling to a simulated subway car where women sit wearing no underpants), and the current fashion of shops that sell the used underwear of junior and senior high school students.[18] Though a commonplace in the sex industry, voyeurism is still packaged as a transgression, as a flirtation with the boundaries of the illicit. As Go Tomohide has written about the sex industry in Japan, it feels *iyarashī* (dirty), which is precisely its purpose and value, he claims, for those who consume it (Go 1981:260).

Is the Japanese notion of *iyashirasa*, however, the same as the Freudian concept of perversion? In the sense that perversion refers back to a standard of normalcy it refuses, I suggest that there is something intentionally perverse about the fantasies so popular and popularized by mass sexuality in Japan. Intended as escape from an everydayness of duty and responsibility, scenarios are crafted as "other" to relationships of production, home, school, and citizenship that are otherwise so central in the lives of at least middle-class Japanese. I note here a construction of fantasy different from that used by such scholars as Kaja Silverman, who describes fantasies in western mass media as relying upon a trope of believability and, consequently, realism. In Silverman's view, making the male penis commensurable with phallic power is a key agenda in mass fantasies in the west (Silverman 1992). In contrast, Japanese sexual storytelling, according to a number of Japanese writing on the subject, relies far more on a convention of fantasy that is compelling because it engenders rather than suspends disbelief. To say this somewhat differently, fantasies of sex are often produced along the lines of abnormal, illicit, transgressive, or dirty encounters that leave certain realities literally off the page and, figuratively, outside representation. For example, in the cartoon story "Like a Sex Doll," which appeared in the ladies' comic *Scandal 20*, marriage is what is manifestly displaced from this tale about passionate but deviant sex. The story concerns a young office woman who, after being forcibly and cruelly raped by her boss, falls into an obsessive and lurid affair with him. Among other acts, the boss shaves off the woman's pubic hair, leaving a visible mark of what she calls her depravity (see Figures 7.9, 7.10). In the eyes of the law, of course, this depubised woman is now "clean." But in the narrative of the comic, the lack of pubic hair is the sign of her being "like a sex doll," and she keeps her shaved pubis hidden from her decent boyfriend by refusing to sleep with him. In the end, nostalgic for the boyfriend she has lost and committed to exchanging her dollness for the realness of marriage and motherhood, she leaves her boss-lover. It is not coincidental, I would say, that she also quits her job, as artificial a role for her as is that of unrestrained lover. Naturalized in the text is that which is not shown—woman at home rather than woman at work or in bed.

The unsaid of this sex story is what is compelling about it: the goodness of marriage, family, and home, whose absence in the text is the very condition for the tale of this woman's sexualization.[19] As the woman is posed in the last frame, toasting her twenty-fifth birthday with a bottle of Coke and smiling with hair neatly combed for the first time in the comic, the reader can imagine that as her pubic hair grows back in, she will become the type of woman who would no longer appear on the pages of a sexual comic. As Angela Carter has said about pornography in the United States and Western Europe, the eroticization of nonnormative acts and relations is seen by authorities to diffuse rather than stimulate the transgression of such state-supported norms as familialism, and such eroticization is banned when the perception is different (Carter 1978). Obscenity laws

FIGURE 7.9   The most realistic image of pubic hair appears on the razor after it has been used to shave the woman.
SOURCE: *20s*, vol. 2, November 1992 (Tokyo: Kasakura Shuppansha), p. 298

in Japan operate on a similar principle. What they legislate against—genital realism—is perceived to threaten state order far more than other constructions of sexual desire—panty shots, female infantilization, misogynistic violence, sadomasochism. And the threat posed by realistic genitalia is not that it is inherently obscene but rather that it is only too "real"—too important and too central to the social realities of national reproduction. Much like the emperor whose symbolic place in the cultural imaginary is staged by keeping him more hidden[20] from the public eye than exposed to it, genitalia as both metaphoric and metonymic of a body politic centered by the reproductions of family, home, and motherhood are veiled as well. Or, to say this differently, by protecting these sites from the sight of the public, the law works to both screen genitalia and embed them with ideological meaning.

FIGURE 7.10   After the woman has been shaved, she is photographed.
Although the vagueness in the pubic area signifies that the hair has been shaved
off, this meaning applies only if one has read the text.
SOURCE: *20s,* vol. 2, November 1992 (Tokyo: Kasakura Shuppansha), p. 299

I use Žižek's notion of the "real" in this context. Following Lacan, he defines the
real as "the rock upon which every attempt at symbolization stumbles"; as "something that persists only as failed, missed, in a shadow," and that "dissolves itself as
soon as we try to grasp it in its positive nature" (Žižek 1989:169). The real is that
which appears to defy representation, that which transcends or is so "essential" to
social life that expressing it by ordinary conventions is not allowed. Thus popular
sexuality is too ordinary for the realm of the "real." In the name of legislating
against obscenity, the law is protecting and constructing a cordon sanitaire—a
territory on the body (both the sexual body and the social body of gendered
power and economic relations)—that stands on the other side of what gets circulated as popular and common entertainment. The taboo against the pubis in public, then, organizes a relationship of difference in terms of which a certain map-
ping of social terrain is laid out: between a social space that is naturalized (home,
family, and work) and one made artificial (leisure, escapism, mass culture) and
between a body that is real (reproducing teleologically for a company, a family, a
state) and a body that is phantasmic (doll-like females and brutish males who
copulate, if at all, in a relationship that does not last). And as Durkheim observed

long ago about such dichotomies, one presupposes the other and both are products of the same law.

Arguing that Japanese obscenity laws produce both realness and fantasy, I use psychoanalytic terms such as "fantasy" and "real" only in the context of material, political, and historical relations that situate their practice. And such practice has hardly stayed still in the almost eighty years that Article 175 has been in place in Japan. Thus, although realism has barely changed in the letter of the law, "realness" certainly has, shifting with moves in the global economy, population density, war, family size, increased urbanization, and so on. What I would emphasize in the 1990s, however, is that there remains an ideology of motherhood and familialism that still grounds (in both a symbolic and real sense) Japaneseness as a national identity and that this involves the role of women as wives, mothers, and domestic mainstays in a way different and beyond that of a western, more "oedipal," model. Women who manage the home (even when they labor outside) ensure the productivities of working men, who are thereby enabled to devote their primary energies to jobs, and of children who, as hard-working students, acquire the skills needed for future generations of workers and mothers. More than anything, I contend, it is this domestic space and the centering of Japan's late capitalism in the labors of mother-centered families that is being covered and veiled by pubic prohibitions. This emphasis on the home accounts for the impulse to otherize sexual leisure, to fashion the commodified forms of mass sexuality as non-domestically perverse. Not only is such sexuality engaged in away from home but not-at-homedness in and of itself is exaggerated as incitement for sexual escapism. When sexual recreation is constructed *as* the other, as bell hooks has written, it must be played out in a realm away from where normative identity is moored. Getting a "bit of the other," then, is getting away, in some sense, from the "self" (hooks 1992).

Postscript

In Japan in the 1990s, this self centered by domestic labor is losing its moorings. Women are working in greater numbers, for more years, and with less inclination to quit at the point of marriage or motherhood. More marriages are ending in divorce, more families are single-parented, and more women are staying single and childless. Official voices use the specter of America's problems—high crime, economic woes, teenage pregnancy, drug addiction—to plead for the retention of Japanese family values. Still, such demographic changes are an ever-increasing reality, reflected in part, I suggest, by the changes in obscenity legislation in 1991.

In the aftermath of Miyazawa's exposure in *Santa Fe*, a new phenomenon, the *hea nūdo* (nude with exposed pubic hair), has become a commonplace. What was once hidden has now permeated the ranks of media recreation, having been brought to the light by shifts in the socioeconomic order. Genital realism, once the symbol for a real of domestic familialism, stands alongside such shifts in material relations as a labor force less dominated by men, a consumership of mass fantasies more participated in by women, and families in which old forms and norms are breaking down. Still, change is never clean, just as ideology is never total. Intermixed with all the photos and cartoons showing pubic hair are the standard images discussed throughout the book—including those of young girls shown to have bodies maturing under girlish clothing—as well as a plethora of various types that blend and transcend old notions of heterosexuality and gender.

That *shōjo* (young females) are so popularized in the public imaginary as a sign of and for escape still refers in the mid-1990s, I would argue, to the role assigned to and assumed by mothers in Japan. And only when the changes that have started to reorganize the matri-centrality of family life proceed even further do I predict that the fixation on nonmaternal young girls will abate and new fantasy conventions take their place.[21]

Notes

INTRODUCTION

1. Field does acknowledge this implication in her work and claims that she does not adhere to any romanticized notion of childhood that existed in previous eras (1995:68–69).

2. According to 1989 statistics.

3. In 1991.

4. Of these, 54.6 percent see their income as supplementing household income; 31.8 percent use their wages for savings (Buckley 1993).

5. In 1989 the average age of marriage was 25.8 for women and 28.5 for men. In the same year the birth rate hit an all-time low at 1.57 average children born (Tanaka 1995).

6. I am indebted to John Treat for his brilliant analysis of this action on the part of the Japanese government as well as of the novel *Kitchen* itself.

7. I use Asada's terminology here, though I dislike its implications of characterizing capitalism in the west as "adult" and capitalism in Japan as "infantile."

CHAPTER 1

1. Following Japanese convention, I present Japanese names with the family name first.

2. See, for example, Spivak (1982), Yamada (1983), Pence (1982), Lorde (1983), hooks (1992), Trinh (1989).

3. On stereotyping and bashing of Japan, see Miyoshi (1991: 62–96).

4. Ruth Benedict, *The Chrysanthemum and the Sword* (1989 [1946]).

5. The contributors include (in *Dirty Looks*) Carol Clover, Lynne Segal, Gertrude Koch, Linda Williams, Jennifer Wicke, Maureen Turim, Bette Gordon and Karyn Kay, Liz Kotz, Laura Kipnis, Lynda Nead, Chris Strayer, Grace Lau, Anne McClintock, and (in *Sex Exposed*) Elizabeth Wilson, Carole Vance, Mandy Merck, Lynne Segal, Kobena Mercer, Anne McClintock, Elizabeth Cowie, Mary McIntosh, Robin Gorna, Carol Smart, Jane Mills, Mery Harriett Gilbert, Linda Williams, Loretta Loach, Gillian Rodgerson, Lynda Nead, and Marybeth Hamilton.

6. So much has been written on this issue. I refer here only to representative works. For the pro-censorship position, Catharine MacKinnon and Andrea Dworkin have been the most vocal and influential proponents. For the anticensorship position, see, for example, Duggan, Hunter, and Vance (1992); Vance (1990, 1992); and the essays by Willis, Califia, Snitow, Hunter, Webster, Ellis, Duggan, and Duggan, Hunter, and Vance in *Caught Looking:*

Feminism, Pornography, and Censorship (F.A.C.T. Book Committee 1992). Many feminists have also written critiques of the MacKinnon-Dworkin position; Drucilla Cornell's (1991, 1993) work is particularly astute.

7. Contributors for *Crossroads* include di Leonardo, Ann Stoler, Margaret Conkey, Sarah Williams, Irene Silverblatt, Susan Gal, Susan Sperling, Elizabeth Povinelli, Jane Guyer, Kay Warren, Susan Bourque, Patricia Zavella, Nadine Peacock, Harold Scheffler, and Rayna Rapp.

8. Some of the articles in these two volumes are classics whose authors include Karen Sacks, Sally Slocum, Kathleen Gough, Susan Harding, Michelle Rosaldo, Gayle Rubin, Patricia Draper, Rayna Rapp, Nancy Chodorow, Louise Lamphere, Jane Collier, Sherry Ortner, Carol Stack, Margery Wolf, Peggy Sanday, and Bridget O'Laughlin.

9. And as Laura Kipnis (1992), among others, has noted, the very privileging of gender often homogenizes the category "woman" by effacing conditions that differentiate women, such as class. This position, in turn, feeds into rather than challenges the hegemony of a bourgeois social order.

10. The Human Area Research Files is a catalog of indexed ethnographic summaries begun in 1937 by George Peter Murdock. By 1967, over 240 cultures were described in the files.

11. Obeyesekere (1981), Herdt (1981, 1982a, 1982b), and Herdt and Stoller (1990).

12. For overviews of the scholarship on sexuality both within anthropology and the social sciences in general see the following three essays in the *Annual Reviews of Anthropology*: "The Cross-Cultural Study of Human Sexuality" by Davis and Whitten (1987), "Lesbian/Gay Studies in the House of Anthropology" by Weston (1993), and "All Made Up" by Rosalind Morris (1995).

13. See, for example, Sedgwick (1985, 1990, 1993); Silverman (1983, 1992); Butler (1990, 1993); Zizek (1989, 1992); and Williams (1989, 1990, 1993a, 1993b).

14. In other genres of mass entertainment, however, such as *bishōnen* comics for adolescent girls (Buckley 1991); the Takarazuka theater, in which females play all the parts, including those of males (Robertson 1989, 1991); and recent literary trends such as the novels by the self-identified *shōjo* (young woman) novelist Yoshimoto Banana (Treat 1993), the boundaries of gender difference are far less clear cut. My own assessment is that there remains a special fetishization of breasts *as* female that crosscuts mass culture generally in Japan. And as I argue elsewhere in this book, this fetish relates to the role played by mothers in late-capitalist Japan. Were the economic order to become less dependent on mother-centered families, the voyeuristic fixation on breasts would fade, I predict.

15. See Lacan (1977, 1982); Lorraine (1990); Rose (1982); Mitchell (1982); Grosz (1990); Freud (1964a, 1964b, 1975).

16. All the data I use to substantiate such claims about Japan are found in the chapters that follow.

17. The issues I introduce here of fetishized sights/sites, ambiguity and ambivalence, maternal rather than paternal body parts organizing an economy (and perhaps a politics) of desire, and voyeurism as a form of mass leisure in Japan at this moment of late capitalism are all ones I take up later in the book. See especially Chapters 2 and 7.

18. Zhang Yingjin makes a similar point about the need to neither abandon nor uncritically use western-based theory in the study of nonwestern cultures. To this end, he advocates what he calls a "dialogic mode of cross-cultural analysis" and adds, "What is at issue here is not that Western theory cannot be applied, but that it should not be so applied as to dominate other cultures" (1994:53).

CHAPTER 2

1. My discussion of *ero manga* is based on my own research (see Chapter 3) as well as that of Buckley (1991), Go (1981), Kusamori (1983), and Ishikawa (1983).

2. Actually Ishikawa's research concerns photographic media rather than cartoon art. See the section "*Manga:* Comics of (not only) Play" in Chapter 3 for a discussion of how the common practice of reading sex comics in public places (i.e., trains) may diffuse rather than encourage masturbation.

3. Ladies' comics appeared in the late 1980s and seem aimed at a readership of office workers, professional women, and college students (Nakano 1990). In two issues I looked at (*Scandal I*, no. 9, and *20's*, November 1992), both stories and images tended to be softer and more romantic than those that characterize *ero manga*. A surprising similarity, however, was the degree of sadomasochism with the female commonly positioned as the submissive (here, however, she is more likely to respond eventually with pleasure). That gazing is still central and still centrally focused on the bodies of females even when the medium is for women suggests both that viewing can be a pleasure for both genders and that the position of viewer is usually coded as male. This raises the possibility of females identifying with the position of male rather than female as they view *ero manga* or children's *manga*.

4. The theory is, to a certain extent, still popular; see, for example, Silverman (1992), Williams (1989), and Gamman and Marshment (1989).

5. See Chapter 3 for further discussion of *ero manga*.

6. "Fantasy might thus be said to confer psychical reality upon the objects which stand in metaphorically for what is sacrificed to meaning—the subject's very 'life'" (Silverman 1992:20). As Silverman also writes, fantasies are "tableaux" in which we imagine objects of desire as well as ourselves in desirable subject positions that differ from those we usually inhabit.

7. See Allison (1994).

8. As mentioned in note 3, I acknowledge that although such practices as *ero manga* may target a male audience, it is certainly possible that women may also be their consumers (yet according to my research [Allison 1994], this is less true for corporate entertainment in places such as hostess clubs). With this caveat, I will continue to use the word "male" for practices that overtly cater to a male audience.

9. As Steven Marcus has pointed out, Freud's 1905 theory of the development of sexuality is one of "overlapping periodicities" and "interlocking phases" (Freud 1975:xxxv). Thus, Freud states that for a nursing child sexual instinct is linked to a sexual object outside the infant's body. He writes that this object is subsequently lost only to be rediscovered at

the time of puberty and genital maturity. "There are thus good reasons why a child sucking at his mother's breast has become the prototype of every relation of love. The finding of an object is in fact a refinding of it" (88).

10. Perversions were defined by Freud as deviations in respect to the sexual aim, which at the time of genital maturity is orgasm effected by the "regions of the body that are designed for sexual union" (1975:16).

11. To be precise, Freud listed three conditions under which scopophilia becomes a perversion: "a) if it is restricted exclusively to the genitals, or b) if it is connected with the overriding of disgust . . . , or c) if, instead of being *preparatory* to the normal sexual aim, it supplants it" (1975:23). Again, this definition of perversion rests on a definition of genital-based sexuality that begins at the time of puberty. Regarding the sexuality enjoyed by pre-pubescent children, scopophilia is *not* discussed by Freud in terms of perversions. At a later point Freud notes the confusion often made between "sexual" and "genital" (46), making a distinction himself between these two terms.

12. To argue that Freud's theory is simple or simplistically biologic is problematic. In his essay on infantile sexuality (1975:39–72), for example, he argues that sexual instincts arise organically but are also influenced by such nonorganic factors as family dynamics, personal events, cultural ideologies, and education. Somewhat inconsistently, however, Freud also states that biology is the determining component and is molded rather than altered by historical or cultural conditions. "One gets an impression from civilized children that construction of these dams is a product of education, and no doubt education has much to do with it. But in reality this development is organically determined and fixed by heredity, and it can occasionally occur without any help at all from education. Education will not be trespassing beyond its appropriate domain if it limits itself to following the lines which have already been laid down organically and to impressing them somewhat more clearly and deeply" (44).

13. As Williams notes, however, Mulvey's tendency (like that of other film theorists such as Christian Metz and Jean-Louis Baudry) is to see the cinematic apparatus as not constructing as much as merely "enhancing . . . perverse desires that already exist in the subject" (1989:45).

14. The increasing proliferation and fetishization of images is, of course, the mark of postmodernism, which though an impassioned subject these days (for example, see Baudrillard [1975], Harvey [1989], and Ewen [1988]) is one too little discussed in terms of gender and power (for a good exception, however, see Bordo [1993]).

15. In this case, I mean in the United States and Western Europe.

16. It should be kept in mind that puberty does not coincide with the oedipal stage. According to the Freudian model, there are three stages to infantile sexuality—oral, anal, and phallic (1975:39–66)—and during the latter (perhaps around age five), the genitals begin to dominate and the organization of sexuality as genital-based begins. Freud emphasizes that "it is not the genitals of both sexes that play a part at this stage, but only the male ones (the phallus)" (1964b:154). Thus the Oedipus phase impacts differently on the two genders. As Freud states it, boys are traumatized by the oedipal drama (desiring the mother, being threatened with castration by the father), and girls are disappointed (lacking a penis, realizing the "inferiority" of the clitoris) (155). Thereafter, both enter a

period of latency from which they emerge at the time of puberty. During puberty, they achieve "the complete organization" of sexuality, which Freud labels the genital phase (155).

17. See, for example, Gamman and Marshment (1989), Trinh (1989), Williams (1989, 1990, 1993a, 1993b), de Lauretis (1990), Gaines (1990a), Erens (1990), Kaplan (1983), Kuhn (1985), and Kent (1985). The point has also been made that when heterosexual men look at heterosexual pornography, for example, their gaze may fall as much on men on the screen as on women (MacDonald 1983; Williams 1989).

18. Gaylyn Studlar also makes the same point, using and exploring the concept of masochism (1988).

19. See, for example, Young (1990), de Lauretis (1987), Butler (1990), Gaines (1990b), Irigaray (1985), Davis (1981), hooks (1981), and Moraga and Anzaldúa (1983).

20. I am not trying to argue that Japanese behavior is always and inevitably "different" from western behavior. That Japan is at a comparable stage of economic and industrial development to the United States, in fact, suggests that there would be much similarity in certain structures and relations of behavior. My point simply is that we should look for these similarities rather than assume them and not disregard the specific cultural, social, historical, and political conditions within which goods such as children's comics are being both produced and consumed.

21. As mentioned earlier, however, the anatomical coding of the characters on the screen does not preclude a female viewer from identifying with a male character or a male viewer from identifying with a female character (see Clover for her discussion of slasher films with heroines who are viewed by an audience of mainly adolescent males who, she argues, gender switch in their positions of identification [1992]).

22. See, for example, Takeuchi's discussion of the controversy surrounding sex comics and the sex element in children's comics that exploded in the early 1990s (1995:181–190).

23. On the issue of females as consumers, see, for example, Skov and Moeran (1995).

24. For further discussion of nightlife discourse, see Allison (1994).

25. As Andrew Gordon has pointed out, however, the commodification of sex has a long history in Japan, going back at least as far as the Tokugawa period (1603–1868). Though Oshima is not explicit on the difference between past and recent forms of sexual commodification, his implication is that this process has intensified since the late 1960s with more people (particularly men) working at jobs that demand longer hours and more totalizing commitments than before and at workplaces that are farther from their homes. Clearly Oshima is making a connection between white-collar work and sexual commodification that impacts also on spouses of (mainly male) white-collar workers.

26. Men go to soaplands to be soaped and sexually serviced in various ways, including genital intercourse. These used to be called *toruko* (for Turkish baths) until the name was changed at the request of the Turkish embassy in Tokyo.

27. *Pinku saron* are establishments that provide sexual services such as fellation and "assisted masturbation."

28. For a discussion of Japanese literature on these issues, see the chapters "Family and Home," "Structure of Japanese Play," and "Male Play with Money, Women, and Sex" in Allison (1994).

29. This structure of sexual distancing is also discussed in Chapter 7.

30. The prioritization of work over family is demanded particularly of white-collar workers, called *sararīman*. For an account of work ideology for *sararīman* in English, see Arai Shinya's novel *Shōshaman: A Tale of Corporate Japan* (1991). In Japanese, Tsuda Masumi's book *Shinsedai Sararīman no Seikatsu to Iken* (The Lives and Opinions of Modern-Generation Salarymen) is based on interviews with three generations of white-collar workers and their wives (1987). The feminization of the home is discussed and analyzed by Yuzawa Yasuhiko, who suggests that the modern Japanese family is one in which the father is no longer "needed" (*otto fuyō jidai*) (1982:70). Even though many women work outside the home (38 percent of the workforce is composed of women who work almost exclusively in lower-level jobs and increasingly in part-time jobs; salaries are 60.2 percent of men's, which drops to 48 percent when part-time workers are included [Hayashi 1995:43]), management of the home is almost exclusively a female rather than a male responsibility. According to the responses of Yuzawa's interviewees (wives, husbands, and children), a man's familial responsibilities are met by and limited to bringing home a paycheck. In the case of the woman, by contrast, responsibilities include everything from cleaning the home and cooking the meals to helping children with homework and balancing the checkbook.

31. The practice of entertaining employees and clients on company expense (*kōsaihi*) was effectively endorsed by the government under a corporate tax law that, between the years 1954 and 1982, allowed the bulk of these expenditures to be written off as tax deductible (Tabe 1986). The practice (although it has been severely affected by the downturn of the bubble economy in 1991–1992) continues today and is most heavily endorsed by trade companies, securities firms, and pharmaceutical businesses (Tabe 1986; Allison 1994).

32. Entrance exams are taken upon entry into private schools as well as by everyone entering high school and college. The period of study preceding these exams (lasting usually from one to three years) is referred to as "exam hell" because of the intense pressure to succeed. Days of single-minded study, cram school sessions, and nights of little sleep are required for success. Mothers I know have canceled social activities and quit part-time jobs while their children studied for exams in order to fully assist them. Mothers who are so involved in the educational careers of their children are called *kyōiku mama*s (education mothers) and are ideologically recognized as good mothers (see Chapter 5 for further discussion.)

33. I thank Andrew Gordon for pointing out this disjuncture between the male centeredness of practices such as corporate entertainment and the higher degree of gender parity in the workplace. Part of my argument, of course, is that this disjuncture is not accidental but rather part of the ideology of male privilege in these practices. That the new genre of women's pornographic magazines (ladies' comics) is geared to working women and has gendered and sexual images that resemble those in *ero manga* for men suggests that the position of worker–sexual consumer remains coded as male, a gender position that both working men and women are expected to identify with.

34. See the references to *sararīman* ideology and identity in note 30. The relationship between work and male subjectivity pertains to other classes and professions but may be particularly enforced by the corporate institution for white-collar workers.

35. High-class hostess clubs on the Ginza or in Akasaka can cost hundreds of dollars for just one hour for one customer. Even so-called second-tier clubs in areas like Roppongi in Tokyo cost close to $100 per hour. Taking a client or an employee to an elegant hostess club is considered a perk of white-collar positions, particularly in certain companies. In the hostess club where I conducted fieldwork (in 1981), 95 percent of all customers charged their bills to the company. These services would be a luxury few men could afford on a routine basis (see Allison 1994).

36. Feminist groups started protesting the danger (*yūgai*) of adult sex comics for children and the prevalence of female nudity and sexual scenes in children's *manga* in the early 1990s. As a result of their efforts, a number of cartoons such as "Angel" in the magazine *Yangu Sandē* were suspended. These actions led to counterprotests by *manga* artists and publishers on the basis of their constitutional rights to free speech. Despite all the uproar, nudity and eroticized scenes and imagery in children's media remain prevalent. (See Takeuchi [1995:174–190] for a summary of feminist efforts to protest *manga;* the *Asahi Shinbun* [January 12, 1993:23] for an account of a junior high school teacher who uses *manga* to enlighten her students about gender; and Yunomae [1995] for an account of other feminist activism against the commodification of sex in Japan.)

37. As previously noted, girls also use *manga* as a diversionary pursuit, and there are many written comics targeted specifically to a female audience.

38. Because the rigidity of these gender differences is not an exact reflection of gender in the labor market (yet *does* reflect more accurately gender roles at home: females managing the child-raising, children's education, and domestic chores), it may be suggested that the gender model in these comic images is a regressive rather than a progressive representation. It must be pointed out again that this particular image (male gazing at a naked female on display) is not the only one encoding gender in *manga.* Some gendered images are much more androgynous, for example, and merge rather than distinguish the two genders (Schodt 1986; Buckley 1991; Jennifer Robertson, personal communication).

39. Again, the *manga* depiction is not an exact reflection of sexuality in the so-called real world. Although much in the way of sexual practices, representations, and discourse does cater to the notion the males are far more sexually inclined than females, articles and letters in women's magazines such as *Fujin Kōron* indicate avid sexual interest on the parts of women. Also, there have been reports of working women traveling overseas to engage in nonmarital and commodified sex, as might a working man (see, for example, Takahashi 1992).

40. See note 16 about the difference between the genital phase (occurring at the time of puberty) and the Oedipus complex (which coincides with the phallic phase and occurs around the age of five) (Freud 1964b:154–155). Although genitals begin to be important during the phallic phase, they are not important in organizing and dominating a person's sexuality until the genital phase (when the "new sexual aim in men consists in the discharge of the sexual products" [Freud 1975:73]).

41. I am perhaps overstating the point. Just because prepubescent children view sexual imagery, it has been suggested to me, doesn't mean that their perception and reading of these images will not change at the time of adolescence. If there is a difference between Japan and western societies, it may be more in the fact that sexual imagery is explicitly

included in formats for children in Japan, whereas in the United States this imagery is more implicit and muted (in, for example, cartoons). Still this difference itself is significant, I am arguing, because a position of voyeur, consumer, and aggressive viewer is installed at so early an age. It is also interesting and significant that Japanese report starting to read certain children's *manga* when children and continuing to read them as teenagers and adults (Adams and Hill 1992:102).

42. The disrupture that Freud emphasizes is the break between children, particularly boys, and their parents, particularly mothers. Speaking of the incest taboo, Freud writes: "Society must defend itself against the danger that the interests which it needs for the establishment of higher social units may be swallowed up by the family; and for this reason, the case of every individual, but in particular of adolescent boys, it seeks by all possible means to loosen their connection with their family—a connection which, in their childhood, is the only important one" (1975:91). One should note that at precisely this point of adolescence when children in a social environment such as that in the United States are distancing themselves from their mothers in a move to establish their own sexuality and identity, Japanese children are being pushed into even closer proximity with their mothers in the period of entrance exam preparation (*jukenbenkyō*).

CHAPTER 3

1. *Kaibutsu* is translated as monster, goblin, hideous creature; and *sensei* is a term of respect used to address, for example, teachers, professors, and doctors. The title could thus be translated into something like Dr. Hideous.

2. *Shūkan Manga Times* reads "Manga for Men" in English on the front. The issue is July 27, 1980 (no. 1247) and its "Kaibutsu-sensei" is the twenty-ninth in this continuing series.

3. I include this description here very purposefully. Far too few scholars writing about sexual (erotic and pornographic) media look at actual texts or do so with careful scrutiny. To avoid falling into the abstraction of "erotic comic books" and so that readers can better follow and judge my analysis in the rest of the chapter, I give this fairly thorough account of one specific comic. "Kaibutsu-sensei" is not, by the way, intended to be representative here of all *ero manga*, though it is, in my opinion, typical of some of the more standard tropes and themes found in the genre as a whole. I offer this account for another reason. For those unfamiliar with Japanese *manga* and those who have not spent much time reading or contemplating comic art, I try to render some of the distinctiveness of *manga* style here—a combination of sparse and direct wording and drawings that caricature the familiar in unfamiliar or unrealistic ways, such as eyes that pop out of heads to show surprise and empty word bubbles that signify speechlessness—as a way of emphasizing how important the medium of representation is to the type and nature of sexual story told in *ero manga*.

4. Such confections would probably have cost no more than 100 or 150 yen at the time, so the man is offering an inflated price.

5. The gender of the victim is not clear but implied, by both the context of the cartoon and that of the *ero manga* itself (which, in the six issues I examined for this chapter, never explicitly showed such an act being done to a male). This image of naked and receptive

buttocks is extremely common in *ero manga* and is often disembodied, leading to various gendered and sexual readings, as I will argue later.

6. "Otoko no hitotte ironna yaru no ne?" The verb *yaru* means "to do," but also "to have sex," and the word *ironna* means both "various" and "sexy"; so the sentence carries at least a double meaning here: Males can do many different things; males can have sex in a variety of ways.

7. As will be elaborated later, males typically consume their *manga* away from home, the inverse of the female reading hers at home. Also, the readers of *ero manga* are overwhelmingly males, so the female, simply by buying and reading this *manga*, is performing a transgressive act.

8. Much smaller than American eggplants, this Japanese eggplant (*nasu*) serves as a masturbatory device and erotic symbol here.

9. English is often used in titles and elsewhere in *manga*. This is said to foster the feeling of otherness, escape, and fantasy being created by the medium.

10. In 1996, this situation appears to be changing somewhat. As observers, including the Japanese critic and intellectual Karatani Kojin, have noted, Japan is currently going through a phase of sanitization. Although public billboards and advertisements showing explicit nudity still remain and there is still a brisk trade in sex comics in train station kiosks, the act of reading sexually graphic materials in public trains is more restrained than in the 1980s.

11. Due to the skyrocketing prices of land, Japanese who work in such urban centers as Tokyo often buy houses in the suburbs. Commutes to and from work take as much as two or three hours one way. These commuters account for the fact that 60 percent of sales of printed mass media (magazines, newspapers, comic books) take place at the kiosks and newsstands of train stations (Beer 1984). (See the "Travel and Borders" section in Chapter 7 for further discussion.)

12. The work of Carol Clover, among others, has shown that gender shifting may be common in the viewing of mass media. Even a medium so clearly marked by gender and sexual preference (straight male) as *ero manga*, that is, could be read and enjoyed by others (women and gay men, for example). Since the late 1980s, the previously mentioned genre of comic book erotica for women called ladies' comics (*redīsu komikku*) has emerged with narratives and images not significantly different from those in *ero manga*. For references to ladies' comics see Chapter 7.

13. See, for example, the work by Tani Barlow and Angela Zito (1994), Judith Farquhar (1994), Margaret Lock (1993), and Lila Abu-Lughod (1986).

14. See Dworkin (1981, 1987) and MacKinnon (1979, 1982, 1987, 1989).

15. These critics (who do not necessarily criticize on postmodernist grounds) include Susan Barrowclough (1982), Linda Williams (1989), Leslie Stern (1992), Angela Carter (1978), Gertrude Koch (1990), Ann Kaplan (1983), Annette Kuhn (1985), Carole Vance (1984, 1992), and Kate Ellis (1992).

16. Examples of such works include F.A.C.T. Book Committee (1992), Pat Califia (on dominance and sadomasochism, 1994), Janice Radway (on harlequin novels, 1984), Tania Modleski (on soap operas, 1982), and Scott MacDonald (a feminist male trying to analyze the pleasure he takes in straight porn, 1983).

17. The first research project was the basis of my doctoral dissertation and later, book (*Nightwork: Sexuality, Pleasure, and Corporate Masculinity in a Tokyo Hostess Club*, 1994), in which I studied the corporate practice of entertaining workers and clients in the highly sexualized and masculinized setting of hostess clubs with the aim of fostering good work relations and "healthy" male egos. The second was almost the inverse: a project (post-doctorate conducted in a middle-class neighborhood in Tokyo for fifteen months in 1987–1988) on matricentric families and homes where (middle-class) men have become virtually absent.

18. The Japanese language has four syllabaries. *Katakana,* the syllabary used to write foreign words, is liberally but by no means exclusively used in *manga.* It is often used in comics to mark action, emotion, suspense, or surprise.

19. I use "evoke" here in the sense that Steven Tyler (1986) does to distinguish it from realism, once attempted and now critiqued, in writing ethnographies.

20. As scholars of postmodernism such as Fredric Jameson and David Harvey have argued, as well as scholars of the Frankfurt School such as Jürgen Habermas, Theodor Adorno, and Max Horkheimer, the lines between the spheres of public and private, home and work, pleasure and labor, become increasingly indistinguishable as capitalism proceeds. See also in this context my work on the use of hostess clubs by Japanese corporations (Allison 1994).

21. Abbot Toba (1053–1140) was so known for his craft in this regard that a school of comic art was named after him—*Tobae.* The still famous *Scroll of Frolicking Animals* and *The Origins of Shigisan* from this time period are usually attributed to him (Tsurumi 1987:31).

22. *Kamishibai* is a form of storytelling in which the teller holds up large picture cards to a crowd of people while relating a story.

23. The fetish, which stands in for what the boy once thought the mother had and cannot bear to realize she lacks—a penis—is more controllable by the boy than the mother ever was. A shoe fetish, for example, can be satisfied by the boy acquiring a shoe that he can always possess and derive pleasure from. A fetishist is narcissistic, Freud notes. So, many say, is the postmodernist subject.

24. Pachinko is a machine-game played with steel balls that a player tries to get into holes. Pachinko parlors are typically large and noisy, and Tada's description of the solitary, immersed player is a stereotypical image. Prizes are usually minimal (towels, soap, cigarettes), and though some say winning is totally arbitrary, others argue that a skilled player can cultivate talent. Blue-collar workers and *sararīman,* as well as housewives and students, are avid players.

25. Nakano laments that the construction of sex even in this venue for women is something other than "beautiful." Consumers, however, seem to have a different opinion, as witnessed by the fact that ladies' comics are one of the fastest-growing genres within the *manga* industry. In 1993, there were sixty titles per month and 10 million issues sold per year (Bukkupēji Kankōkai 1994).

26. I am following here Rosalind Coward's definitions of sex, sexuality, and sexual identity (1983). Sexuality is the representation of activities surrounding sensual aims and

gratifications, sex is the act in which sensual aims and gratifications are enacted, and sexual identity is the public representation of sensual aims and objectives as integrated into the personality. In these terms it could be said that there are in Japan, as elsewhere, multiple types of sex, multiple sexualities, and different possibilities for sexual identity. My aim here is to unravel what construction(s) of all of these are being encoded with the *ero manga*.

27. I use the word "gender" here instead of "sexual identity" because division of labor instead of sexual preference is more important to the cultural constructedness of female and male in Japan.

28. Laura Kipnis (1992) analyzes *Hustler* magazine for its messages about class, arguing, correctly I believe, that just because porno is overtly about sex does not limit its meaning, pleasure, or ideological work to that level. In the case of *Hustler*, she argues, its stories, editorializing, and photos challenge conventions of propriety in far more ways than merely sexual ones, and it is this characteristic that makes it subversive of bourgeois norms.

29. Until 1991, the state upheld rigorous obscenity laws against the display of genitalia and pubic hair. Since that time, the laws have begun to ease; crotches can now be more realistically shown, although in *manga,* there is still an inhibition against doing so. See Chapter 7 for elaboration.

30. I use "his" here because males are the targeted audience for *ero manga* and the primary readers. I do realize, however, that there may be women who also read *ero manga*.

31. One of the classic statements regarding dominance in this context is John Berger's (1972); I outline his theory in Chapter 2. See also Sarah Kent (1985) for an analysis of why this "dominating" look is so difficult to duplicate on the pages of straight female erotica such as *Playgirl*.

32. A Japanese friend has told me that women often use the word *iya* in the throes of sexual passion, and it is not necessarily used as an expression of discomfort or discontent. Outside a sexual context, however, "awful" *is* the meaning of *iya,* so its female-specific usage during sex is, if not literal, revealing of gender ideology.

33. Ōshima's 1976 film *In the Realm of the Senses* (*Ai no Korīda*) also develops this theme: A male is killed in the act of sexual strangulation by a sexually voracious female. Based on the true story of Abe Sada, the film has never been shown in Japan due, according to the courts, to its explicit display of genitalia and pubic hair (see Lehman 1988; Kimoto 1983).

34. The Japanese anthropologist Wagatsuma Hiroshi once identified a parallel set of behaviors (sucking a breast, then raping or otherwise forcibly violating the woman) as characterizing Japanese pornographic film in contrast to genres of pornography found in other cultures (personal communication).

35. In this regard, *ero manga* is far more rigid about both sex and gender constructions than other genre such as *bishōnen manga* (aimed at teenage girls), where androgynous characters (whose "true" identity is often concealed throughout much of the plot) are common and sexual penetration is subordinated to other forms of interpersonal contact such as kissing, caressing, and oral sex. According to Buckley (1991), even adult women who have married and become housewives find subversive pleasure in *bishōnen manga*.

36. Places of labor that are commuted to are mainly work, school, and *juku* (cram school). It should be noted that many schoolchildren from elementary school students on

up commute to school on public transportation in such urban centers as Tokyo and Osaka. Vast numbers of Japanese children also attend *juku* (or other supplemental schooling such as *yobikō*) after school, particularly for the one or two years preceding entrance exams, taken (at the least and latest) upon entering high school.

37. This is not to say that there is no monitoring, either legal or social, of sexually explicit materials. What Kimoto (1983) calls a system of "self control" (*jishukisei*) operates, according to him, at four levels: Recommendations (to ban or at least label certain publications with a red slip indicating their unsuitability for readers under eighteen years of age) are made to the publishers by (1) the police department, (2) local self-governing bodies (*jichitai*), and (3) certain employee associations. Further, (4) the publishers take certain measures (for example, setting up their own ethics committees) to monitor themselves. How efficacious all this monitoring is, however, is questionable. Labeling certain materials as sexually explicit often increases rather than decreases their sales, for example, and large companies often avoid publishing erotica themselves only to do so under the operation of a smaller firm they have purchased. For more discussion of monitoring and censorship see Chapter 7.

38. *Gekiga,* created in the 1960s, was a genre of comics whose storytelling was considered more dramatic.

39. Sato argues further that the presence of a porno culture in Japan is the direct result of strict controls over the sexuality of Japanese youth (from teens to early twenties). Japanese of these ages must study so hard that they have no outlet for their pent-up sexuality.

40. How hyperpresent and constantly enforced these values are in a work-group situation has often been written about. See, for example, the accounts of Thomas Rohlen (1974) and Dorinne Kondo (1990), who describe specific practices in which, for example, fellow workers were made to expose weaknesses, emotions, and personal histories as a device to solidify work relations. See also my work on hostess clubs (1994), where I make the same point about parties of men who sing, flirt, get drunk, and joke with one another as a means of building *ningenkankei* (social relations).

41. I deal so extensively with this issue of matricentric families and the resentments as well as dependencies they create in males (as sons as well as fathers-husbands) elsewhere that I devote little space to it here. For my analysis of mother-son relationships in light of how they affect practices, representations, and fantasies of sexuality, see especially Chapters 2 and 6. For an elaboration on the nitty-gritty of mother-child relationships, see Chapters 4 and 5. I take it as a given in this chapter that the rage inspiring the attacks on women in *ero manga* stems mainly from the resentment boys feel at being so dependent on their mothers. I also take it as a given that such violence is a convenient and familiar vehicle for expressing a multiplicity of other frustrations whose sources lie elsewhere.

42. *Labien* 12(December):1–38. The comic is entitled "Maia, Daisanwa/Aigan" (Maia, the Third Story of a Pet).

43. Nongenital sex also resonates with pregenital sex, the type of sexuality a child can express with his mother.

44. For discussion of meanings associated with female breasts, see Chapter 1; for similar discussion regarding female genitals, see Chapter 7.

45. Mothers may not only encourage a relationship of dependence but also use that relationship to discipline their children into regimens of study. Being forced to perform by

means of a mother's devotedness and "love," children often react with feelings of rage or ambivalence that have multiple expressions, including real acts of violence against mothers. The latter, in fact, are a far more common form of domestic violence than parents abusing children.

CHAPTER 4

1. As Dorinne Kondo has pointed out, however, these cuisinal principles may be conditioned by factors of both class and circumstance. Her *shitamachi* (more traditional area in Tokyo) informants, for example, adhered only casually to this coding, and other Japanese she knew followed them more carefully when preparing food for guests rather than family and when eating outside rather than inside the home (Kondo 1990:61–62).

2. Rice is often, if not always, included in a meal; it may substantially as well as symbolically constitute the core of the meal. When served at a table it is put in a large pot or electric ricemaker and spooned into a bowl, still no bigger than the many other containers from which a person eats. In an *obentō*, rice may be in one, perhaps the largest, section of a multisectioned *obentō*, box, yet it will be arranged and served with a variety of other foods. In a sense rice provides the syntactic and substantial center to a meal, yet the presentation of the food rarely emphasizes this core. The rice bowl is refilled rather than heaped, as in the preformed *obentō* box, and rice is often embroidered, supplemented, or covered with other foods.

3. Japanese until recently both have endured a high price for rice at home and resisted American attempts to export rice to Japan in order to stay domestically self-sufficient in this national food qua cultural symbol. And for a long time, rice was the only foodstuff in which Japanese maintained self-sufficient production.

4. The primary sources on education I use here are Horio (1988), Duke (1986), Rohlen (1983), and Cummings (1980).

5. Neither the state's role in overseeing education nor a system of standardized tests is a new development in post–World War II Japan. What is new is the national standardization of tests and the intensified role the state has thus assumed in overseeing them. See Dore (1965) and Horio (1988).

6. Boocock (1989) differs from Tobin (1989) on this point and asserts that the institutional differences are insignificant. Her essay on the preschool system in Japan describes extensively how both *yōchien* and *hoikuen* are administered (*yōchien* are under the authority of the Monbushō and *hoikuen* are under the authority of the Koseishō—Ministry of Health and Welfare) and how both feed into the larger system of education. She emphasizes diversity: Though certain trends are common among preschools, differences in teaching styles and philosophies are plentiful as well.

7. According to Rohlen (1989), families are incapable of indoctrinating the child into this social pattern of *shūdan seikatsu* by their very structure and particularly by the relationship (of indulgence and dependence) between mother and child. For this reason and the importance placed on group structures in Japan, the nursery school's primary objective, argues Rohlen, is teaching children how to assimilate into groups. For further discussion of this point see also Peak (1989), Lewis (1989), and Sano (1989) and the entire issue

of the *Journal of Japanese Studies* (vol. 15, no. 1) that is devoted to Japanese preschool education. These articles, including Boocock's, are published in this issue.

8. For a succinct anthropological discussion of these concepts see Hendry (1987: 39–41). For an architectural study of Japan's management and organization of space in terms of such cultural categories as *uchi* and *soto*, see Greenbie (1988).

9. Endless studies, reports, surveys, and narratives document the close tie between women and home, domesticity and femininity, in Japan. A recent international survey conducted for a Japanese housing construction firm, for example, polled working wives in three cities, finding that 97 percent (of those polled) in Tokyo prepared breakfast for their families almost daily (compared with 43 percent in New York and 34 percent in London); 70 percent shopped for groceries on a daily basis (3 percent in New York, 14 percent in London); and only 22 percent had husbands who assisted or were willing to assist with housework (62 percent in New York, 77 percent in London) (quoted in "Burdens of Working Wives," 1991). For a recent anthropological study of Japanese housewives in English, see Imamura (1987), in Japanese "Josei no Genzai to Mirai" (1985), Miraishakai (1979), and Ohirasōri no Seifukenkyūkai (1980).

10. My comments pertain directly, of course, to only the women I observed, interviewed, and interacted with at the one private nursery school serving middle-class families in urban Tokyo. The profusion of *obentō*-related materials in the press plus the revelations made to me by Japanese and observations made by other researchers in Japan (see, for example, Tobin [1989] and Fallows [1990]), however, substantiate this discussion among women as a more general phenomenon.

11. To illustrate this preoccupation and conscientiousness: During the time when my son was not eating all his *obentō*, many mothers gave me suggestions, one mother lent me a magazine, his teacher gave me a full set of *obentō* cookbooks (one per season), and another mother gave me a set of small, frozen food portions she had made in advance for future *obentō*s.

12. My son's teacher, Hamada-sensei, cited this explicitly as one of the reasons the *obentō* was such an important training device for nursery school children. "Once they become *ichinensei* [first-graders] they'll be faced with a variety of food, prepared without elaboration or much spice, and will need to eat it within a delimited time period."

13. An anonymous reviewer of this chapter questioned whether such emphasis placed on consumption of food in nursery school leads to food problems and anxieties in later years. Although I have heard that anorexia is a phenomenon now in Japan, I question its connection to nursery school *obentō*s. Much of the meaning of the latter, as I interpret it, has to do with the interface and connection between production and consumption, and its gender linkage comes from the production end (mothers making it) rather than the consumption end (children eating it). Hence although control is taught through food, it is not a control linked primarily to females or bodily appearance, as anorexia may tend to be in U.S. culture.

14. Fujita (1989) argues, from her experience as a working mother of a day-care (*hoikuen*) child, that the substance of these daily talks between teacher and mother is intentionally insignificant. Her interpretation is that the mother is not to be overly involved in or too informed about school matters.

15. *Boku* is a personal pronoun that males in Japan use as a familiar reference to themselves. Those in close relationships with males—mothers, for example—can use *boku* in the third person to refer to their sons. Its reference in this context is telling.

16. In the upper third grade of the nursery school (*nenchōgumi* class; children aged five to six) my son attended, children were ordered to bring their *obentō* with chopsticks and not forks and spoons (considered easier to use) and in the traditional *furoshiki* (piece of cloth that wraps items inside and is double tied to close it) instead of the easier-to-manage *obentō* bags with drawstrings. Both *furoshiki* and chopsticks (*o-hashi*) are considered traditionally Japanese, and their use marks not only greater effort and skills on the part of the children but their enculturation into being Japanese.

17. For the mother's role in the education of her child see, for example, White (1987). For an analysis by a Japanese of the intense dependence created and cultivated in a child on the mother more generally, see Doi (1971). For Japanese sources on the mother-child relationship and the ideology (some say pathology) of Japanese motherhood, see Yamamura (1971), Kawai (1976), Kyutoku (1981), Sōrifu Seihonentaisaku Honbunhen (1981), Kadeshobō Shinsha (1981). Fujita's account (1989) of the ideology of motherhood at the nursery school level is particularly interesting and relevant in this connection.

18. Women are entering the labor market in increasing numbers, yet the proportion to do so for part-time work (legally constituting as much as thirty-five hours per week but without the benefits accorded to full-time workers) has also increased. The choice of part-time over full-time employment has much to do with a woman's simultaneous and almost total responsibility for the domestic realm ("Josei no Gensai to Mirai" 1985; see also Kondo 1990).

19. As Fujita points out (1989:72–79), working mothers are treated as a separate category of mothers, and nonworking mothers are expected, by definition, to be mothers full time.

20. Nakane's much quoted text on Japanese society states this male position in structuralist terms (1970). Though dated, see also Vogel (1963) and Rohlen (1974) for descriptions of the social roles for middle-class, urban Japanese males. For a succinct recent discussion of gender roles within the family, see Lock (1990).

CHAPTER 5

1. Compulsory education stops at ninth grade; all students who go on to high school take entrance exams.

2. For a critique of this principle, particularly from the perspective of the damage it wreaks upon children, see Horio (1988).

3. NHK is also the national (government sponsored) television station.

4. The appellations "sensei" and "san" are used when referring to people one knows personally. Thus I do not use "sensei" here.

5. Boocock (1989) and Tobin (1989) describe some of the differences, both real and perceived, between nursery schools and day-care centers (*hoikuen*). Because entrance into the latter is determined by local municipal offices on the basis of a mother's work outside the home (Boocock states that the determination is made on the basis of need, but our

family's "need" was denied in 1987 because I did not have a job that took me to an office for more than thirty-seven hours a week), day-care centers do not presume or demand a mother's involvement in her child's education, as do nursery schools. This may be one of the major differences between the two; Boocock argues that the differences in pedgagogy, care, and student organization are far less minor than is commonly imagined.

6. See also Fujita (1989) on the role of mothers demanded in preschool education. For other scholarship on Japanese preschools see Tobin (1989), Hendry (1986), and the entire winter 1989 (vol. 15, no. 1) issue of the *Journal of Japanese Studies,* entitled "Social Control and Early Socialization." Thomas Rohlen's article, "Order in Japanese Society: Attachment, Authority, and Routine," is particularly useful, and his analysis of the emphasis on routines within the classroom dovetails with the emphasis placed on a mother's monitoring of daily routines that I discuss here.

7. According to 1987–1988 statistics put out by the Japanese government and gathered by Mary Brinton, 48.6 percent, or over 16 million, of adult women work. They work in professional and technical occupations at a rate similar to women in other industrialized countries, but only 8 percent attain managerial positions. In clerical, sales, and service occupations, Japanese women work at the lowest rate compared to other industrialized countries. About one-third of women's jobs are part time (and 70 percent of part-time work is conducted by women). Wages for women are 57.6 percent of men's. A government white paper put out in 1987 reported that women still manage the bulk of all housework in families where both adults have jobs outside the home (Brinton 1993:1–23).

8. Interviewing one-on-one seemed to make people uneasy, so I arranged groups of between three and six women who would convene usually at my house for sessions that lasted as long as four hours. Most of these groups met more than once, and one group met for a total of twelve sessions.

9. This is a fictitious name. Yōchien = nursery school.

10. The interview usually takes place months before the new school year, which begins in April. In our case, David had been accepted in absentia because a friend whose child was the only other "foreigner" to attend Yamaguchi Yōchien wrote a letter presenting our case. The interview for us was then pro forma and constituted basically an introductory meeting.

11. These included seven skills the child should be able to accomplish without a mother's help (including getting up and going to bed according to a schedule, eating a meal, going to the toilet, washing oneself, dressing) and three additional goals (develop a positive attitude about going to school, abandon babytalk, and learn the route to school [by going the same route everyday]) (*Guidebook,* p. 1).

12. The "o" preceding *obentō* is the honorific. Both *obentō* and *bentō* are used to refer to the boxed lunch.

13. At our school, the *kaban* were yellow shoulder bags with the school's insignia printed on the front. Children could put their *bentō* bags and other small items, including memos and school directives sent from the class, in these.

14. At Yamaguchi Yōchien children wore uniforms to school and changed into smocks upon entering the classroom.

15. Unlike scholars such as Aida, I regard such mergences as worker-man and student-child as compelled by very concrete institutions such as corporate and educational prac-

tices. In Aida's view, these behaviors emerge out of Japanese culture and are merely picked up, rather than instilled by, institutional policy.

16. Actually, the mergence of a man with his work is also enabled by the domestic work that women perform as wives and mothers. Men can stay late at work only because they have wives who are tending to the home and children; men who participate in these responsibilities assume, by definition, a different relationship to their place of work.

17. School runs six days a week in Japan. At Yamaguchi Yōchien class ran until 1:30 P.M. every day except for Monday and Saturday, which were short days (no-lunch days) ending at 11:30 A.M.

18. Uniforms are bought through the school in two sets: one for spring-summer and one for fall-winter. There is a jacket and short pants or skirt for winter and pants or skirt with suspenders for summer. Long-sleeved shirts are worn in the winter and short-sleeved in the summer. Hats change as well: felt for winter and straw for summer. Uniforms are changed on a designated day for both seasons and unless the weather is extremely unseasonal, the uniform schedule is adhered to.

19. These requests came either directly or indirectly through handouts from school, discussions with a child's teacher, or advice given by the principal.

20. As mentioned in Chapter 4, these events are the Dance Festival (Bon Odori) held in summer, Sports Day (Undōkai) held in fall, and Winter Assembly (Seikatsu Happyōkai), all of which entail rigorous training and preparation on the part of the children for approximately six weeks before the event.

21. There is almost an unwritten understanding that children should return home at 5:00 P.M. from playdates or playing outside their homes, which is also the time that women often set out to do their shopping for dinner. In the neighborhood where we lived, a chime went off at 5:00 P.M. It was transmitted from the school and could be heard for blocks around. Friends in other neighborhoods reported the same phenomenon.

22. Many said, however, that they would get up later when their husbands got home, usually to make them something to eat.

23. There was actually much discussion about gender roles in our group interviews. About one-third of the women mentioned a desire for their husbands to participate more fully in child-raising and wished that they could be liberated more often from the home and its duties. About the same percentage of women said they wished to work when their children became older, and virtually all the others stated that they would pursue some activity—charity, hobby, further education—at some later point. Still, none expressed a longing to exchange their own lives as mothers with those of their husbands as workers.

24. A teacher in the third grade eventually got him to participate again by refusing to believe the boy's statement that he was totally inept.

25. The implication was that the mother should be practicing with her child at home, a suggestion that was also made to me when David had similar trouble with jump-roping.

CHAPTER 6

1. Police records figure incest only incidentally (in the life histories of adolescent boys caught for delinquency, for example, where maternal incest has been found to be fairly

common [Kinjō and Nakatani 1983:287]), and statistics that report incest are unavailable or unreliable.

2. Such descriptions are formulated, for example, as the excessive attention mothers focus on their children and the extended dependence of children on their mothers (Kyutoku 1981; Kawai 1976; Aoi 1974).

3. In 1978, for example, there were 130 such calls out of 16,218 received (Kakinuma 1980).

4. Kakinuma writes as if she is merely using the counselor's words and not representing the story in her own voice. Having visited Hinin Sōdanshitsu myself and been denied access to such incest cases, I wonder if Kakinuma was really given them and if not, why she fails to note this in her article.

5. Translations throughout are mine.

6. This argument has been made by such scholars as David Schneider, who, known for his scholarship on kinship, refuted its very terminology in the 1980s for its presumption of universal forms (1984).

7. Many feminists have made this argument. See, for example, Rubin (1973).

8. Amano Chihoko, writing as a feminist, has argued that in Kosawa's rendering of the Ajase myth, the father's role is important, if marginal. The familial dynamics here are still as a threesome (mother, father, child) rather than a dyad (mother and child), which is the reading Okonogi Keigo, also a Japanese psychoanalyst, has given the Ajase myth. According to Amano, Okonogi altered the Ajase myth to further marginalize the presence and role of the father as a means of calling Japan matricentric and critiquing it for being a "fatherless society." Amano challenges these assertions, suggesting that Japan in the 1990s is far less matricentric or fatherless than Okonogi claims (Amano 1995).

9. In a survey conducted in 1982, 71.1 percent of Japanese agreed with the notion that men should be the primary workers in a family and women, the primary homekeepers and childraisers. Men do assist women in domestic chores, but their assistance falls off steeply when their wives stay at home, and even when their wives work, research conducted by Takahashi Michiko in the mid-1980s has shown that such help is mainly limited to child-related activities such as sharing meals, bathing, or taking children to school (Takahashi 1989).

10. Butler argues similarly for the behavior of gay males as performed in the drag balls Jennie Livingston documented in her film *Paris Is Burning* (1993:132).

11. Sano Yōko also makes this point about the mother who deprives her son of a sexual future (1991).

12. See Andrew Gordon's important book *Postwar Japan as History* (1993), in particular the essays by Dower, Cummings, Kelly, Ivy, Uno, and Buckley.

13. See Iwao (1993) and Ueno (1988). These accounts and others, such as the More sex survey conducted in 1986, report that one out of six married women has experienced an extramarital affair.

CHAPTER 7

1. The book included another collection by Shinoyama entitled *Water Fruit*, photos in the May issues of the magazines *An-An* and *Geijutsu Shinchō* and in the December pub-

lication of Madonna's book *Sex* with all but four of her nudes intact (Heibonsha 1992:186–187; Shūeisha 1992; Kamei 1991:242–245).

2. Significantly, the foreign word "hair" (*hea*) was used in this context rather than the Japanese word for pubic hair (*inmō*), which is created from the characters for shadows (hiddenness, darkness) and hair.

3. In a survey conducted by the *Yomiuri Shinbun* in November 1994, for example, 67 percent of the respondents were against *hea nūdo*. By age and gender, reactions broke down as follows. Against *hea nūdo* were 45 percent of men and 77 percent of women in their twenties, 52 percent of men and 88 percent of women in their thirties, 60 percent of men and 89 percent women in their forties, 76 percent of men and 92 percent of women in their fifties, 85 percent of men and 94 percent of women in their sixties, and 91 percent of men and 99 percent of women in their seventies. Also, 33 percent of all readers stated that they would absolutely not read media with *hea nūdo* in them.

4. As is often noted, however, those who self-identify as middle class are approximately 90 percent of the population, making the ideal, if not the reality, of white-collar work heavily broad based. See Kelly (1993).

5. Kimoto Itaru (1983) is a lawyer and legal scholar and Okudaira Yasuhira (quoted in Ihaya 1991:8) is a professor of law at International Christian University.

6. In this case, these markers have been written in by the publishers themselves, a common practice of self-censorship intended to appease the authorities. My suggestion is that there is also a sexual aesthetic being constructed here that depends as much upon concealing as revealing certain scenes.

7. This photo by Kanō Tenmei appeared in his magazine *Za Tenmei*.

8. The photographer Kanō Tenmei shoots women in poses that reveal as much of their pubic areas as possible ("Trouble/Toraburu" 1994).

9. For feminist critiques of Lacan see, for example, Flax (1990) and Gallop (1982, 1985).

10. The Supreme Court articulated its opinion on the standards of obscenity in three major cases it heard: the translation and distribution of *Lady Chatterley's Lover* (1957), two portions of *In Praise of Vice* by de Sade (1969), and the reissuing of a story by Nagai Kafū entitled "Yojōhan" (1980). In each case it clarified its standards, achieving its clearest exposition in 1980. At that time it stated that obscenity should be judged according to five criteria: (1) the relative boldness, detail, and general style of a work's depiction of sexual behavior, (2) the proportion of the work taken up with the sexual description, (3) the place assumed by sex within the intellectual content of the work as a whole, (4) the degree to which artistry and thought content mitigate the sexual excitement induced by the writing, and (5) the relationship of the sexual portrayals to the structure and plot of the story (Beer 1984:353).

11. The Eirin started operating in 1957 and was institutionalized with a code of approval in 1959. All films are reviewed by its committee. If passed, a film receives a code of approval; if refused, it cannot be shown at theaters belonging to the Theater Owners Association. Occasionally Eirin-approved movies have been given warnings by the police or charged with obscenity and confiscated. In 1971–1972 four such incidents occurred, leading to a revision

of Eirin standards (Beer 1984; Kimoto 1983). For details on how the Eirin revised its standards, see a special issue of *Juristo* (no. 5, October 1976).

12. The RBA bans the sale of a publication at any of its newsstands if an obscenity violation is suspected. If the police seize a publication, the RBA bans the next three publications (Beer 1984).

13. NHK is the national television network. Its guidelines demand that sex be treated with seriousness, without "loss of dignity," and in a manner so as not to glamorize "unwholesome" relationships between women and men. Imports such as *Emmanuelle* pass these standards (Beer 1984:339).

14. A number of very successful efforts to ban and modify sexual images in the mass media, notably comics either directed or accessible to children, were made in the early 1990s by women's groups (see Takeuchi 1995:181–190). Despite these efforts, however, sexual imagery remains pronounced in Japanese mass media, including that targeted to children.

15. This story was related to me by Jennifer Robertson.

16. Myth, to Barthes, means taking a set of terms with denotative meaning, emptying this signification, and filling it with a new, higher order of connotative meaning (Barthes 1972:109–159).

17. In Oe Kenzaburō's book *A Personal Matter*, anal sex is a critical feature.

18. When sold, such underpants are called, among other terms, *pantsu* or *burusera* (*buru* refers to bloomers; *sera* refers to the sailor uniforms that female high school students wear). For an article about *burusera shoppu* (shops that sell *burusera*) and the *burusera būmu* (the boom in *burusera*), see Mizuno (1994).

19. This is a point also made by Nakano Akira (1990) in his analysis of ladies' comics.

20. Tanizaki Jun'ichirō, the novelist and essayist, made a similar argument in the 1920s about the Japanese aesthetic of shadows, which he believed was vulgarized and destroyed by the adoption of western customs, habits, and technology at the time of Japan's modernization (1977). Ueno Chizuko (1992), a feminist anthropologist, has similarly argued for a Japanese organization of desire around hidden rather than exposed flesh. Ueno traces this pattern through the postwar history of underwear and its rapid commodification and commodity fetishization during this time, stressing also the sites underwear provides for management and surveillance: mothers washing their sons' underwear and wives buying their husbands' underwear.

21. There are signs that the borders between fantasy and "reality" are beginning to break down. When I was visiting Japan in summer 1995, a number of my friends suggested that the perpetrators of the poison gas attacks on the trains in Tokyo had been raised on *manga* culture and took for reality a scenario that should have been relegated to the level of fantasy. That is, instead of reading about public violence in a *manga* on a train, that space where such fantasies are commonly consumed, they executed this scenario *as* a reality and on the trains.

References

Abu-Lughod, Lila. 1986. *Veiled Sentiments: Honor and Poetry in Bedouin Society*. Berkeley: University of California Press.

———. 1990. "Can There Be a Feminist Ethnography?" *Women and Performance: A Journal of Feminist Theory* 5(1):7–27.

———. 1993. *Writing Women's Worlds: Bedouin Stories*. Berkeley: University of California Press.

Adams, Kenneth Alan, and Lester Hill Jr. 1992. "Fantasy Themes in Japanese Comics." *Journal of Popular Culture* 25:99–128.

Aida, Yuji. 1972. *Nihonjin no Ishiki Kōzō* (The Structure of Japanese Consciousness). Tokyo: Kōdansha.

Alcoff, Linda. 1991. "The Problem of Speaking for Others." *Cultural Critique* 20 (winter):5–32.

Allison, Anne. 1994. *Nightwork: Sexuality, Pleasure, and Corporate Masculinity in a Tokyo Hostess Club*. Chicago: University of Chicago Press.

Althusser, Louis. 1971. "Ideology and Ideological State Apparatuses." In *Notes Toward an Investigation in Lenin and Philosophy and Other Essays*. New York: Monthly Review, pp. 111–123.

Amano, Chihoko. 1995. "Ajase Konpurekkusu Kenshō (Verification of the Ajase Complex). *New Feminism Review* 6:152–157.

Amano, Ikuo. 1989. "The Dilemma of Japanese Education Today." In J. Shields, ed., *Japanese Schooling: Patterns of Socialization, Equality, and Political Control*. University Park: Pennsylvania State University Press.

Anzaldúa, Gloria. 1983. "Speaking in Tongues: A Letter to Third World Women Writers." In C. Morraga and G. Anzaldúa, eds., *This Bridge Called My Back: Writings by Radical Women of Color*. New York: Kitchen Table: Women of Color Press, pp. 165–174.

Aoi, Kazuo. 1974. "Gendai no Boshikankei to Seinen no Shakaitekiō" (Present-Day Social Adaptation in the Relationship Between Mothers and Youth). *Seikyōiku Kenkyū* 8.

Aokī, Yayoi. 1986. *Bosei to wa Nani ka?* (What Is Motherhood?). Tokyo: Kaneko Shobō.

Arai, Shinya. 1991. *Shōshaman: A Tale of Corporate Japan*. Chieko Mulhern, trans. Berkeley: University of California Press.

Arita, Michio, and Yamaoka Shunsuke. 1992. "Karōji Shōkōgun" (The "Overworked Child" Syndrome). *Asahi Journal* (March 20):11–16.

Asada, Akira. 1989. "Infantile Capitalism and Japan's Postmodernism: A Fairy Tale." In Masao Miyoshi and H. D. Harootunian, eds., *Postmodernism and Japan*. Durham and London: Duke University Press, pp. 273–278.

Asahi Shinbunstra. 1995. *Chiezō* (Knowledge Handbook). Tokyo: Asahi Shinbunsha.

Asanuma, Kaoru. 1987. *"Ganbari" no Kōzō* (Structure of "Ganbari"). Tokyo: Kitsugawa Kōbunkan.

Babcock, Barbara. 1993. "Feminisms/Pretexts: Fragments, Questions, and Reflections." *Anthropological Quarterly* 66(2):59–66.

Barlow, Tani, and Angela Zito. 1994. *Body, Subject and Power in China*. Chicago: University of Chicago Press.

Barrett, Michele. 1988. *Women's Oppression Today: The Marxist/Feminist Encounter*. New York: Verso.

Barrowclough, Susan. 1982. "Not a Love Story." *Screen* 23(5):26–38.

Barthes, Roland. 1972(1957). *Mythologies*. Annette Lavers, trans. New York: Noonday Press.

———. 1982. *Empire of Signs*. Richard Howard, trans. New York: Farrar, Straus and Giroux.

Baudrillard, Jean. 1975. *The Mirror of Production*. M. Poster, trans. St. Louis: Telos Press.

———. 1981. *For a Critique of the Political Economy of the Sign*. St. Louis: Telos Press.

Beer, L. W. 1984. *Freedom of Expression in Japan: A Study in Comparative Law, Politics, and Society*. Tokyo: Kōdansha.

Behar, Ruth. 1993. "Introduction. Women Writing Culture: Another Telling of the Story of American Anthropology." *Critique of Anthropology* 13(4):307–325.

———. 1995. "Introduction: Out of Exile." In Ruth Behar and Deborah A. Gordon, eds., *Women Writing Culture*. Los Angeles and London: University of California Press, pp. 1–32.

Benedict, Ruth. 1989(1946). *The Chrysanthemum and the Sword*. Boston: Houghton Mifflin.

Benjamin, Jessica. 1988. *The Bonds of Love: Psychoanalysis, Feminism, and the Problem of Domination*. New York: Pantheon Books.

Berger, John. 1972. *Ways of Seeing*. London: Penguin Books.

Bettelheim, Bruno. 1962. *Symbolic Wounds: Puberty Rites and the Envious Male*. New York: Collier Books.

Bhabha, Homi. 1992. "The Other Question: Difference, Discrimination and the Discourse of Colonialism." In R. Ferguson, M. Gever, M. Trinh, and C. West, eds., *Out There: Marginalization and Contemporary Cultures*. Cambridge: MIT Press, pp. 71–88.

Boocock, Sarane Spence. 1989. "Controlled Diversity: An Overview of the Japanese Preschool System." *Journal of Japanese Studies* 15(1):41–66.

Bordo, Susan. 1993. *Unbearable Weight: Feminism, Western Culture, and the Body*. Berkeley: University of California Press.

Bornhoff, Nicholas. 1991. *Pink Samurai: Love, Marriage and Sex in Contemporary Japan*. New York: Basic Books.

Bowen, Eleanor (aka Laura Bohannan). 1964. *Return to Laughter*. Garden City, N.Y.: Doubleday.

Brinton, Mary. 1993. *Women and the Economic Miracle: Gender and Work in Postwar Japan*. Berkeley, Los Angeles, and London: University of California Press.

Brownmiller, Susan. 1975. *Against Our Will: Men, Women and Rape*. London: Secker and Warbury.

Buckley, Sandra. 1991. "'Penguin in Bondage': A Graphic Tale of Japanese Comic Books." In C. Penley and A. Ross, eds., *Technoculture*. Minneapolis: University of Minnesota Press, pp. 163–193.

———. 1993. "Altered States: The Body Politics of 'Being-Woman.'" In A. Gordon, ed., *Postwar Japan as History*. Berkeley: University of California Press, pp. 347–372.

Bukkupēji Kankōkai. 1994. *Bukku Pēji; Hon no nen Kan* (Book Page: Annual Edition). Tokyo: Bukkupēji Kankōkai.

"Burdens of Working Wives Weigh Heavily in Japan." 1991. *Chicago Tribune*, January 27, section 6:7.

Buruma, Ian. 1984. *Behind the Mask: On Sexual Demons, Sacred Mothers, Transvestites, Gangsters, and Other Japanese Cultural Heroes*. New York: Pantheon Books.

Butler, Judith. 1990. *Gender Trouble: Feminism and the Subversion of Identity*. New York: Routledge.

———. 1993. *Bodies That Matter: On the Discursive Limits of "Sex."* New York: Routledge.

Califia, Pat. 1994. *Public Sex: The Culture of Radical Sex*. Pittsburgh: Cleis Press.

Canby, Vincent. 1989. "What's So Funny About Japan?" *New York Times Magazine*, June 18, section 6:26.

Carter, Angela. 1978. *The Sadeian Woman and the Ideology of Pornography*. New York: Harper Colophon Books.

Chodorow, Nancy. 1978. *The Reproduction of Mothering: Psychoanalysis and the Sociology of Gender*. Berkeley and Los Angeles: University of California Press.

———. 1989. *Feminism and Psychoanalytic Theory*. New Haven: Yale University Press.

Cixious, Hélène. 1980. "The Laugh of the Medusa." In E. Marks and I. deCourtivron, eds., *New French Feminisms*. Amherst: University of Massachusetts Press, pp. 245–264.

Clifford, James. 1988. "On Ethnographic Authority." In *The Predicament of Culture: Twentieth-Century Ethnography, Literature, and Art*. Cambridge: Harvard University Press, pp. 21–54.

Clifford, James, and George Marcus, eds. 1986. *Writing Culture: The Poetics and Politics of Ethnography*. Berkeley: University of California Press.

Clover, Carol J. 1992. *Men, Women, and Chain Saws: Gender in the Modern Horror Film*. Princeton: Princeton University Press.

Comaroff, Jean and John. 1991. *Of Revelation and Revolution: Christianity, Colonialism, and Consciousness in South Africa*. Volume 1. Chicago: The University of Chicago Press.

Cornell, Drucilla. 1991. *Beyond Accommodation: Ethical Feminism, Deconstruction, and the Law*. New York: Routledge.

———. 1993. *Transformations*. New York: Routledge.

Coward, Rosalind. 1983. *Patriarchal Precedents: Sexuality and Social Relations*. London: Routledge and Kegan Paul.

Cummings, Bruce. 1993. "Japan's Position in the World System." In A. Gordon, ed., *Postwar Japan as History*. Berkeley: University of California Press, pp. 34–63.

Cummings, William K. 1980. *Education and Equality in Japan*. Princeton: Princeton University Press.

Davis, Angela. 1981. *Woman, Race, and Class*. New York: Random House.

Davis, D., and R. Whitten. 1987. "The Cross-Cultural Study of Human Sexuality." *Annual Reviews of Anthropology* 16:69–98.

de Lauretis, Teresa. 1984. *Alice Doesn't: Feminism, Semiotics, Cinema.* Bloomington: Indiana University Press.

———. 1987. *Technologies of Gender: Essays on Theory, Film, and Fiction.* Bloomington: Indiana University Press.

———. 1990. "Rethinking Women's Cinema: Aesthetics and Feminist Theory." In P. Evans, ed., *Issues in Feminist Film Criticism.* Bloomington: Indiana University Press, pp. 288–308.

de Lauretis, Teresa, ed. 1986. *Feminist Studies/Critical Studies.* Bloomington: Indiana University Press.

de Lauretis, Teresa, and Stephen Heath, eds. 1980. *The Cinematic Apparatus.* New York: St. Martin's Press.

Deleuze, Gilles, and Felix Guattari. 1983(1972). *Anti-Oedipus: Capitalism and Schizophrenia.* R. Hurley, M. Seem, and H. Lane, trans. Minneapolis: University of Minnesota Press.

di Leonardo, Micaela, ed. 1991. *Gender at the Crossroads of Knowledge: Feminist Anthropology in the Postmodern Era.* Berkeley: University of California Press.

Dinnerstein, Donna. 1976. *The Mermaid and the Minotaur: Sexual Arrangements and Human Malaise.* New York: Harper & Row.

Doane, Mary Ann. 1983. "Gilda: Epistemology as Striptease." *Camera Obscura* 11:7–27.

———. 1990a. "Film and the Masquerade: Theorizing the Female Spectator." In P. Evans, ed., *Issues in Feminist Film Criticism.* Bloomington: Indiana University Press, pp. 41–57.

———. 1990b. "Technophilia: Technology, Representation, and the Feminine." In M. Jacobus, E. Fox Keller, S. Shuttleworth, eds., *Body/Politics.* New York: Routledge, pp. 163–176.

Doi, Takeo. 1971. *The Anatomy of Dependence: The Key Analysis of Japanese Behavior.* John Becker, trans. Tokyo: Kōdansha.

"'Dokusho Shūkan' Honsha Seron Chōsa" (Head Office Public Opinion Survey on "Reading Week"). 1994. *Yomiuri Shinbun,* November 11, section 12:18.

Dore, Ronald P. 1958. *City Life in Japan.* Berkeley: University of California Press.

———. 1965. *Education in Tokugawa Japan.* London: Routledge and Kegan Paul.

Dower, John. 1993. "Peace and Democracy in Two Systems: External Policy and Internal Conflict." In A. Gordon, ed., *Postwar Japan as History.* Berkeley: University of California Press, pp. 3–33.

Duggan, Lisa, Nan D. Hunter, and Carole S. Vance. 1992. "False Promises." In F.A.C.T. Book Committee, ed., *Caught Looking: Feminism, Pornography, and Censorship.* East Haven, Conn.: LongRiver Books, p. 72.

Duke, Benjamin. 1986. *The Japanese School: Lessons for Industrial America.* New York: Praeger.

Dworkin, Andrea. 1981. *Pornography: Men Possessing Women.* London: Women's Press.

———. 1987. *Intercourse.* New York: Free Press.

Ellis, Kate. 1992. "I'm Black and Blue." In F.A.C.T. Book Committee, ed., *Caught Looking: Feminism, Pornography, and Censorship*. East Haven, Conn.: LongRiver Books, pp. 38–47.

Erens, Patricia, ed. 1990. *Issues in Feminist Film Criticism*. Bloomington: Indiana University Press.

Ewen, Stuart. 1988. *All Consuming Images: The Politics of Style in Contemporary Culture*. New York: Basic Books.

F.A.C.T. Book Committee, ed. 1992. *Caught Looking: Feminism, Pornography, and Censorship*. East Haven, Conn.: LongRiver Books.

Fallows, Deborah. 1990. "Japanese Women." *National Geographic* 177(4):52–83.

Farquhar, Judith. 1994. "Eating Chinese Medicine." *Cultural Anthropology* 9(4):471–497.

Ferguson, R. 1992. "Introduction: Invisible Center." In R. Ferguson, M. Gever, M. Trinh, and C. West, eds., *Out There: Marginalization and Contemporary Cultures*. Cambridge: MIT Press, pp. 9-18.

Field, Norma. 1991. *In the Realm of a Dying Emperor: A Portrait of Japan at Century's End*. New York: Pantheon Books.

————. 1995. "The Child as Laborer and Consumer: The Disappearance of Childhood in Contemporary Japan." In Sharon Stephens, ed., *Children and the Politics of Culture*. Princeton: Princeton University Press, pp. 51–78.

Flax, Jane. 1990. *Thinking Fragments: Psychoanalysis, Feminism, and Postmodernism in the Contemporary West*. Berkeley: University of California Press.

Foucault, Michel. 1980(1976). *The History of Sexuality. Vol. I: An Introduction*. R. Hurley, trans. New York: Random House.

Frazer, James G. 1959. *The Golden Bough: A New Abridgement of the Classical Work*. New York: Criterion Books.

Freud, Sigmund. 1961(1927). "Fetishism." In *Standard Edition of the Complete Psychological Works of Sigmund Freud*, James Strachey, trans., vol. 19. London: Hogarth Press, pp. 147–157.

————. 1964a(1925). "Some Psychical Consequences of the Anatomical Distinction Between the Sexes." In *Standard Edition*, vol. 19. London: Hogarth Press, pp. 248–260.

————. 1964b(1940). "The Development of the Sexual Function." In *Standard Edition*, vol. 23, pp. 152–156.

————. 1975(1905). *Three Essays on the Theory of Sexuality*. J. Strachey, trans. New York: Basic Books.

Fujita, Mariko. 1989. "'It's All Mother's Fault': Childcare and the Socialization in Japanese Day-Care Centers." *Journal of Japanese Studies* 15(1):67–92.

Gaines, Jane. 1990a. "Women and Representation: Can We Enjoy Alternative Pleasure?" In P. Erens, ed., *Issues in Feminist Film Criticism*. Bloomington: Indiana University Press, pp. 75–93.

————. 1990b. "White Privilege and Looking Relations: Race and Gender in Feminist Film Theory." In P. Erens, ed., *Issues in Feminist Film Theory*. Bloomington: Indiana University Press, pp. 197–215.

Gallop, Jane. 1982. *The Daughter's Seduction: Feminism and Psychoanalysis*. Ithaca: Cornell University Press.

———. 1985. *Reading Lacan*. Ithaca: Cornell University Press.

Gamman, Lorraine, and Margaret Marshment, eds. 1989. *The Female Gaze: Women as Viewers of Popular Culture*. Seattle: Real Comet Press.

Gates, Henry Louis. 1987. "Authority, (White) Power and the (Black) Critic." *Cultural Critique* 0882-4371(fall):19–46.

Gendai Hyōronsha. 1980. *Hikisakareta Sei* (Sex That Has Been Torn to Pieces). Tokyo: Gendai Hyōronsha.

Gibson, Pamela Church, and Roman Gibson, eds. 1993. *Dirty Looks: Women, Pornography, Power*. London: BFI.

Ginsburg, Faye, and Anne Lowenhaupt Tsing. 1990. *Uncertain Terms: Negotiating Gender in American Culture*. Boston: Beacon Press.

Gluck, Carol. 1993. "The Past in the Present." In A. Gordon, ed., *Postwar Japan as History*. Berkeley: University of California Press, pp. 64–98.

Go, Tomohide. 1981. "Gendai Eromanga Tenbō" (View of Erotic Comic Books Today). *Manga Ronsō*, special issue of *Bessatsu Takarajima* 13:260–262.

Gordon, Andrew, 1993. "Contests for the Workplace." In A. Gordon, ed., *Postwar Japan as History*. Berkeley: University of California Press, pp. 373–394.

Goux, Jean-Joseph. 1990. *Symbolic Economies: After Marx and Freud*, trans. Jennifer Gage. Ithaca: Cornell University Press.

Greenbie, Barrie B. 1988. *Space and Spirit in Modern Japan*. New Haven: Yale University Press.

Griffin, Susan. 1981. *Pornography and Silence: Culture's Revenge Against Women*. London: Women's Press.

Grosz, Elizabeth. 1990. *Jacques Lacan: A Feminist Introduction*. London: Routledge.

Gupta, A., and James Ferguson. 1992. "Beyond 'Culture': Space, Identity, and the Politics of Difference." *Cultural Anthropology* 7(1):6–23.

Habermas, Jürgen. 1989. *The Structural Transformation of the Public Sphere: An Inquiry into a Category of Bourgeois Society*. T. Burger with F. Lawrence, trans. Cambridge: MIT Press.

Haraway, Donna. 1991. *Simians, Cyborgs, and Women: The Reinvention of Nature*. New York: Routledge.

Harootunian, H. D. 1989. "Visible Discourses/Invisible Ideologies." In Masao Miyoshi and H. D. Harootunian, eds., *Postmodernism and Japan*. Durham and London: Duke University Press, pp. 63–92.

Harris, Marvin. 1968. *The Rise of Anthropological Theory*. New York: Columbia University Press.

Hartmann, Heidi. 1981. "The Unhappy Marriage of Marxism and Feminism: Towards a More Progressive Union." In Lydia Sargent, ed., *Women and Revolution: A Discussion of the Unhappy Marriage of Marxism and Feminism*. Boston: South End Press.

Harvey, David. 1989. *The Condition of Postmodernity: An Enquiry into the Origins of Cultural Change*. Cambridge: Basil Blackwell.

Haug, Wolfgang Fritz. 1986(1971). *Critique of Commodity Aesthetics: Appearance, Sexuality and Advertising in Capitalist Society.* R. Bock, trans. Minneapolis: University of Minnesota Press.

Hayashi, Yoko. 1995. "Legal Issues in Employment." *Ampo* 25(4):42–45.

Heath, Stephen. 1981. *Questions of Cinema.* Bloomington, Ind.: Schoken Books.

Heibonsha. 1992. *Heibon Hyakka Nenkan* (Heibon Annual Encyclopedia). Tokyo: Heibonsha.

Hendry, Joy. 1986. *Becoming Japanese: The World of the Preschool Child.* Honolulu: University of Hawaii Press.

———. 1987. *Understanding Japanese Society.* London: Croom Helm.

Herdt, Gilbert. 1981. *Guardians of the Flute.* New York: McGraw-Hill.

———. 1982a. *The Sambia: Ritual and Gender in New Guinea.* New York: Holt, Rinehart & Winston.

Herdt, Gilbert, ed. 1982b. *Rituals of Manhood: Male Initiation in Papua New Guinea.* Berkeley: University of California Press.

Herdt, Gilbert, and Robert Stoller. 1990. *Intimate Communications: Erotics and the Study of Culture.* New York: Columbia University Press.

hooks, bell. 1981. *Ain't I a Woman! Black Women and Feminism.* Boston: South End Press.

———. 1992. *Black Looks: Race and Representation.* Boston: South End Press.

Horio, Teruhisa. 1988. *Educational Thought and Ideology in Japan: State Authority and Educational Freedom.* S. Platzer, trans. Tokyo: University of Tokyo Press.

Horkheimer, Max, and Theodor Adorno. 1991(1972). *Dialectic of Enlightenment.* J. Cummings, trans. New York: Continuum.

Horney, Karen. 1967. *Feminine Psychology.* Boston: Routledge & Kegan Paul.

Ihaya, Manako. 1991. "Obscenity and Censorship Still Flourish in Japan." *Japan Times Weekly International Edition*, September 2–8:8.

Imamura, Anne E. 1987. *Urban Japanese Housewives: At Home and in the Community.* Honolulu: University of Hawaii Press.

Irigaray, Luce. 1985. *This Sex Which Is Not One.* C. Porter, trans. Ithaca: Cornell University Press.

Ishikawa, Hiroyoshi. 1983. "Porunogurafī" (Pornography). *Juristo* 25:228–233.

Ivy, Marilyn. 1993. "Formations of Mass Culture." In A. Gordon, ed., *Postwar Japan as History.* Berkeley: University of California Press, pp. 239–258.

Iwao, Sumiko. 1993. *The Japanese Woman: Traditional Image and Changing Reality.* New York: Free Press.

Jameson, Fredric. 1984. "Postmodernism, or the Cultural Logic of Late Capitalism." *New Left Review* 146:53–92.

"Josei no Genzai to Mirai" (The Present and Future of Women). 1985. *Juristo zokei Sōgōtokushu* (special issue of *Juristo*) 39.

Kadeshobō Shinsha. 1981. *Hahaoya* (Mother). Tokyo: Kadeshobō Shinsha.

Kakinuma, Miyuki. 1980. "Boshisōkan Gensō no Kyōjitsu" (The Truth and Falsehood of the Fantasy of Mother-Child Incest). *Gendai no Me* 2(1105):88–93.

Kamei, Shunsuke. 1991. "Madonna Shashinshū 'Sex' o Yomu" (Reading Madonna's Photo Collection, "Sex"). *Chūō Kōron* (February):242–245.

Kamewada, Takeru. 1981. "Sei no Kitsuonshatachi" (Sexual Stutterers). *Manga Ronsō*, special issue of *Bessatsu Takarajima* 13:132–137.

Kanō, Masanao. 1986. "Changing Perspectives on the Family in Post-war Japan." *Review of Japanese Culture and Society* 1(1):78–84.

Kaplan, Ann. 1983. *Women and Film: Both Sides of the Camera*. New York: Methuen.

Kawai, Hayao. 1976. *Bosei Shakai Nihon no Byōri* (The Pathology of the Motherhood Society—Japan). Tokyo: Chūō Kōronsha.

———. 1988. *The Japanese Psyche: Major Motifs in the Fairy Tales of Japan*. Kawai Hayao and Sachiko Reese, trans. Dallas: Spring Publications.

Kawashima, Yoko. 1995. "Female Workers: An Overview of Past and Current Trends." In Kumiko Fujimura-Fanselow and Atsuko Kameda, eds., *Japanese Women: New Feminist Perspectives on the Past, Present, and Future*. New York: The Feminist Press, pp. 271–294.

Kelly, William. 1993. "Finding a Place in Metropolitan Japan: Ideologies, Institutions, and Everyday Life." In A. Gordon, ed., *Postwar Japan as History*. Berkeley: University of California Press, pp. 189–238.

Kennedy, Duncan. 1993. *Sexy Dressing Etc.: Essays on the Power and Politics of Cultural Identity*. Cambridge and London: Harvard University Press.

Kennedy, Elizabeth L. 1995. *Boots of Leather, Slippers of Gold: The History of a Lesbian Community*. New York: Routledge.

Kent, Sarah. 1985. "The Erotic Male Nude." In S. Kent and J. Morreau, eds., *Women's Images of Men*. London: Writers and Readers, pp. 75–105.

Kimoto, Itaru. 1983. "Jishukisei ka no Porunogurafī Shuppan" (The Publication of Pornography Under Self-Control). *Juristo* 25:299–306.

Kinjō, Kiyoko, and Nakatani, Kizuko. 1983. "Hanzai o Meguru Seisabetsu" (Gender Discrimination Surrounding Crimes). *Juristo* 25:269–287.

Kipnis, Laura. 1992. "(Male) Desire and (Female) Disgust: Reading *Hustler*." In L. Grossberg, C. Nelson, and P. Treichler, eds., *Cultural Studies*. New York: Routledge, pp. 373–391.

Kirby, Vicki. 1989. "Capitalising Difference: Feminism and Anthropology." *Australian Feminist Studies* 9:1–24.

———. 1993. "Feminisms and Postmodernisms: Anthropology and the Management of Differerence." *Anthropological Quarterly* 66(3)(July):127–133.

Kobayashi, Naoki. 1970. "Zadankai" (Roundtable). *Juristo* 1372:19–42.

Koch, Gertrude. 1990. "The Body's Shadow Realm: On Pornographic Cinema." *Jump-Cut* 35:17–29.

Kondo, Dorinne. 1990. *Crafting Selves: Power, Gender and Discourses of Identity in a Japanese Workplace*. Chicago: University of Chicago Press.

Kristeva, Julia. 1980. *Desire in Language: A Semiotic Approach to Literature and Art*. L. Roudiez, ed. T. Gora, A. Jardine, L. Roudiez, trans. New York: Columbia University Press.

Kuhn, Annette. 1985. *The Power of the Image: Essays on Representation and Sexuality*. London: Routledge and Kegan Paul.

Kusamori, Shinichi. 1983. "Mizu no Ranpi" (The Dissipation of Water). *Juristo* 25: 234–241.

Kyutoku, Shigemori. 1981. *Bogenbyō* (Disease Rooted in Motherhood), vol. 2. Tokyo: Sanmāku Shuppan.

Lacan, Jacques. 1977(1966). *Écrits: A Selection*. A. Sheridan, trans. London: Tavistock.

———. 1982(1977). *Feminine Sexuality*. J. Rose and J. Mitchell, eds. J. Rose, trans. New York: W. W. Norton.

Laclau, Ernesto, and Chantal Mouffe. 1990(1985). *Hegemony and Socialist Strategy: Towards a Radical Democratic Politics.* London: Verso Press.

Laplanche, J., and J. B. Pontalis. 1968. "Fantasy and the Origins of Sexuality." In Victor Burgin and Cora Kaplan, eds., *Formations of Fantasy.* London and New York: Methuen, pp. 5–34.

Lehman, Peter. 1988. *"In the Realm of the Senses:* Desire, Power, and the Representation of the Male Body." *Genders* 2:91–110.

Lévi-Strauss, Claude. 1975. *The Elementary Structures of Kinship.* R. Needham, ed. J. Bell and J. Von Struner, trans. Boston: Beacon Press.

Lewis, Catherine C. 1989. "From Indulgence to Internalization: Social Control in the Early School Years. *Journal of Japanese Studies* 15(1):139–157.

Lock, Margaret. 1990. "Restoring Order to the House of Japan." *Wilson Quarterly* 14(4):42–49.

———. 1993. *Encounters with Aging: Mythologies of Menopause in Japan and North America.* Berkeley: University of California Press.

Lorde, Audre. 1983. "The Master's Tools Will Never Dismantle the Master's House." In C. Morraga and G. Anzaldúa, eds., *This Bridge Called My Back: Writings by Radical Women of Color.* New York: Kitchen Table: Women of Color Press, pp. 98–101.

———. 1992. "Age, Race, Class, and Sex: Women Redefining Difference." In R. Ferguson, M. Gever, M. Trinh, and C. West, eds., *Out There: Marginalization and Contemporary Cultures.* Cambridge: MIT Press, pp. 281–288.

Lorraine, Tasmin. 1990. *Gender, Identity, and the Production of Meaning.* Boulder: Westview Press.

Lurie, Susan. 1980. "Pornography and the Dread of Women: The Male Sexual Dilemma." In L. Lederer, ed., *Take Back the Night: Women on Pornography.* New York: Bantam Books, pp. 152–167.

Lutz, Catherine. 1990. "The Erasure of Women's Writing in Sociocultural Anthropology." *American Ethnologist* 17(4):611–627.

———. 1995. "The Gender of Theory." In Ruth Behar and Deborah A. Gordon, eds., *Women Writing Culture.* Los Angeles and London: University of California Press, pp. 249–266.

MacCormack, Carol, and Marilyn Strathern, eds. 1980. *Nature, Culture, and Gender.* Cambridge: Cambridge University Press.

MacDonald, Scott. 1983. "Confessions of a Feminist Porn Watcher." *Film Quarterly* 36(3):10–17.

Mackie, Vera. 1988. "Feminist Politics in Japan." *New Left Review* 167:53–71.

Mackie, Vera, and Sandra Buckley. 1985. "Women in the New Japanese State." In Gavan Mc-Cormack and Yoshio Sugimoto, eds., *Democracy in Japan.* Melbourne: Hale & Iremonger.

MacKinnon, Catharine. 1979. *Sexual Harassment and the Working Woman: A Case of Sex Discrimination.* New York: Putnam.

———. 1982. "Feminism, Marxism, Method and the State: An Agenda for Theory." *Signs* 7(3)(spring):515–544.

———. 1984. "Not a Moral Issue." *Yale Law and Policy Review* 2(321):320–345.

———. 1987. *Feminism Unmodified: Discourses on Life and Law.* New Haven: Yale University Press.

———. 1989. *Toward a Feminist Theory of the State.* Cambridge: Harvard University Press.

Maeda, Shinjiro. 1980. "Sekkusu to Hō to Shakai" (Sex, Law, and Society). *Juristo* 12:71–80.

Malinowski, Bronislaw. 1922. *Argonauts of the Western Pacific.* London: Routledge.

———. 1929. *The Sexual Life of Savages in North-western Melanesia.* New York: Routledge.

Marcus, George, and Michael Fischer. 1986. *Anthropology as Cultural Critique: An Experimental Moment in the Human Sciences.* Chicago: University of Chicago Press.

Marcus, Steven. 1975. "Introduction." In S. Freud, *Three Essays on the Theory of Sexuality.* New York: Basic Books, pp. xix–xli.

Marcuse, Herbert. 1966(1955). *Eros and Civilization: A Philosophical Inquiry into Freud.* Boston: Beacon Press.

Marx, Karl. 1978. "Capital, Volume One." In Robert Tucker, ed., *The Marx-Engels Reader.* New York: W. W. Norton, pp. 294–438.

———. 1978. "Economic and Philosophic Manuscripts of 1844." In Robert Tucker, ed., *The Marx-Engels Reader.* New York: W.W. Norton, pp. 66–125.

Marx, Karl, and Friedrich Engels. 1970(1947). *The German Ideology.* C. J. Arthur, ed. New York: International.

Mascia-Lees, Frances, Patricia Sharpe, and Colleen Ballerino Cohen. 1989. "The Postmodernist Turn in Anthropology: Cautions from a Feminist Perspective." *Signs* 15(1):7–33.

McClintock, Anne. 1990. "Porn in the U.S.A.: A Story Without a Climax." *Voice Literary Supplement* 84:16–17.

Mead, Margaret. 1928. *Coming of Age in Samoa: A Psychological Study of Primitive Youth for Western Civilization.* New York: W. Morrow.

———. 1963(1935). *Sex and Temperament in Three Primitive Societies.* New York: Morrow Quill Paperbacks.

Metz, Christian. 1974. *The Imaginary Signifier.* C. Britton, trans. Bloomington: Indiana University Press.

Miraishakai. 1979. "Shufu to Onna" (Housewives and Women). In *Kinitachishi Kōmininkan Shimindaigaku Seminā no Kiroku* (Record of the Citizen's University Seminar at the Public Hall of Kunitachi City). Tokyo: Miraisha.

Mitchell, Juliet. 1982. "Introduction—I." In *Feminine Sexuality.* Jacques Lacan. J. Rose, trans. New York: W. W. Norton, pp. 1–26.

Mitchell, Richard. 1983. *Censorship in Imperial Japan*. Princeton: Princeton University Press.

Mitchell, W.J.Y. 1995. "Postcolonial Culture, Postimperial Criticism." In B. Ashcroft, G. Griffiths, and H. Tiffin, eds., *The Post-Colonial Studies Reader*. London: Routledge, pp. 475–479.

Miyoshi, Masao. 1991. *Off Center: Power and Culture Relations Between Japan and the United States*. Cambridge: Harvard University Press.

Mizuno, Reiko. 1994. "Pantsu o Katte Iru nowa Dareda?" (Who Is Buying Pants?). *Bessatsu Takarajima* 196:184–190.

Mizuta, Noriko. 1995. "Musume ni yoru Hahamonogatari kara Haha ni yoru Monogatari" (From Mother's Stories by Daughters to Stories by Mothers). In Kanō Mikiyo, ed., *New Feminism Review*, vol. 6. Tokyo: Gakuyō Shobō, pp. 254–261.

Modleski, Tania. 1982. *Loving with a Vengeance: Mass-Produced Fantasies for Women*. Hamden, Conn.: Archon Books.

Moore, Henrietta L. 1988. *Feminism and Anthropology*. Minneapolis: University of Minnesota Press.

Moraga, Cherrie, and Gloria Anzaldúa, eds. 1983. *This Bridge Called My Back: Writings by Radical Women of Color*. New York: Kitchen Table: Women of Color Press.

Morgan, Robin. 1979. *Going Too Far*. New York: Random House.

Morris, Rosalind C. 1995. "All Made Up: Performance Theory and the New Anthropology of Sex and Gender." *Annual Reviews of Anthropology* 24:567–592.

Mouer, Ross, and Yoshio Sugimoto. 1986. *Images of Japanese Society: A Study in the Social Construction of Reality*. London: Routledge and Kegan Paul.

Mulvey, Laura. 1975. "Visual Pleasure and Narrative Cinema." *Screen* 16(3).

Murakami, Ryū. 1994. *Kōin Roka Bēbi* (Coin Locker Babies). S. Snyder, trans. Tokyo: Kōdansha.

Nakane, Chie. 1970. *Japanese Society*. Berkeley: University of California Press.

Nakano, Akira. 1990. "Redīsu Komikku no Yokubō o Yomu" (Reading the Desire of Ladies' Comics). *Hon no Zasshi* 12:72–76.

Nakatani, Kino, and Kinjō Seiko. 1982. "Zadankai: Hanzai o Meguru Seisabetsu" (Roundtable: Gender Discrimination Surrounding Crime). *Juristo* 25:269–287.

Narabayashi, Yoshi. 1983. "Zadankai" (Roundtable). *Juristo* 25:8–26.

Newton, Esther. 1972. *Mother Camp: Female Impersonators in America*. Chicago: Chicago University Press.

"Nihonjin no Sugao: Honsha Seron Chōsa Jūnen" (The Unpainted Face of the Japanese: Ten Years of Public Survey Reports"). 1988. *Asahi Shinbun*, morning edition, February 3:12.

Nohara, Hiroko. 1994. "Kōshi te Watashitachi Fūfu wa Sekkusuresu ni Natta (This Is How We Husbands and Wives Became Sexless). *Fujin Kōron* 79(5):128–135.

Obeyesekere, Gananath. 1981. *Medusa's Hair*. Chicago: University of Chicago Press.

Ohirasōri no Seifukenkyūkai (Prime Minister Ōhira's Governmental Research Group). 1980. "Katei Kiban no Jujitsu" (The Fullness of Family Foundations). Tokyo: Ōkurashō Insatsukyoku.

Okonogi, Keigo. 1978. "The Ajase Complex of the Japanese (1)." *Japan Echo* 5(4):88–105.

———. 1979. "The Ajase Complex of the Japanese (2)." *Japan Echo* 6(1):104–118.

Ortner, Sherry B., and Harriet Whitehead. 1981. *Sexual Meanings: The Cultural Construction of Gender and Sexuality.* Cambridge: Cambridge University Press.

Ōshima, Nagisa. 1983. "Fūzoku to Hanzai no Aida" (Between Crime and Custom). *Juristo* 25:55–58.

———. 1981. "Bunka.Sei.Seiji" (Culture.Sex.Politics). *Juristo* 5401:19–40.

———. 1988. *Cinema, Censorship, and the State: The Writings of Nagisa Ōshima.* A. Michelson, ed. D. Lawson, trans. Cambridge: MIT Press.

Peak, Lois. 1989. "Learning to Become Part of the Group: The Japanese Child's Transition to Preschool Life." *Journal of Japanese Studies* 15(1):93–123.

———. 1991. *Learning to Go to School in Japan: Transition from Home to Preschool Life.* Berkeley: University of California Press.

Pence, Elizabeth. 1982. "Racism—A White Issue." In G. Hull, P. Scott, and B. Smith, eds., *All the Women Are White and All the Blacks Are Men But Some of Us Are Brave: Black Women's Studies.* Old Westbury, N.Y.: Feminist Press.

Radway, Janice. 1984. *Reading the Romance: Women, Patriarchy, and Popular Literature.* Chapel Hill: University of North Carolina Press.

Ragland-Sullivan, Ellie. 1982. "Jacques Lacan: Feminism and the Problem of Gender Identity." *sub-stance* 36:6–20.

Rapp (Reiter), Rayna, ed. 1975. *Toward an Anthropology of Women.* New York: Monthly Review Press.

Regelman, Karen. 1993. "Will Tokyo Tame 'Crying Game'?" *Variety* (March 22):1, 68.

Richie, Donald. 1985. *A Taste of Japan.* Tokyo: Kōdansha.

Robertson, Jennifer. 1989. "Gender-Bending in Paradise: Doing 'Female' and 'Male' in Japan." *Genders* 5:50–69.

———. 1991. "Theatrical Resistances, Theatres of Restraint: The Takarazuka Revue and the 'State Theatre' Movement." *Anthropological Quarterly* 64(4)(October):165–177.

Rohlen, Thomas. 1974. *For Harmony and Strength: Japanese White Collar Organization in Anthropology.* Berkeley: University of California Press.

———. 1983. *Japan's High Schools.* Berkeley: University of California Press.

———. 1989. "Order in Japanese Society: Attachment, Authority, and Routine." *Journal of Japanese Studies* 15(1):5–40.

Rosaldo, Michelle, and Louise Lamphere, eds. 1973. *Woman, Culture and Society.* Stanford: Stanford University Press.

Rose, Jacqueline. 1982. "Introduction—II." In Jacques Lacan, *Feminine Sexuality.* J. Rose, trans. New York: W. W. Norton.

Ross, Andrew. 1989. *No Respect: Intellectuals and Popular Culture.* New York: Routledge.

Rubin, Gayle. 1973. "Traffic in Women: Notes on the 'Political Economy' of Sex." In R. Rapp, ed., *Toward an Anthropology of Women.* New York: Monthly Review Press, pp. 157–210.

———. 1984. "Thinking Sex: Notes for a Radical Theory of the Politics of Sexuality." In C. Vance, ed., *Pleasure and Danger*. Boston: Routledge & Kegan Paul, pp. 267–319.

Rubin, Jay. 1984. *Injurious to Public Morals: Writers and the Meiji State*. Seattle: University of Washington Press.

Said, Edward. 1978. *Orientalism*. New York: Random House.

———. 1989. "Representing the Colonized: Anthropology's Interlocutors." *Critical Inquiry* 15(winter):205–225.

Saikō Saibansho. 1958. "Judgment upon Case of Translation and Publication of Lady Chatterley's Lover and Article 175 of the Penal Code." In *Series of Prominent Judgments of the Supreme Court upon Questions of Constitutionality, No. 2*. Tokyo: General Secretariat, Supreme Court of Japan.

Sanday, Peggy. 1990. *Fraternity Gang Rape: Sex, Brotherhood, and Privilege on Campus*. New York: New York University Press.

Sano, Toshiyuki. 1989. "Methods of Social Control and Socialization in Japanese Day-Care Centers." *Journal of Japanese Studies* 15(1):125–138.

Sano, Yōko. 1991. "Freud to Kleenex" (Freud and Kleenex). *Hon no Zasshi* 94:94–5.

Sato, Tadao. 1981. "Teizoku Bunka to wa Nani ka?" (What Is Low Culture?). *Manga Ronsō*, special issue of *Bessatsu Takarajima* 13:62–71.

Schilling, Mark. 1992. "Worshipping the Naked Goddess: The Media, Mores, and Miyazawa Rie." *Japan Quarterly* 39(2):218–224.

Schneider, David. 1984. *A Critique of the Study of Kinship*. Ann Arbor: University of Michigan Press.

Schodt, Frederick. 1986. *Manga! Manga! Manga! The World of Japanese Comics*. New York: Kōdansha.

Sedgwick, Eve. 1985. *Between Men: English Literature and Male Homosocial Desire*. New York: Columbia University Press.

———. 1990. *Epistemology of the Closet*. Berkeley: University of California Press.

———. 1993. *Tendencies*. Durham, N.C.: Duke University Press.

Segal, Lynne, and Mary McIntosh, eds. 1993. *Sex Exposed: Sexuality and the Pornography Debate*. New Brunswick, N.J.: Rutgers University Press.

Shields, James J. Jr., ed. 1989. *Japanese Schooling: Patterns of Socialization, Equality, and Political Control*. University Park: Pennsylvania State University Press.

Shinoyama, Kishin. 1991a. *Santa Fe*. Tokyo: Asahi Shuppansha.

———. 1991b. *Water Fruit*. Tokyo: Asahi Shuppansha.

Shinoyama, Yasuko. 1980. "Musuko Kawaisa yueni Kurutta Ichiya" (The Night I Went Crazy on Account of My Son's Cuteness), part 2 of "Boshi Sōkan: Kindan no Kairaku ni Oborete" (Mother-Child Incest: Drowning in Forbidden Happiness). *Fujin Kōron* 66(1):341–344.

Shostak, Marjorie. 1983. *Nisa: The Life and Words of a !Kung Woman*. New York: Random House.

Shūeisha. 1992. "Masumedia." In *Imidasu* (a statistical yearbook). Tokyo: Shūeisha.

Shufunotomo. 1980. *Obentō 500 Sen* (500 *Obentō* Selections). Tokyo: Shufunotomo.

———. 1981. *365 Nichi no Obentō Hyakka* (365-Day *Obentō* Encyclopedia). Tokyo: Shu-funotomo.

Silverberg, Miriam. 1993. "Remembering Pearl Harbor, Forgetting Charlie Chaplin, and the Case of the Disappearing Western Woman: A Picture Story." *positions* 1(1) (spring):24–76.

Silverman, Kaja. 1981. *The Subject of Semiotics*. Oxford: Oxford University Press.

———. 1983. "*Histoire d'O*: The Story of a Disciplined and Punished Body." *enclitic* 7(2)(fall):63–81.

———. 1992. *Male Subjectivity at the Margins*. New York: Routledge.

Skov, Lise, and Brian Moeran. 1995. *Women, Media and Consumption in Japan*. Richmond, Surrey, UK: Curzon Press.

Smith, Barbara. 1985. "Toward a Black Feminist Criticism." In J. Newton and D. Rosenfelt, eds., *Feminist Criticism and Social Change*. New York: Methuen, pp. 3–18.

Smith, Robert, and Ella Wiswell. 1982. *The Women of Suye Mura*. Chicago: University of Chicago Press.

Sōrifu Seishonen-taisaku Honbunhen. 1981. *Nihon no Kodomo to Hahaoya: Kokusai-hikaku* (Japanese Mothers and Children: International Comparisons). Tokyo: Sōrifu Seishonen-taisaku Honbunhen.

Spiro, Melford. 1982. *Oedipus in the Trobriands*. Chicago: University of Chicago Press.

———. 1987. *Culture and Human Nature: Theoretical Papers of Melford E. Spiro*. Chicago: University of Chicago Press.

Spivak, Gayatri. 1982. "The Politics of Interpretations." *Critical Inquiry* 9(1).

———. 1988. "Can the Subaltern Speak?" In C. Nelson and L. Grossberg, eds., *Marxism and the Interpretation of Culture*. London: Macmillan, pp. 271–313.

Stacey, Judith. 1988. "Can There Be a Feminist Ethnography?" *Women's Studies International Forum* 11(1):21–27.

Stern, Leslie. 1992. "Body as Evidence." In *The Sexual Subject: A Screen Reader in Sexuality*. New York: Routledge, pp. 197–222.

Strathern, Marilyn. 1984a. "Domesticity and the Denigration of Women." In D. O'Brien and S. Tiffany, eds., *Rethinking Women's Roles: Perspectives from the Pacific*. Berkeley: University of California Press.

———. 1984b. "Subject or Object? Women and the Circulation of Valuables in Highlands New Guinea." In R. Hirschon, ed., *Women and Property, Women as Property*. London: Croom Helm, pp. 158–175.

———. 1987a. "Producing Difference: Connections and Disconnections in Two New Guinea Highlands Kinship Systems." In J. Collier and S. Yanagisako, eds., *Gender and Kinship: Essays Toward a Unified Analysis*. Stanford: Stanford University Press, pp. 271–300.

———. 1987b. "An Awkward Relationship: The Case of Feminism and Anthropology." *Signs* 12(2):276–292.

———. 1988. *The Gender of the Gift: Problems with Women and Problems with Society in Melanesia*. Berkeley: University of California Press.

Studlar, Gaylyn. 1988. *In the Realm of Pleasure: Von Sternberg, Dietrich, and the Masochistic Aesthetic*. Urbana: University of Illinois Press.

Tabe, Shirō. 1986. *Kigyō Kōsaihi to Zeijitsumu Jōhō* (Practical Information About Taxes and Enterprise Company Expense). Tokyo: Zeimu Keirikyōkai.

Tada, Michitarō. 1974. *Asobi to Nihonjin* (Play and the Japanese). Tokyo: Chikuma Shobō.

Takahashi, Shiro. 1992. "Onna no Ko ga Nūdo ni Narru nowa Makudonarudo no Baito to Onnaji" (Becoming Nude for a Female Is the Same as Part-time Work at MacDonald's). *Bessatsu Takarajima* 107:131–134.

Takahashi, Michiko. 1989. "Working Mothers and Families." *Review of Japanese Culture and Society* 3(1):21–30.

Takeuchi, Osamu. 1995. *Sengo Manga 50 Nenshi* (A 50-Year History of Postwar Comics). Tokyo: Chikuma Raburarī.

Tanaka, Kazuko. 1995. "Work, Education, and the Family." In Kumiko Fujimura-Fanselow and Atsuko Kameda, eds., *Japanese Women: New Feminist Perspectives on the Past, Present, and Future*. New York: The Feminist Press, pp. 295–308.

Tanazawa, Naoko, Horiba Kiyoko, and Takayoshi Rumiko. 1988. "Josei, Gengo, Sozo" (Women, Original Language, Creation). *Shin Nihonbun* 469.

Tanizaki, Jun'ichirō. 1977. *In Praise of Shadows*. Thomas J. Harper and Edward G. Seidensticker, trans. New Haven, Conn.: Leete's Island Books.

Tobin, Joseph J. 1989. "Komatsudani: A Japanese Preschool." In J. Tobin, D. Wu, and D. Davidson, eds., *Preschool in Three Cultures: Japan, China, and the United States*. New Haven: Yale University Press, pp. 12–71.

Treat, John Whittier. 1993. "Yoshimoto Banana Writes Home: Shōjo Culture and the Nostalgic Subject." In *Journal of Japanese Studies* 19(2):353–387.

———. 1995. "Yoshimoto Banana's *Kitchen*, or the Cultural Logic of Japanese Consumerism." In Lise Skov and Brian Moeran, eds., *Women, Media and Consumption in Japan*. Richmond, Surrey, U.K.: Curzon Press, pp. 274–298. Conference, February, University of Texas, Austin.

Trinh, T. Minh-ha. 1989. *Woman, Native, Other: Writing Postcoloniality and Feminism*. Bloomington: Indiana University Press.

"Trouble/Toraburu: Tenmei Tokusen 'Bokki Saseru Shasshin'" (Tenmei's Special—"I Give Erections"). 1994. *Focus* 32(August 10):30–33.

Tsuda, Masumi. 1987. *Shinsedai Sararīman no Seikatsu to Iken* (The Lives and Opinions of Modern-Generation Salarymen). Tokyo: Tokyo Keizai Shinpo.

Tsurumi, Shunsuke. 1987(1984). *A Cultural History of Post-War Japan 1945–1980*. London and New York: KPI.

Tyler, Stephen. 1986. "Post-modern Ethnography: From Document of the Occult to Occult Documentation." In J. Clifford and G. Marcus, eds., *Writing Culture: The Poetics and Politics of Ethnography*. Berkeley: University of California Press, pp. 122–140.

Ueno, Chizuko. 1988. *Onna Asobi*. Tokyo: Gakuyo Shobo.

———. 1987. "The Position of Japanese Women Reconsidered." *Current Anthropology* 28(4):75–84.

———. 1992. *Sukāto no Shita no Gekijo* (Theater in the Skirt). Tokyo: Kawade Bunko.

———. 1995. "Orientarizumu to Jendā" (Orientalism and Gender). In Kano Mikiyo, ed., *New Feminism Review*, vol. 6. Tokyo: Gakayo Shobō, pp. 108–131.

Uno, Kathleen. 1993. "The Death of 'Good Wife, Wise Mother'?" In A. Gordon, ed., *Postwar Japan as History*. Berkeley: University of California Press, pp. 293–324.

Vance, Carole. 1990. "Negotiating Sex and Gender in the Attorney General's Commission on Pornography." In F. Ginsburg and A. Tsing, eds., *Uncertain Terms: Negotiating Gender in American Culture*. Boston: Beacon Press, pp. 118–136.

———. 1992. "The Pleasure of Looking: The Attorney General's Commission on Pornography Versus Visual Images." *Fiction International* 22:205–238.

Vance, Carole, ed. 1984. *Pleasure and Danger*. Boston: Routledge & Kegan Paul.

Vogel, Ezra. 1963. *Japan's New Middle Class: The Salaryman and His Family in a Tokyo Suburb*. Berkeley: University of California Press.

Wagatsuma, Hiroshi, and Fukuda Yoshiya. 1983. "Zadankai: Ningen no Sei" (Roundtable: Human Sexuality). *Juristo* 25:8–26.

Watney, Simon. 1989. *Policing Desire: Pornography, AIDS, and the Media*. Minneapolis: University of Minnesota Press.

West, Cornell. 1992. "The New Cultural Politics of Difference." In R. Ferguson, M. Gever, Trinh, M., and C. West, eds., *Out There: Marginalization and Contemporary Cultures* Cambridge: MIT Press, pp. 19–38.

Weston, Kath. 1993. "Lesbian/Gay Studies in the House of Anthropology." *Annual Reviews of Anthropology* 22:339–367.

White, Merry. 1987. *The Japanese Educational Challenge: A Commitment to Children*. New York: Free Press.

Williams, Linda. 1989. *Hard Core: Power, Pleasure, and the "Frenzy of the Visible."* Berkeley: University of California Press.

———. 1990. "'Something Else Besides a Mother': *Stella Dallas* and the Maternal Melodrama." In P. Erens, ed., *Issues in Feminist Film Criticism*. Bloomington: Indiana University Press, pp. 137–162.

———. 1993a. "Pornographies On/Scene, or Diff'rent Strokes for Diff'rent Folks." In L. Segal and M. McIntosh, eds., *Sex Exposed*. New Brunswick, N.J.: Rutgers University Press, pp. 233–265.

———. 1993b. "Second Thoughts on *Hard Core*: American Obscenity Law and the Scapegoating of Deviance." In P. Gibson and R. Gibson, eds., *Dirty Looks: Women, Pornography, Power*. London: BFI, pp. 176–191.

Yamada, Mitsuye. 1983. "Speaking in Tongues: A Letter to Third World Women Writers." In C. Morraga and G. Anzaldúa, eds., *This Bridge Called My Back: Writings by Radical Women of Color*. New York: Kitchen Table: Women of Color Press, pp. 165–174.

Yamamura, Yoshiaki. 1971. *Nihonjin to Haha: Bunka toshite no Haha no Kannen ni tsuite no Kenkyū* (The Japanese and Mother: Research on the Conceptualization of Mother as Culture). Tokyo: Tōyō Shuppansha.

Yamauchi, Toshiko. 1981. "Hahako maredo Otoko to Onna no Shiawase to Osore" (Fearing the Happiness of Man and Woman Although We're Mother and Child), part 2 of "Boshi Sōkan: Kindan no Kairaku ni Oborete" (Mother-Child Incest: Drowning in Forbidden Happiness). *Fujin Kōron* 66(1):344–348.

Yoda, Akira. 1981. *Otoko ni totte Onna to wa Nani ka?* (To Men, What Are Women?). Tokyo: Nihon Jitsugyō Shuppan.

Yoshimura, Takashi. 1987. "Yōji no Jiritsu o Hayameru Natsu no Shitsuke Sakusen" (Strategies for Summer Discipline That Facilitate the Independence of Children). *NHK Okāsan no Kenkyūshitsu* 8:26–39.

Young, Iris Marion. 1990. *Throwing Like a Girl and Other Essays in Feminist Philosophy and Social Theory*. Bloomington: Indiana University Press.

Yunomae, Tomoko. 1995. "Commodified Sex: Japan's Pornographic Culture." *Ampo* 25(4), 26(1):55–59.

Yuzawa, Yasuhiko. 1982. "Katei ni Okeru otto no Yakuwari" (The Husband's Role in the Family). In *Gendai Seikyōiku Kenkyū*. Tokyo: Nihon Seikyōiku Kyōkai.

Zhang, Yingjin. 1994. "Rethinking Cross-Cultural Analysis: The Questions of Authority, Power, and Difference in Western Studies of Chinese Films." *Bulletin of Concerned Asian Scholars* 26(4):44–54.

Žižek, Slavoj. 1989. *The Sublime Object of Ideology*. London: Verso.

———. 1992. *Enjoy Your Symptom! Jacques Lacan in Hollywood and Out*. New York: Routledge.

About the Book and Author

Erect-nippled, cartoonish breasts floating, like clouds, across a children's television program; sexually explicit scenes of rape and brutality mainstreamed in mass-marketed, highly accessible comic books for both children and adults; food in children's lunch boxes meticulously sculpted to look like Zen monks (hard-boiled egg) or octopuses (wieners); everyday stories of mother-son incest; and, in the face of rampant pornography, the incongruence of obscenity laws prohibiting the visibility of pubic hair in public media—this book provides a thoughtful analysis of the varied culture of sex and sexuality, power relations, and gender dynamics in contemporary Japan.

Anne Allison, author of *Nightwork: Sexuality, Pleasure, and Corporate Masculinity in a Tokyo Hostess Club,* spent five years in Japan. The observations she made and the fieldwork she conducted there form the foundation for this book.

Anne Allison teaches anthropology at Duke University and now lives in Durham, North Carolina.

Index